The History of the Khalifahs
who took the right way

The History of the Khalifahs
who took the right way

3rd Revised edition

a translation of the chapters on
al-Khulafa' ar-Rashidun
from
Tarikh al-Khulafa'
of

Jalal ad-Din as-Suyuti
Translated by Abdassamad Clarke

Ta-Ha Publishers Ltd.

Copyright © 1415/1995, Abdassamad Clarke.

Reprinted : 1996, 1998
Second Edition: 2001
Reprinted 2004
Third Revised Edition 2008
Reprinted: 2011, 2017, 2021

Published by:	Ta-Ha Publishers Ltd.
	Unit 4, The Windsor Centre,
	Windsor Grove,
	London, SE279NT
Website:	www.tahapublihers.com
E-mail:	support@tahapublishers.com

All rights reserved. No part of this publication may be reproduced, stored in any retrieval system, or transmitted in any form or by any means, electronic or otherwise, without written permission of the publishers.

By:	Jalal ad-Din as-Suyuti
General Editor:	Mr Afsar Siddiqui
Translated, typeset and cover by:	Abdassamad Clarke

A catalogue record of this book is available from the British Library

ISBN-13: 978 1 84200 097 7(Paperback)

Printed and Bound by IMAK Ofset, Turkey

Contents

Preface to the First Edition	xi
Preface to the Second Edition	xii
Preface to the Third Edition	xvi
Abu Bakr as-Siddiq	1
His name and affectionate nickname	3
His birth and early life	6
Abu Bakr was the most abstinent of men in the *Jahiliyyah*	7
His description	8
His acceptance of Islam	8
His companionship and expeditions	11
His bravery and that he was the bravest of the Companions	13
His spending his wealth on the Messenger of Allah and that he was the most generous of the Companions	14
His knowledge and that he was the most knowledgeable of the Companions and the most intelligent of them	18
His memorisation of the Qur'an	22
That he was the most eminent of the Companions and the best of them	23
Section	26
Those *ayat* which have been revealed in praise of him or in affirmation of him or other matters concerning him	27
The *hadith* related on his merit coupled with ʿUmar, apart from what has already been mentioned	29
The *hadith* related on his merit alone apart from what	

has already been mentioned	33
That which has been related from the Companions and the right-acting early generations on his merit	40
Section	42
The *hadith* and *ayat* which indicate his *khilafah*, and the words of the *imams* on that	43
The oath of allegiance to him	51
That which happened in his *khilafah*	59
The collection of the Qur'an	64
The things in which he was first	65
Section	68
Some examples of his forbearance and humility	68
Section	69
His final illness, his death, his last testament and his appointment of ʿUmar as *khalifah*	69
What *hadith* with chains of transmission have been related from him	77
That which is narrated from as-Siddiq in commentary on the Qur'an	87
What is narrated from as-Siddiq of traditions which stop short at him, sayings, judgements, *khutbahs*, and prayers	88
His words indicative of the strength of his fear of his Lord	100
That which is narrated from him in interpretation of dreams	101
A point of interest	102
Section	102
Section	103
ʿUMAR IBN AL-KHATTAB	107
The reports on his acceptance of Islam	108
His emigration	115
The *hadith* on his merit, other than those already quoted in the chapter on as-Siddiq	116
Sayings of the Companions and first generations on him	120
Section	123

The agreements of (the views of) ʿUmar (with subsequent confirmatory revelations of Qurʾan)	123
His miracles	127
Some particulars of his biography	131
His description	134
His *khilafah*	134
The things in which he was first	141
Some accounts of him and of his judgements	143
Section	154
Those of the Companions who died during his days	155
ʿUTHMAN IBN ʿAFFAN	157
The *hadith* related on his merit apart from what have already been quoted	161
His *khilafah*	164
An observation	166
Section	178
The things in which ʿUthman was first	179
The notables who died during the time of ʿUthman	180
ʿALI IBN ABI TALIB	181
The *hadith* related on his merit	184
The pledge of allegiance to ʿAli for the *khilafah* and what came about from that	190
Some fragments of accounts of ʿAli, his judgements and his words	194
His commentary on the Qurʾan	205
Some fragments of his astonishingly concise words	206
Those notable people who died during his time	208
AL-HASAN IBN ʿALI	209
GLOSSARY OF ARABIC TERMS	219
APPENDIX: ON THE IMAMATE	227
BIBLIOGRAPHY	232

بسم الله الرحمن الرحيم

Preface to the First Edition

May Allah bless the Prophet, his Family and Companions and grant them peace

This is a new translation of the chapters on *al-Khulafa' ar-Rashidun* from as-Suyuti's *Tarikh al-Khulafa'*. These chapters shine with a genuine light.

I have continued beyond the first four *khulafa'* to include al-Hasan ibn ʿAli ibn Abi Talib, may Allah be pleased with him, because he was the fifth of the *khulafa'* and he legitimately transferred the *khilafah* to Muʿawiyah, may Allah be pleased with him.

The translation lacks the majority of references to the books which are the sources of the *hadith* quoted, because whoever is interested will find the Arabic text easily available.

Furthermore the translation stays as close as possible to the original Arabic at the risk of a slight awkwardness in the English. Where necessary I have added within parentheses whatever seemed necessary for an understanding of the book.

The history outlined in these pages is further illuminated by a work which is even greater than it, but is itself an exposition that assumes a knowledge of what is in these pages, that is *al-ʿAwasim min al-Qawasim* ('Defence Against Disaster') by Qadi Abu Bakr ibn al-ʿArabi, may Allah show him mercy. Whereas as-Suyuti gives the most authentic traditions relating to these *khilafahs*, Qadi Abu Bakr lays bare the real significance of many of the events which as-Suyuti so expertly relates.

Preface to the Second Edition

Living as we do in 'later times' if not necessarily 'last times', it is fruitful to bear in mind Imam Malik's saying, may Allah be merciful to him, "Only what was right for the first of this *ummah* will be right for the last of it." This is even more clear to us 'late ones', since the fantasy of evolution, progress and development is increasingly being exposed for the hollow fiction it is.

The best of mankind and the best generations of humanity have already lived and passed on. We who are alive now hope to model ourselves on them, and so this book will be of greatest value to those who take it in hand as an aid and inspiration for establishing a just and illuminated civilisation in the present age.

Having realised the greatness of these men, the first *khulafa'*, may Allah be pleased with them, it is also vital for the reader to grasp the greatness of the most recent *khulafa'*, the Osmanli (Uthmaniyyah or Ottomans). Their history is proof that the khalifate of Islam has endured right down to our own day, since the demise of the Uthmaniyyah (1923) is, historically speaking, only yesterday. It is important to realise this – otherwise we may become trapped in the helpless idealism of those who romanticise the *Khulafa' ar-Rashidun* and then regard the rest of Islamic history as a continuing and irreversible decline, rather than as a series of cycles of emergence, greatness, decline and renewal as natural and as breathtaking as the life-cycle of a flower. To counter that false picture of decline, I can recommend nothing better for the reader than *Osmanli history, 1289-1922: based on Osmanli sources* by Professor Mehmet Maksudoglu.

Preface

It is clear from the whole texture of the lives of the great men painted so graphically within the pages of the book now in your hands, that they were not building a so-called 'Islamic state' – but that rather they typified the very form of prophetic Islamic governance, which has nothing in common with the modern bankers' control technique that is statism. This is confirmed by the work of Professor Maksudoglu, who was the first to refuse to refer to the Osmanlis as the Ottoman 'Empire', and who went on to conclude that neither were they a 'state', since a state is a fictitious entity that legislates, whereas a *dawlah*[1] brings Allah's revealed *ahkam* (judgement-rulings) into effect.[2]

It remains to draw the reader's attention to Shaykh Abdalqadir as-Sufi's book, *The Return of the Khalifate*, which exposes in most extraordinary detail the actual technique used to destroy the most recent khalifate of Islam – the names of the principle parties, the dates, and the sums of money involved. It was not by military conquest or superior technology that the destruction occurred, but by means of an unstoppable, exponentially growing, usurious debt which was presented to the Osmanlis as the only means of achieving a developed technology and systems culture.

The creation of that debt, owed to entities hostile to the *ummah*, can only have been possible in the ambience of supportive *fatwas* made from within the *ummah* by ʿ*ulama* of modernist persuasion – *fatwas* which are now seriously in doubt, because it is so clear that they completely fail to consider the inherent nature and intrinsic worthlessness of the money used, the deceptions involved and the underlying objective – while simultaneously either displaying a

---

[1] *Dawlah's* root meaning signifies a 'turn of fortune', revealing a dynamic concept utterly opposed to the static concept of 'state'; it is organic growth as opposed to concrete and plastic.

[2] Also in accordance with the Professor's work, we follow him in not translating *fath* as 'conquest' but as 'opening [to Islam]', and the *Fath Makkah* as 'the Opening of Makkah [to Islam]' rather than the 'Conquest of Makkah'.

profound ignorance of the true nature and undoubted sophistication and superiority of the *fiqh* of Islamic commerce or being beguiled by their own superficial mastery of that very sophistication into devising means to circumvent the *fiqh* and permit usury. Today, only a few well-paid Islamic bankers, associated intellectuals and *'ulama'* still seek to maintain that what Allah has forbidden is permitted as long as the interest rate being charged is 'reasonable' and described as 'Islamic' or falsely concealed as a 'legitimate service charge' or a 'profit-sharing transaction'.

The Osmanli debt was based on nothing more complicated than writing some numbers on pieces of paper and then subjecting them to a compound mathematical formula in order to make them grow. The Osmanli were caught in the same trap that continues to ensnare most of us today, and which is perpetuated by our acceptance of the quite sinister power we have unwittingly handed over to a group of shadowy people to print money and then charge interest for its use, thus creating their wealth out of nothing, at our expense.

If that were the entire story, then it would only be bad news, but Shaykh Abdalqadir also draws attention to the logical corollary: a return to the Muslims' traditional bi-metal currency as being the correct and only way out of transitory decline after this 'second interregnum' in the Osmanli Khalifate. This remedy confirms the words with which we began: "Only what was right for the first of this *ummah* will be right for the last of it."

Contrary to those whose concept of the restoration of the khalifate is akin to the idea of building a house starting with the chimney and then proceeding to build roof, walls, floors and finally foundations, we see its restoration proceeding from the re-laying of the foundations of Islam, i.e. a return to the *halal* and non-usurious modes of transacting in Islam, first and foremost using the currency of the Muslims, the gold dinar and silver dirham, an important element of which will be the use of the e-dinar, a non-usurious utilisation of the Internet (http://www.edinar.com) according to the *fiqh* of transactions.

Preface

The most significant aspect of this initiative, and one which is an individual obligation on every Muslim man and woman, is the restoration of the dormant pillar of *zakat*, collected by *zakat* collectors – empowered by *amirs* – in gold dinars and silver dirhams, as was done by our Prophet, may Allah bless him and grant him peace, and all the *khulafa'* who followed after, throughout history, until shortly before our own time.

This re-invigoration of the collection and distribution of *zakat*, combined with the concomitant cleansing of usury from the economic practice of the Muslims, will *insha'Allah* inexorably bring about a revival of the inner and social riches of Islam – in parallel with the inevitable self-destruction of the usurious monetarist system that has so enslaved mankind and polluted the earth during the last centuries.

In that programme we will need constantly to bear in mind the luminous human and spiritual qualities that the Islam of the Last Messenger, may Allah bless him and grant him peace, brings about in the people who actually live it as exemplified by these noble men, the Khalifahs who took the right way.[3]

This book is in honour of the khalifate to come; may Allah make it shine as brightly as those which have been.

Abdassamad Clarke
Charlottenlund, Denmark
Rabi' ath-Thani 1422/June 2001

---

[3] *Rashidun* is translated as "who took the right way" as opposed to "rightly guided" since although the latter passive sense is the correct translation of *mahdiyyun*, *rashidun* has the more active sense indicated.

Preface to the Third Edition

Little was meant to have changed in this edition apart from a slight expansion of the appendix and the placement in the footnotes of some text previously located in parentheses in the body of the book, but then we restored as-Suyuti's own accounts of the sources of his *hadith* and narrations. It is probably the greatest indication of the profound changes that have taken place in the interim since its first publication, when it was felt unnecessary and perhaps even burdensome to the reader to include that material. The reader must on his part follow the author in his careful explication of this science and not reduce it to the simplistic search for only traditions from the two *Sahih* collections.

After extensive research I found no reason to revise the footnote about the death of al-Hasan, may Allah be pleased with him, and the alleged hand of Yazid in it.

Ironically, this book is being widely cited by Shi'ah sources because of its luminous chapter on Sayyiduna 'Ali ibn Abi Talib, may Allah honour his face, but it would be a serious mistake to take that chapter out of the context of all of these *Khulafa'* and Companions, may Allah be pleased with all of them without exception. As-Suyuti's penetrating insight is best illustrated by the fact that the chapter on Sayyiduna Abu Bakr as-Siddiq, may Allah be pleased with him, is equal in volume to all of the other chapters combined, and contains proof after proof of his uniquely high standing and his prior right to the *khalifate*, many of them transmitted from Sayyiduna 'Ali ibn Abi Talib, may Allah honour his face.

Preface

   Finally, I have included the Arabic text of the *duʿa* taught by the Messenger of Allah, may Allah bless him and grant him peace, to al-Hasan in a dream, as it is a part of the last words from him, may Allah bless him and grant him peace, in the book, and for the blessing of this wonderful *duʿa*.

Abdassamad Clarke, Norwich
Tuesday 4th Rajab 1429/8th July 2008

Abu Bakr as-Siddiq
may Allah be pleased with him

Abu Bakr as-Siddiq, may Allah be pleased with him, was the *khalifah* of the Messenger of Allah, may Allah bless him and grant him peace. His name was ʿAbdullah ibn Abi Quhafah ʿUthman ibn ʿAmir ibn ʿAmr ibn Kaʿb ibn Saʿd ibn Taym ibn Murrah ibn Kaʿb ibn Luʾayy ibn Ghalib al-Qurashi at-Taymi, whose genealogy connects to that of the Messenger of Allah, may Allah bless him and grant him peace, in Murrah.

An-Nawawi said in his *Tahdhib*: What I have said, that the name of Abu Bakr as-Siddiq was ʿAbdullah, is correct and well known. It is said also that his name was ʿAteeq, but the truth upon which the generality of the men of knowledge agree is that ʿAteeq (the one set free) was an affectionate nickname and not his own name and he was given that name on account of his having been set free from the Fire as has been narrated in the *hadith* of at-Tirmidhi; and it is also said, on account of his face's ʿitaqah, that is to say its goodness and beauty, as Musʿab ibn az-Zubayr, al-Layth ibn Saʿd and a whole group said; and it has also been said that it is because there is nothing in his genealogy to be found fault with.

Musʿab ibn az-Zubayr and others said, 'The *ummah* agree unanimously on his being named as-Siddiq because he hastened to affirm the Messenger of Allah, may Allah bless him and grant him peace, and adhered steadfastly to truthfulness, and he was not remiss nor did he hesitate in any state or condition. He made exalted stands in Islam, among which was his story on the Night of the *Isra'*, his steadfastness and his replying to the *kuffar* about it.

There is also his emigration with the Messenger of Allah, may Allah bless him and grant him peace, leaving his family and children, and his remaining by the Prophet, may Allah bless him and grant him peace, in the Cave and on the rest of the journey (of the Hijrah). Then there are his words on the Day of Badr, and on the Day of Hudaybiyyah when the matter of delaying entry into Makkah seemed unclear to others. There is his weeping when the Messenger of Allah, may Allah bless him and grant him peace, said, "Allah has given a slave the choice between this life and the next (and he has chosen the next)." Later there is his steadfastness on the day of the death of the Messenger of Allah, may Allah bless him and grant him peace, his addressing the people and his stilling them. There is his undertaking the matter of the oath of allegiance for the benefit of the Muslims, and then his diligence in sending the army of Usamah ibn Zaid to Syria and his determination on that. Then there is the stand he took over those who reneged (on their Islam) and his exchange of views with the other Companions until he overcame their arguments with his proofs, and Allah expanded their breasts as He had expanded his breast to the reality and truth, which was to fight the renegades. Then there is his equipping the armies to go to Syria to conquer it and his support of them. Then he sealed all of that by an important action which was one of his best deeds and most majestic of his virtues – his appointment of ᶜUmar, may Allah be pleased with him, as *khalifah* of the Muslims, (and his perceptiveness concerning him, his bequeathing to him, and his entrusting the *ummah* to Allah, so that Allah, the Mighty and Exalted, made him succeed among them as the best *khalifah*, and for ᶜUmar, who was one of his good actions, were realised the establishment of Islam, the strengthening of the *deen* and the fulfilment of the promise of Allah, the Exalted, that He would make it manifest over the *deen*, all of it.) How many qualities, stations and virtues of as-Siddiq there are which just cannot be numbered.'

The above is from an-Nawawi.

I say: I want to expand upon the introduction to as-Siddiq somewhat, mentioning about him much that I have discovered of his life, and to arrange that in sections.

His name and affectionate nickname

Ibn Kathir said that all admit that his name was ʿAbdullah ibn ʿUthman, except for the narration of Ibn Saʿd on the authority of Ibn Sirin which asserts his name to have been ʿAteeq whereas the truth is that that was his affectionate nickname. Then there is some disagreement as to the time of his being so named, and the reason for it; for some say that it was on account of the ʿitaqah of his countenance, that is, its beauty – but Abu Nuʿaym al-Fadl ibn Dukayn said that it was on account of his priority in merit – and also it is said on account of the nobility of his pedigree, that is its purity, as there is nothing in his lineage that can be accounted a stain; and it is said too he was first so named and afterwards called ʿAbdullah.

At-Tabarani narrated that al-Qasim ibn Muhammad questioned ʿA'ishah, may Allah be pleased with her, as to the name of Abu Bakr, and she replied, 'ʿAbdullah.' Then he said, 'The people call him ʿAteeq.' She answered, 'Abu Quhafah had three sons whom he named ʿAteeq, Muʿtaq and Muʿaytaq.'

Ibn Mandah and Ibn ʿAsakir narrated that Musa ibn Talhah said: I said to my father Talhah, 'Why was Abu Bakr called ʿAteeq?' He said, 'His mother had no son surviving and when she gave birth to him, she faced towards the House (the Kaʿbah) with him and exclaimed, "O Allah if this one is ʿAteeq (free) from death then give him to me."'

At-Tabarani narrated that Ibn ʿAbbas said: He was only called ʿAteeq because of the beauty of his face.

Ibn ʿAsakir narrated that ʿA'ishah, may Allah be pleased with her, said, 'Abu Bakr's name which his family called him by was ʿAbdullah, but the name ʿAteeq became the dominant usage.' In a version, 'But the Prophet, may Allah bless him and grant him peace, called him ʿAteeq.'

Abu Yaʿla, Ibn Saʿd and al-Hakim, who declared it *sahih*, narrated that ʿA'ishah, may Allah be pleased with her, said, 'By Allah, I was in my house one day and the Messenger of Allah, may Allah bless him and grant him peace, and his companions were in the courtyard, a curtain between me and them. Abu Bakr came up and the Prophet, may Allah bless him and grant him peace, said, "Whoever is pleased to look upon one who is free from the Fire then let him look upon Abu Bakr." The name which his family knew him by was ʿAbdullah but ʿAteeq became the dominant usage.'

At-Tirmidhi and al-Hakim narrated that ʿA'ishah, may Allah be pleased with her, said, 'Abu Bakr entered upon the Messenger of Allah, may Allah bless him and grant him peace, who said, "Abu Bakr, you are the one Allah has freed from the Fire." From that day he was known as ʿAteeq."

Al-Bazzar and at-Tabarani narrated with an excellent *isnad* that ʿAbdullah ibn az-Zubayr said, 'Abu Bakr's name was ʿAbdullah, then the Messenger of Allah, may Allah bless him and grant him peace, said to him, "You are Allah's freed one from the Fire." So he was known as ʿAteeq.'

As for the name as-Siddiq, it is said about it, 'He was given the affectionate nickname in the *Jahiliyyah*, because of the truthfulness for which he was known' as Ibn Musdi mentioned. It has been said also, 'Because of his haste in affirming the Messenger of Allah, may Allah bless him and grant him peace, in that of which he informed.'

Ibn Ishaq narrated that al-Hasan al-Basri and Qatadah said: The first time that he became known for it was the morning after the Night of the *Isra'*.

Al-Hakim narrated in the *Mustadrak* that ʿA'ishah, may Allah be pleased with her, said: The idolaters came to Abu Bakr and said, 'What do you think of your Companion? He claims that he was taken this night to Bait al-Maqdis (Jerusalem).' He replied,

'Did he say that?' They said, 'Yes.' He said, 'He has definitely told the truth. I believe and affirm him in matters more remote than that: the news from heaven in the early part of the morning and in the evening.' For that reason he was called as-Siddiq. Its *isnad* is excellent, and that has also been narrated from *hadith* of Anas and Abu Hurayrah, for which Ibn ʿAsakir gave *isnads*, and Umm Hani', which was narrated by at-Tabarani.

Saʿid ibn Mansur narrated in his *Sunan*: Abu Maʿshar narrated that Wahb the freed slave of Abu Hurayrah said: When the Messenger of Allah, may Allah bless him and grant him peace, returned on the night in which he was made to travel (to Jerusalem), and he was at Dhu Tuwa, he said, 'Jibril, my people will not believe me.' He (Jibril) said, 'Abu Bakr will believe you, and he is as-Siddiq.'

Al-Hakim narrated in the *Mustadrak* that an-Nazzal ibn Sabrah said: We said to ʿAli: 'Amir al-Mu'minin, tell us about Abu Bakr.' He said, 'That man, Allah named him as-Siddiq on the tongue of Jibril and on the tongue of Muhammad, may Allah bless him and grant him peace. He was the deputy of the Messenger of Allah, may Allah bless him and grant him peace, for the prayer; he was contented with him for our *deen* and so we were pleased with him for our worldly affairs.' Its *isnad* is excellent.

Ad-Daraqutni and al-Hakim narrated that Abu Yahya said: I cannot count the number of times that I heard ʿAli say upon the *minbar*, 'Truly Allah named Abu Bakr through the tongue of His Prophet, a *siddiq*.'

At-Tabarani narrated with an excellent *sahih isnad* that Hakim ibn Saʿd said: I heard ʿAli say, and he swore upon it, 'Allah definitely revealed from heaven the name of Abu Bakr, as-Siddiq.'

In the *hadith* of Uhud, 'Be still, for there are only upon you a Prophet, a *siddiq* and two martyrs.'

'Abu Bakr's mother was the daughter of his father's paternal uncle (she was his father's cousin). Her name was Salma bint Sakhr ibn

ʿAmir ibn Kaʿb. She was given the *kunyah* (surname) Umm al-Khayr (Mother of good),' said az-Zuhri as narrated by Ibn ʿAsakir.

His birth and early life

He was born two years and some months after the birth of the Prophet, may Allah bless him and grant him peace, and he died when he was sixty-three years old.

Ibn Kathir said: As for that which Khalifah ibn al-Khayyat narrated that Yazid ibn al-Asamm said, that the Prophet, may Allah bless him and grant him peace, said to Abu Bakr, 'Am I older (*akbar* – also greater) or you?' And he said, 'You are greater than me but I have more years than you,' it is a *mursal* (attributed directly to the Prophet without mention of the Companion from whom it was heard) *ghareeb* (unusual, in having a single reporter at some stage of the *isnad*) tradition, and what is well known is the opposite (i.e. the Prophet, may Allah bless him and grant him peace, was older), and it is true only of al-ʿAbbas (that he was some years older than the Prophet, may Allah bless him and grant him peace).

His early life was in Makkah, which he only left for trade, and he had great wealth among his people, complete manliness, and munificence, and courtesy among them, as Ibn ad-Daghniyyah said, 'You join ties of kinship, you are truthful, you attain what others are denied, you support those in need, you help in difficult times, and you are hospitable to the guest.'

An-Nawawi said: He was one of the chiefs of Quraysh in the *Jahiliyyah*, one of their counsellors, beloved among them, and the wisest in the direction of their affairs. Then when Islam came he preferred it over everything else, and entered into it perfectly and completely.

Az-Zubayr ibn Bakkar and Ibn ʿAsakir narrated that Maʿruf ibn Kharrabudh said: Abu Bakr as-Siddiq, may Allah be pleased with him, was one of ten men of Quraysh who united pre-eminence in *Jahiliyyah* and Islam. He had responsibility for the settlement of blood-money and debts. That was because Quraysh had no king to whom all affairs could be referred. Rather in each tribe there was a general area of responsibility which resided in its chief; so that Banu Hashim had responsibility for giving (the pilgrims) to drink, and feeding them (by collecting from the tribes of Quraysh), meaning that no-one ate or drank except from their food and drink. Banu ʿAbd ad-Dar had responsibility for being the doorkeepers and guardians (of the Kaʿbah) and for the banner and council, i.e. no-one could enter the House without their permission, and whenever Quraysh fastened on the banner of war, the Banu ʿAbd ad-Dar bound it for them, and whenever they assembled together for a matter, either to confirm or annul it, their assembly could not be anywhere but in the House of Council, nor decided upon except there, and it belonged to Bani ʿAbd ad-Dar.'

Abu Bakr was the most abstinent of men in the *Jahiliyyah*
Ibn ʿAsakir narrated with a *sahih isnad* that ʿA'ishah, may Allah be pleased with her, said: By Allah, Abu Bakr never spoke poetry (i.e. he never 'composed' poetry) either in the *Jahiliyyah* or in Islam, and he and ʿUthman gave up drinking wine in the *Jahiliyyah*.

Abu Nuʿaym narrated with an excellent *isnad* that she said, may Allah be pleased with her: Abu Bakr had forbidden himself wine in the *Jahiliyyah*.

Ibn ʿAsakir narrated that ʿAbdullah ibn az-Zubayr said: Abu Bakr never ever spoke poetry.

Ibn ʿAsakir narrated that Abu'l-ʿAliyyah ar-Riyahi said: It was said to Abu Bakr as-Siddiq in a gathering of the companions of the Messenger of Allah, may Allah bless him and grant him peace, 'Did you drink wine in the *Jahiliyyah*?' He said, 'I seek refuge in Allah.' Someone said, 'Why?' He replied, 'I tried to protect my honour and guard my manliness, for whoever drinks wine will lose his honour and his manliness.' He said: That reached the Messenger of Allah, may Allah bless him and grant him peace, and he said, 'Abu Bakr has told the truth, Abu Bakr has told the truth,' twice. It is a *mursal ghareeb hadith* in both *isnad* and text.

His description

Ibn Sa'd narrated that 'A'ishah, may Allah be pleased with her, said that a man said to her, 'Describe Abu Bakr to us.' She said, 'A fair man, of slender build, thin cheeked and with a stoop; he could not keep his lower garment from slipping over his loins; gaunt-faced, eyes deep-set, with a prominent forehead, and the backs of his hands fleshless. This is his description.'

He narrated that 'A'ishah, may Allah be pleased with her, said that Abu Bakr used to dye [his hair and beard] with henna and indigo (*katam*).

He narrated that Anas said: The Messenger of Allah, may Allah bless him and grant him peace, went to Madinah and there was no-one among his companions having hair of mixed white and black except Abu Bakr, so he dyed it with henna and indigo (*katam*).

His acceptance of Islam

At-Tirmidhi and Ibn Hibban, in his *Sahih*, narrated that Abu Sa'id al-Khudri said: Abu Bakr said, 'Am I not the most suitable of people for it (the *khilafah*)? Am I not the first to accept Islam? Am I not the one of such-and-such? Am I not the one of such-and-such?'

Ibn 'Asakir narrated by way of al-Harith who related that 'Ali, may Allah be pleased with him, said: The first among men to accept Islam was Abu Bakr.

Ibn Abi Khaythamah narrated with a *sahih isnad* that Zaid ibn Arqam said: The first to perform the prayer with the Prophet, may Allah bless him and grant him peace, was Abu Bakr as-Siddiq.

Ibn Sa'd narrated that Abu Arwa ad-Dawsi the Companion, may Allah be pleased with him, said: The first to accept Islam was Abu Bakr as-Siddiq.

At-Tabarani narrated in the *Kabir* and 'Abdullah ibn Ahmad [Ibn

Hanbal] narrated in the *Zawa'id az-Zuhd* that ash-Sha'bi said: I asked Ibn 'Abbas, 'Who was the first person to accept Islam?' He said, 'Abu Bakr as-Siddiq. Did you not hear the words of Hassan?:

> "When you recall the distress of a trusted brother, then remember your brother Abu Bakr for what he did.
> The best of creation, most fearfully obedient of them, and the most just, except for the Prophet, and the most certain to fulfil what he has undertaken,
> The second, the follower whose assembly is praised, and the first of the men of they who affirmed the Messenger.'"

Abu Nu'aym narrated that Furat ibn as-Sa'ib said: I asked Maymun ibn Mihran, 'Is 'Ali better in your view or Abu Bakr and 'Umar?' He shook until his staff fell from his hand and replied, 'I never thought that I would live to a time when anyone would be compared with them. Their good deeds belong to Allah! They were the head of Islam.' I said, ''Ali was the first to accept Islam or Abu Bakr?' He said, 'By Allah, Abu Bakr believed in the Prophet, may Allah bless him and grant him peace, at the time of Buhayra the monk when he passed by him.'

There is a disagreement as to him and Khadijah (which of them was first to accept Islam) until (it is said that) he married her to him, may Allah bless him and grant him peace, and all of that before the birth of 'Ali.

A whole group of the Companions and the Followers said that he was the first to accept Islam, and some of them claimed that there was a consensus on that. It has been said, 'The first to accept Islam was 'Ali.' It has also been said, 'Khadijah.' The reconciliation between these apparently conflicting statements is that Abu Bakr was the first man to accept Islam, 'Ali was the first of the children to accept Islam, and Khadijah was the first woman to accept Islam. The first to reconcile it in this way was the Imam Abu Hanifah, may Allah be merciful to him.

Ibn Abi Shaybah and Ibn ʿAsakir narrated that Salim ibn Abi'l-Jaʿd said: I said to Muhammad ibn al-Hanafiyyah, 'Was Abu Bakr the first person to accept Islam?' He said, 'No.' I said, 'So how did Abu Bakr excel and precede others so much so that no-one else is mentioned but Abu Bakr?' He said, 'Because he was the best of them in Islam from the moment he accepted Islam until the moment he met his Lord.'

Ibn ʿAsakir narrated with an excellent *isnad* that Muhammad ibn Saʿd ibn Abi Waqqas said to his father Saʿd, 'Was Abu Bakr the first of you to accept Islam?' He said, 'No. More than five people accepted Islam before him, but he was the best of us in Islam.'

Ibn Kathir said: It is clear that the people of his house, may Allah bless him and grant him peace, believed before anyone; his wife Khadijah, his freed slave Zaid, Zaid's wife Umm Ayman, ʿAli and Waraqah.

Ibn ʿAsakir narrated that ʿIsa ibn Yazid said: Abu Bakr as-Siddiq said, 'I was sitting in the courtyard of the Kaʿbah and Zaid ibn ʿAmr ibn Nufayl was seated, then Umayyah ibn Abi's-Salt passed by him and said, "How are you, seeker after good?" He said, "Well." He said, "And have you found?" He said, "No," so he said,

"Every *deen* on the Day of Rising, except that which Allah has decreed, will perish.

"But as for this Prophet who is awaited, will he be from us or from you?" And I had not heard before that of a prophet who was awaited and who would be sent. So I went to Waraqah ibn Nawfal who used to look much towards heaven, and was much astonished of heart. I stopped him and told him the story. He said, "Yes, my nephew. We are the people of books and sciences, but this Prophet who is awaited is from the midst (noblest) of the Arabs genealogically – and I have a knowledge of genealogy – and your people are midmost (noblest) of the Arabs in terms of lineage." I said, "Uncle, and what will the Prophet say?" He said, "He will say what is said to him, except that he will not oppress nor be oppressed nor seek the oppression (of anyone)." So that when the Messenger of Allah, may Allah bless him and grant him peace, was sent I believed in him and affirmed him.'

Ibn Ishaq said: Muhammad ibn ʿAbd ar-Rahman ibn ʿAbdullah ibn al-Husayn at-Tamimi narrated to me that the Messenger of Allah, may Allah bless him and grant him peace, said, 'I have never invited anyone to Islam except that he had an aversion to it, and irresolution and deliberation, except for Abu Bakr. He did not delay when I reminded him and he was not irresolute.' Al-Bayhaqi said: This was because he used to see the proofs of the prophethood of the Messenger of Allah, may Allah bless him and grant him peace, and hear the traces of it before his invitation (to Islam), so that when he invited him he had already reflected and thought about it, and he submitted and accepted Islam at once.

Then he [al-Bayhaqi] narrated that Abu Maysurah said that the Messenger of Allah, may Allah bless him and grant him peace, used to hear someone calling him when he went out, 'Muhammad!' When he heard the voice he would turn back in flight and he told it in confidence to Abu Bakr who was his friend in *Jahiliyyah*.

Abu Nuʿaym and Ibn ʿAsakri narrated that Ibn ʿAbbas said: The Messenger of Allah, may Allah bless him and grant him peace, said, 'I never spoke to anyone about Islam but that they refused me and rejected my words except for the son of Abu Quhafah. I never spoke to him about something but that he accepted it and was steadfast in it.

Al-Bukhari narrated that Abu'd-Darda' said: The Messenger of Allah, may Allah bless him and grant him peace, said, 'Will you leave me my companion? (Will you leave me my companion?) I said, "People, I am the Messenger of Allah to you all," and you said, "You are lying." Abu Bakr said, "You have told the truth."'

His companionship and expeditions

The *ʿulama* say: Abu Bakr accompanied the Prophet, may Allah bless him and grant him peace, from the moment he accepted Islam until his death, not leaving him in a journey or in residence, except for that which he, may Allah bless him and grant him peace, authorised him to go out on, such as the Hajj and fighting expeditions. He was present at all the battles with him, emigrated with him, leaving his family and children, longing for Allah and His Messenger, may Allah bless him and grant him peace. He was his close companion in the cave. He, exalted is He, said, '*The second of two when the two of them were in the cave, when he said to his companion, "Do not be sad. Truly Allah is with us."*' (Qur'an 9: 40). He undertook to help the Messenger of Allah, may Allah bless him and grant him peace, more than once. He gave splendid service in the battles, and was firm on the Day of Uhud and the Day of Hunayn when all of the people had fled, as we will show in the section on his bravery.

Ibn ʿAsakir narrated that Abu Hurayrah said: The angels made each other to rejoice on the Day of Badr, saying, 'Do you not see as-Siddiq with the Messenger of Allah, may Allah bless him and grant him peace, in the shelter?'

Abu Yaʿla, al-Hakim and Ahmad narrated that ʿAli said: The Messenger of Allah, may Allah bless him and grant him peace, said to me and Abu Bakr on the Day of Badr, 'With one of you is Jibril and with the other is Mika'il.'

Ibn ʿAsakir narrated that Ibn Sirin said that ʿAbd ar-Rahman ibn Abi Bakr was, on the Day of Badr, with those who associate partners with Allah. When he (later) accepted Islam he said to his father, 'You were exposed to me (*ahdafta*) as a target on the Day of Badr, but I turned away from you and did not kill you.' Abu Bakr said, 'However, if you had been exposed to me as a target I would not have turned away from you.' Ibn Qutaybah said: The meaning of *ahdafta* is *ashrafta* – you were high or open, exposed and close. Thus it is said of a tall building, '*Hadaf* (literally – target).'

His bravery and that he was the bravest of the Companions

Al-Bazzar narrated in his *Musnad* that ʿAli said, 'Tell me who is the bravest of men?' They said, 'You.' He said, 'As for me, I never encountered anyone but that I took my due from him, but tell me who is the bravest of men?' They said, 'We don't know. Who is it?' He said, 'Abu Bakr. On the Day of Badr we made a shelter from the sun for the Messenger of Allah, may Allah bless him and grant him peace, and then we said, "Who will be with the Messenger of Allah, may Allah bless him and grant him peace, so that none of the idolaters may fall upon him?" By Allah, none of us drew near except for Abu Bakr who brandished a sword over the head of the Messenger of Allah, may Allah bless him and grant him peace. No-one fell upon him but that he in turn fell upon him. So he is the bravest of men.' ʿAli, may Allah be pleased with him, said: I saw the Messenger of Allah, may Allah bless him and grant him peace, and Quraysh grabbed him. One held him and another threw him down and they were saying, 'Are you the one who has made the gods into one god?' By Allah, none of us approached except Abu Bakr, striking this one, and restraining that one, and throwing down another, saying, 'Woe to you! Will you kill a man because he says, "My Lord is Allah?"' Then ʿAli raised a cloak which he was wearing and wept until his beard was wet and said, 'I adjure you by Allah! Is the believer of the people of Firʿawn better or Abu Bakr?' People were silent. He said, 'Will you not answer? By Allah, an hour of Abu Bakr is better than a thousand hours of the like of the believer of the people of Firʿawn. He was a man who concealed his *iman*, and this was a man who was open about his *iman*.'

Al-Bukhari narrated that ʿUrwah ibn az-Zubayr said: I asked ʿAbdullah ibn ʿAmr ibn al-ʿAs about the worst thing that the idolaters did to the Messenger of Allah, may Allah bless him and grant him peace. He said, 'I saw ʿUqbah ibn Abi Muʿayt who came to the Prophet, may Allah bless him and grant him peace, while he was praying, and he placed his cloak about his neck and seriously tried to throttle him. Then Abu Bakr came and defended him and said, "Would you kill a man because he says, 'My Lord is Allah,' and he has come to you with clear signs from your Lord?'"

Al-Haytham ibn Kulayb narrated in his *Musnad* that Abu Bakr said, 'On the Day of Uhud everyone fled from the Messenger of Allah, and I was the first to return.' The rest of the *hadith* is in the *Musnad* which al-Haytham ibn Kulayb narrated.

Ibn ʿAsakir narrated that ʿAʾishah, may Allah be pleased with her, said: When the companions of the Prophet, may Allah bless him and grant him peace, gathered, and they were thirty-eight men, Abu Bakr pressed upon the Messenger of Allah, may Allah bless him and grant him peace, to be open and public. He said, 'Abu Bakr, we are few.' Abu Bakr wouldn't stop urging the Messenger of Allah, may Allah bless him and grant him peace, until the Messenger of Allah, may Allah bless him and grant him peace, made things public. The Muslims went into every corner of the Mosque (of Makkah), every man among his own kinsfolk, and Abu Bakr stood up among the people addressing them, so that he was the first public speaker to invite people to Allah and His Messenger. The idolaters leapt upon Abu Bakr and the Muslims, and they beat them, in every corner of the Mosque, very severely. The conclusion of this *hadith* will come in the biography of ʿUmar, may Allah be pleased with him.

Ibn ʿAsakir narrated that ʿAli, may Allah be pleased with him, said: When Abu Bakr accepted Islam, he was open about his Islam and he invited people to Allah and to His Messenger, may Allah bless him and grant him peace.

His spending his wealth on the Messenger of Allah and that he was the most generous of the Companions

Allah, exalted is He, says, '*And he will be averted from it (the Fire) who has the most fearful obedience, the one who gives his wealth purifying himself,*' (Qur'an 92: 17-21) to the end of the *surah*. Ibn al-Jawzi said: They agree unanimously that this was revealed about Abu Bakr.

Ahmad narrated that Abu Hurayrah said: The Messenger of Allah, may Allah bless him and grant him peace, said, 'No wealth ever benefited me as did the wealth of Abu Bakr.' Abu Bakr wept and said, 'Are I and my wealth for any but you, Messenger of Allah?' Abu Ya'la narrated that 'A'ishah, may Allah be pleased with her, narrated the like of it as a *marfu' hadith*. Ibn Kathir said: And it is narrated in *hadith* of 'Ali, Ibn 'Abbas, Anas, Jabir ibn 'Abdullah and Abu Sa'id al-Khudri, may Allah be pleased with all of them. Al-Khateeb narrated it from Sa'id ibn al-Musayyab as a *mursal hadith* and added, 'And the Messenger of Allah, may Allah bless and grant peace to him and his family, used to make use of the wealth of Abu Bakr as he did of his own wealth.'

Ibn 'Asakir narrated by various routes that 'A'ishah, may Allah be pleased with her, and 'Urwah ibn az-Zubayr said: Abu Bakr, may Allah be pleased with him, accepted Islam on the day that he did and he had forty thousand dinars (and in a wording – forty thousand dirhams) and he spent them on the Messenger of Allah, may Allah bless him and grant him peace.

Abu Sa'id ibn al-A'rabi narrated that Ibn 'Umar, may Allah be pleased with both of them, said: Abu Bakr accepted Islam, may Allah be pleased with him, on the day that he did, and in his house there were forty thousand dirhams. Then he emigrated to Madinah and he had nothing but five thousand dirhams. He had spent all of that on freeing slaves and helping the cause of Islam.

Ibn 'Asakir narrated that 'A'ishah, may Allah be pleased with her, said that Abu Bakr freed seven (slaves) each one of whom was being tortured for the sake of Allah.

Ibn Shahin narrated in *as-Sunnah*, al-Baghawi in his *tafsir* and Ibn 'Asakir that Ibn 'Umar said: I was with the Prophet, may Allah bless him and grant him peace, and Abu Bakr as-Siddiq was with him, and he had on a large (coarse goatskin) cloak which he had fastened over his breast with a skewer, and then Jibril, peace be upon him, descended upon him and said, 'Muhammad, how is it that I see Abu Bakr and he has on a large (coarse goatskin) cloak which he has fastened over his breast with a skewer?' He said, 'Jibril, he spent his wealth upon me before the Opening (of Makkah to Islam).' He said, 'Allah sends greetings of peace to him and says to say to him, "Are you pleased with Me in this poverty of yours or displeased?" Abu Bakr said, 'Am I displeased with my Lord? I am pleased with my Lord. I am pleased with my Lord. I am pleased with my Lord.' It is unusual (*ghareeb*) and its *isnad* is very weak. Abu Nuʿaym narrated the same from Abu Hurayrah and Ibn Masʿud and their *isnads* are also weak. Ibn ʿAsakir narrated the like of it from a *hadith* of Ibn ʿAbbas.

Al-Khateeb narrated with an *isnad* which is also weak that Ibn ʿAbbas, may Allah be pleased with both of them, related from the Prophet, may Allah bless him and grant him peace, that he said, 'Jibril, peace be upon him, descended upon me and he had on a large piece of coarse cloth fastened on him, so I said to him, "Jibril, what is this?" He said, "Allah, exalted is He, has ordered the angels that they should fasten in the heaven as Abu Bakr fastens on earth."' Ibn Kathir said: This is very much to be rejected (*munkar*)[4]. If it were not that many people hand down this one and the one before it, it would be better to completely avoid them.

Abu Dawud and at-Tirmidhi narrated that ʿUmar ibn al-Khattab said: The Messenger of Allah, may Allah bless him and grant him peace, ordered us to give *sadaqah* and that agreed with the property that I had so I said, 'Today I will outdo Abu Bakr if I am ever to outdo him,' and I brought half of my wealth. The Messenger of Allah, may Allah bless him and grant him peace, said, 'What have

---

[4] *Munkar* means, even in the cases of *hadith* which have sound *isnads*, that the content of the *hadith* contradicts known *ayat* of the Qur'an or the texts of other better known *hadith* or known principles of the *deen*.

you left for your family?' I said, 'I have left the like of it.' Then Abu Bakr came with everything that he had, and he said, 'Abu Bakr, what have you left for your family?' He said, 'I have left for them Allah and His Messenger.' I said, 'I will never ever outdo him in anything.' At-Tirmidhi said, '[This *hadith*] is *hasan sahih*.'

Abu Nuʿaym narrated in *al-Hilyah* that al-Hasan al-Basri said that Abu Bakr came to the Prophet, may Allah bless him and grant him peace, with his *sadaqah* and concealed it. He said, 'Messenger of Allah, this is my *sadaqah*, and, Allah can return to me (for more).' Then ʿUmar came with his *sadaqah* openly and said, 'Messenger of Allah, this is my *sadaqah* and I can return to Allah (for more).' The Messenger of Allah, may Allah bless him and grant him peace, said, 'The difference between your two *sadaqahs* is the same as the difference between your words.' Its *isnad* is excellent, but it is a *mursal*.

At-Tirmidhi narrated that Abu Hurayrah said: The Messenger of Allah, may Allah bless him and grant him peace, said, 'We have never been under obligation to anyone but that we have repaid him, except for Abu Bakr, for he has put obligations on us which Allah will repay him for on the Day of Rising. No-one's wealth has ever benefited me as has Abu Bakr's wealth.'

Al-Bazzar narrated that Abu Bakr as-Siddiq, may Allah be pleased with him, said: I came with my father Abu Quhafah to the Prophet, may Allah bless him and grant him peace, who said, 'You should have left the shaykh until I could come to him.' I said, 'Rather it is more correct that he should come to you.' He said, 'We would rather be protective of him for the favours for which we are obliged to his son.'

Ibn ʿAsakir narrated that Ibn ʿAbbas said: The Messenger of Allah, may Allah bless him and grant him peace, said, 'No-one has shown greater favour to me than Abu Bakr. He shared himself and his wealth with me and he married me his daughter.'

His knowledge and that he was the most knowledgeable of the Companions and the most intelligent of them

An-Nawawi said, in his *Tahdhib*, and from his own writing I transmit: Our companions proved the vastness of his knowledge by his words, may Allah be pleased with him, in the well established *hadith* which is in the two *Sahih* collections, 'By Allah, I will fight whoever distinguishes between *salah* and *zakat*. By Allah, if they refuse me as much as the halter of a camel which they used to pay to the Messenger of Allah, may Allah bless him and grant him peace, I will fight them over their refusal.' Shaykh Abu Ishaq saw a proof, in this and other things, in his *Tabaqat*, that Abu Bakr as-Siddiq, may Allah be pleased with him, was the most knowledgeable of the Companions, because they all failed to understand the judgement on this issue except for him, then it became clear to them because of his discussions with them that his words were the correct position, so they came back to that.

We have transmitted that Ibn ʿUmar was asked, 'Who used to give *fatwa* for people at the time of the Messenger of Allah, may Allah bless him and grant him peace?' He said, 'Abu Bakr and ʿUmar, may Allah be pleased with them. I don't know of anyone other than them.'

The two Shaykhs (al-Bukhari and Muslim) narrated that Abu Saʿid al-Khudri said: The Messenger of Allah, may Allah bless him and grant him peace, addressed people and said, 'Allah, the Blessed and Exalted, has given a slave the choice between the world and that which is with Him. That slave has chosen that which is with Allah, exalted is He.' Then Abu Bakr wept and said, 'We would ransom you with our fathers and mothers.' We were astonished at his weeping because the Messenger of Allah informed about a slave who had been given a choice. But the Messenger of Allah, may Allah bless him and grant him peace, was the one given the choice, and Abu Bakr was the most knowledgeable of us. The Messenger of Allah, may Allah bless him and grant him peace, said, 'The most generous of people to me with his company and his wealth is Abu Bakr. If I were to take an intimate friend other than my Lord I would have taken Abu Bakr, but there is the brotherhood of Islam and its affection. Let no door remain open but for the door of Abu Bakr.'

The above is all the words of an-Nawawi.

Ibn Kathir said: As-Siddiq, may Allah be pleased with him, was the best read of the Companions, meaning that he was the most knowledgeable of them in the Qur'an, because he, may Allah bless him and grant him peace, put him forward as *imam* of the prayer for the Companions, may Allah be pleased with him and them, along with his words, 'The best read in the Book of Allah will lead the people.'

At-Tirmidhi narrated that 'A'ishah, may Allah be pleased with her, said: The Messenger of Allah, may Allah bless him and grant him peace, said, 'It is not fitting for a people among whom is Abu Bakr that another than him should lead them (as *imam*: the word having the meaning of both leading, and leading the prayer).'

He was, along with that, the most knowledgeable in the *Sunnah*. When the Companions referred to him on several occasions, he produced transmissions of sunnahs from the Prophet, may Allah bless him and grant him peace, he had memorised and which he produced at the moments when they were needed, and which they didn't have. How could that not be when he had persevered in accompanying the Messenger, may Allah bless him and grant him peace, from the very beginning of his being sent until his death? Along with that he was one of the most intelligent of the slaves of Allah and one of the most comprehending. However, there are not many *hadith* traced back with a chain of transmission to him, only because of the short time he lived and the speed of his death after the Prophet, may Allah bless him and grant him peace. If he had lived for long, his narrations would have been very extensive. None of the transmitters left a *hadith* that he transmitted without narrating it. But none of the Companions from his time, needed to transmit from him what they shared with him in the narration of, so they only transmitted from him what they themselves didn't have.

Abu'l-Qasim al-Baghawi narrated that Maymun ibn Mihran said: Abu Bakr, when a dispute was brought to him, used to look in the Book of Allah. Then if he found there the basis for a judgement between the disputants he would give judgement on that basis. If there was nothing in the Book and he knew a *Sunnah* on that matter from the Messenger of Allah, may Allah bless and grant him and his family peace, he would give judgement by that. If he could not find the right way he would go out and ask the Muslims, and say, 'Such and such has come to me, so do you know whether the Messenger of Allah, may Allah bless him and grant him peace, gave any judgement on that?' Perhaps a group would gather around him, everyone of them mentioning a judgement of the Messenger of Allah, may Allah bless him and grant him peace. Abu Bakr would say, 'Praise belongs to Allah Who has put among us those who preserve and memorise from our Prophet.' If he was unable to find a *Sunnah* about it from the Messenger of Allah, may Allah bless him and grant him peace, he would gather the leaders and the best of the people and seek their counsel. If they would agree on a view he would give judgement by that. ʿUmar, may Allah be pleased with him, used to do that. If he was unable to find some way in the Qur'an and the *Sunnah*, he would look to see if Abu Bakr had given a judgement on it. If he found that Abu Bakr had already given judgement on it he would pass judgement on the basis of that judgement. If not, he would call the leaders of the Muslims and if they would agree unanimously on a matter he would give judgement on that basis.

As-Siddiq, may Allah be pleased with him, was, along with that, the most knowledgeable in the genealogies of the Arabs, particularly of Quraysh. A shaykh of the *Ansar* said: Jubayr ibn Mutʿim used to be the most knowledgeable of Quraysh in the genealogies of Quraysh and of the Arabs in general and he used to say, 'I only took genealogies from Abu Bakr as-Siddiq, and Abu Bakr as-Siddiq was the most learned in genealogy of the Arabs.'

Along with that, as-Siddiq had reached the limit in the interpretation of dreams. He used to interpret dreams in the time of the Messenger of Allah, may Allah bless him and grant him peace. Muhammad ibn Sirin, and he was the foremost in this knowledge by general consensus, said: Abu Bakr was the most able of this *ummah* after the Prophet, may Allah bless him and grant him peace, to draw a meaning (from a dream). Ibn Sa'd narrated it.

Ad-Daylami narrated in *Musnad al-Firdaws* and Ibn 'Asakir narrated that Samurah said: The Messenger of Allah, may Allah bless him and grant him peace, said, 'I have been commanded to interpret the dream (and to tell it or teach it) to Abu Bakr.'

Ibn Kathir said: He was one of the clearest and most eloquent of people. Az-Zubayr ibn Bakkar said: I heard one of the people of knowledge saying, 'The most eloquent of those of the Companions of the Messenger of Allah who gave the *khutbah* were Abu Bakr and 'Ali ibn Abi Talib, may Allah be pleased with both of them.' In the *hadith* of *as-Saqifah* we will relate the words of 'Umar, may Allah be pleased with him. He was one of the most knowing of mankind of Allah and the most fearful of Him. Some of his words on that and on the interpretation of dream and some of his *khutbahs* we will place together in an independent section.

One of the proofs that he was the most knowledgeable of the Companions is the *hadith* of the Treaty of Hudaybiyyah when 'Umar asked the Messenger of Allah, may Allah bless him and grant him peace, 'For what reason should we accept disgrace in our *deen*?' The Prophet, may Allah bless him and grant him peace, answered him. Then he went to Abu Bakr and asked him the same question that he had asked the Messenger of Allah, may Allah bless him and grant him peace, and he answered him just as the Prophet, may Allah bless him and grant him peace, had answered him, word for word. Al-Bukhari and others narrated it.

Along with that, he was the most penetrating of the Companions in his views and the most perfect of them in intellect. Tamam ar-Razi narrated in his *Fawa'id* and Ibn ᶜAsakir narrated that ᶜAbdullah ibn ᶜAmr ibn al-ᶜAs said: I heard the Messenger of Allah, may Allah bless him and grant him peace, saying, 'Jibril came to me and said, "Allah orders you to seek the counsel of Abu Bakr."'

At-Tabarani, Abu Nuᶜaym and others narrated that Muᶜadh ibn Jabal told that when the Prophet, may Allah bless him and grant him peace, wanted to send Muᶜadh to the Yemen he sought the counsel of men of his companions among whom were Abu Bakr, ᶜUmar, ᶜAli, Talhah, az-Zubayr and Usayd ibn Hudayr. The people talked and every man had his own view. He said, 'What do you think, Muᶜadh?' I (Muᶜadh) said, 'I think the same as that which Abu Bakr said.' The Prophet, may Allah bless him and grant him peace, said, 'Allah dislikes in the heaven that Abu Bakr should make a mistake.' Ibn Abi Usamah related it in his *Musnad*, 'Allah, in the heaven, dislikes that Abu Bakr as-Siddiq should make a mistake on the earth.' Sahl ibn Saᶜd as-Saᶜidi said: The Messenger of Allah, may Allah bless him and grant him peace, said, 'Allah dislikes that Abu Bakr should make a mistake.' The men who transmitted it are all trustworthy.

His memorisation of the Qur'an

An-Nawawi said in his *Tahdhib*: As-Siddiq was one of the Companions who memorised all of the Qur'an.

A large group have mentioned this also, of them Ibn Kathir in his *tafsir*. As for the tradition of Anas, 'Four gathered together (i.e. memorised entirely) the Qur'an in the time of the Messenger of Allah, may Allah bless him and grant him peace,' what he meant was 'of the *Ansar*' as I made clear in the book *al-Itqan*. As for that which ash-Shaᶜbi said, 'Abu Bakr as-Siddiq, may Allah be pleased with him, died without gathering (memorising) all of the Qur'an,' it is rejected, or it can be interpreted that he meant by 'gathering', i.e. in a *mushaf* with the organisation (of *surahs* and *ayat*) which ʿUthman gave it, may Allah be pleased with him.

That he was the most eminent of the Companions and the best of them

The people of the *Sunnah* are unanimous that the best of mankind after the Messenger of Allah, may Allah bless him and grant him peace, were Abu Bakr, then ʿUmar, then ʿUthman, then ʿAli, then the rest of the ten (who were given the good news of the Garden by the Prophet, may Allah bless him and grant him peace), then the rest of the people of Badr, then the rest of the people of Uhud, then the rest of the people of the oath of allegiance (of Hudaybiyyah), then the rest of the Companions. Abu Mansur al-Baghdadi relates that there is consensus on this.

Al-Bukhari narrated that Ibn ʿUmar said, 'We were choosing between people in the time of the Messenger of Allah, may Allah bless him and grant him peace, so we chose Abu Bakr, then ʿUmar (ibn al-Khattab), then ʿUthman (ibn ʿAffan) may Allah be pleased with them all.' At-Tabarani added, in *al-Kabir*, 'And the Prophet came to know of that but did not deny it.'

Ibn ʿAsakir narrated that Ibn ʿUmar said: We, while the Messenger of Allah, may Allah bless him and grant him peace, was among us, used to prefer Abu Bakr, ʿUmar, ʿUthman and ʿAli.

Ibn ʿAsakir narrated that Abu Hurayrah said: We, the gatherings of the Companions of the Messenger of Allah, may Allah bless him and grant him peace, while we were considerable numbers, used to say, 'The best of this *ummah* after its Prophet are Abu Bakr, then ʿUmar, and then ʿUthman,' and then we would be silent.

At-Tirmidhi narrated that Jabir ibn ʿAbdullah said: ʿUmar said to Abu Bakr, 'O best of mankind after the Messenger of Allah, may Allah bless him and grant him peace.' Abu Bakr said, 'If you say that, then I heard him saying, "The sun has not risen over a better man than ʿUmar."'

Al-Bukhari narrated that Muhammad ibn ʿAli ibn Abi Talib said: I said to my father, 'Who is the best of mankind after the Prophet, may Allah bless him and grant him peace?' He said, 'Abu Bakr.' I said, 'Then who?' He said, 'ʿUmar.' I was afraid that he would say ʿUthman so I said, 'Then you?' He said, 'I am nobody but a man among the Muslims.'

Ahmad and others narrated that ʿAli said: The best of this *ummah* after our Prophet are Abu Bakr and ʿUmar. Adh-Dhahabi said: This is *mutawatir*[5] from ʿAli, so may Allah curse *ar-Rafidah* (literally 'the rejectors' i.e. the *Shiʿah*), how ignorant they are!

At-Tirmidhi and al-Hakim narrated that ʿUmar ibn al-Khattab said: Abu Bakr, our master, the best of us and the most beloved to the Prophet, may Allah bless him and grant him peace, said, '…'

Ibn ʿAsakir narrated that ʿAbd ar-Rahman ibn Abi Layla said that ʿUmar ascended the *minbar* and said, 'Definitely the best of this *ummah* after our Prophet is Abu Bakr. Whoever says anything else is an inventor of falsehood. May there be upon him that which is upon the inventor of falsehood.' He also narrated that Ibn Abi Layla said: ʿAli said, 'Anyone who prefers me over Abu Bakr and ʿUmar, I will lash with the *hadd* punishment due to the inventor of falsehood.'

ʿAbd ar-Rahman ibn Humayd, in his *Musnad*, and Abu Nuʿaym and others narrated with different paths of transmission that Abu'd-Dardaʾ, said that the Messenger of Allah, may Allah bless him and grant him peace, said, 'The sun has not risen nor has it set over anyone better than Abu Bakr, unless he were a prophet.' In a differently worded version, '…over any of the Muslims, after the prophets and messengers, better than Abu Bakr.' It has also been transmitted as a *hadith* of Jabir, in its wording is, 'The sun has not risen over anyone of you better than him.' At-Tabarani and others narrated it. There are other texts which support it from other angles

---

[5] Narrated by a large number of people directly from him to other people so that it reached later generations from large numbers of people.

and which require that it be a *sahih* or *hasan hadith*. Ibn Kathir indicated that his judgement was that it is sound.

At-Tabarani narrated that Salamah ibn al-Akwaʿ said: The Messenger of Allah, may Allah bless him and grant him peace, said, 'Abu Bakr as-Siddiq is the best of mankind, unless it be a prophet.' And in *al-Awsat* that Saʿd ibn Zurarah said: The Messenger of Allah, may Allah bless him and grant him peace, said, 'The *Ruh al-Quds*, Jibril, informed me that, "The best of your *ummah* after you is Abu Bakr."'

The two Shaykhs ʿAmr ibn al-ʿAs said: I said, 'Messenger of Allah, which of the people is most beloved to you?' He said, 'ʿA'ishah.' I said, 'Of the men?' He said, 'Her father.' I said, 'Then who?' He said, 'Then ʿUmar ibn al-Khattab.' This *hadith* has been narrated without, 'Then ʿUmar,' in narrations of Anas, Ibn ʿAmr and Ibn ʿAbbas.

At-Tirmidhi, an-Nasa'i and al-Hakim narrated that ʿAbdullah ibn Shaqiq said: I said to ʿA'ishah, 'Which of the companions of the Messenger of Allah were most beloved to the Messenger of Allah, may Allah bless him and grant him peace?' She said, 'Abu Bakr.' I said, 'Then who?' She said, 'Then ʿUmar.' I said, 'Then who?' She said, 'Abu ʿUbaydah ibn al-Jarrah.'

At-Tirmidhi and others narrated that Anas said: The Messenger of Allah, may Allah bless him and grant him peace, said about Abu Bakr and ʿUmar, 'These two are the lords of the mature adults of the people of the Garden, of the first ones and the last ones, except for the prophets and the messengers.' He recorded the like of it from ʿAli.

In this section there are *hadith* from Ibn ʿAbbas, Ibn ʿUmar, Abu Saʿid al-Khudri and Jabir ibn ʿAbdullah.

At-Tabarani narrated in *al-Awsat* that ʿAmmar ibn Yasir said: Whoever preferred anyone of the companions of the Messenger of Allah, may Allah bless him and grant him peace, over Abu Bakr and ʿUmar has belittled the *Muhajirun* and the *Ansar*.

Ibn Sa'id narrated that az-Zuhri said: The Prophet, may Allah bless him and grant him peace, said to Hassan ibn Thabit, 'Have you said anything about Abu Bakr?' He said, 'Yes.' He said, 'Say it and I will listen.' He said,

> 'And the "*second of the two*" in the glorious cave,
>   The enemy went round about it when he ascended the mountain.
> The love of the Messenger of Allah (for him) they already knew,
>   Of people he held not equal any man.'

And the Prophet, may Allah bless him and grant him peace, laughed until his back teeth were visible, then said, 'You have told the truth, Hassan; he is as you say.'

Section

Ahmad and at-Tirmidhi narrated that Anas ibn Malik said: The Messenger of Allah, may Allah bless him and grant him peace, said, 'The most merciful of my *ummah* towards my *ummah* is Abu Bakr, the most severe of them in the matter of Allah is 'Umar, the most truly modest of them is 'Uthman, the most knowledgeable of them of the *halal* and the *haram* is Mu'adh bin Jabal, the most knowledgeable in the laws of inheritance is Zayd ibn Thabit, the best read of them (in Qur'an reading) is Ubayy ibn Ka'b, and every *ummah* has a trusted one and the trusted one of this *ummah* is Abu 'Ubaydah ibn al-Jarrah.' Abu Ya'la narrated it from the *hadith* of Ibn 'Umar and added (in his narration) to it, 'and the most decisive of them (as *Qadi*) is 'Ali.' Ad-Daylami narrated it in *Musnad al-Firdaws* from a *hadith* of Shaddad ibn Aws who added to it, 'and Abu Dharr is the most abstinent of my *ummah* and the most truthful of them, Abu'd-Darda' is the most given to worship of my *ummah* and has the most fearful obedience of them, and Mu'awiyah ibn Abi Sufyan is the most forbearing of my *ummah* and the most liberally generous.'

Our Shaykh al-Khafiji was asked about these distinguishing

characteristics and whether they negated the ones previously given and he replied that there was no contradiction.

Those *ayat* which have been revealed in praise of him or in affirmation of him or other matters concerning him

Know that I have seen a book written by one of the scholars on the names of those about whom Qur'an was revealed but it was not accurate or comprehensive, so I composed on that subject a copious, comprehensive and accurate book and I excerpt from it here that which pertains to as-Siddiq, may Allah be pleased with him.

Allah, exalted is He, says, '*The second of the two when the two of them were in the cave, when he said to his companion, "Do not be sad, truly Allah is with us." So Allah sent down His tranquillity upon him.*' (Qur'an 9: 40) The Muslims are unanimously agreed that the companion who is mentioned here is Abu Bakr, and there will come a tradition from him on it.

Ibn Abi Hatim narrated that Ibn ᶜAbbas said, about His words, exalted is He, '*Then Allah sent down His tranquillity upon him,*' he said, 'upon Abu Bakr. (As for) the Prophet, may Allah bless him and grant him peace, tranquillity was always upon him.'

Ibn Abi Hatim narrated that Ibn Masᶜud said that Abu Bakr bought Bilal from Umayyah ibn Khalf and Ubayy ibn Khalf with a cloak and ten pieces of silver (approximately an ounce each), then set him free for the sake of Allah. Then Allah revealed, '*By the night when it covers…*' up to His words, '*… truly your endeavours are different,*' (Qur'an 96: 1-4) meaning the endeavours of Abu Bakr, Umayyah and Ubayy.

Ibn Jarir narrated that ᶜAmir ibn ᶜAbdullah ibn az-Zubayr said: Abu Bakr used to set free (slaves) upon (their acceptance of) Islam, in Makkah. He would set free old women and women generally whenever they accepted Islam. His father said, 'Son, I see you freeing weak people. Why do you not free strong men who would stand with you, protect you and repel (attackers) from you.' He said, 'Father,

I wish for that which is with Allah.' He ('Amir) said: Some of my family told me that this *ayah* was revealed about him, '*So as for he who gives and has fearful obedience …*' (Qur'an 96: 5-21) to its end.

Ibn Abi Hatim and at-Tabarani narrated that 'Urwah said that Abu Bakr as-Siddiq, may Allah be pleased with him, freed seven, each of whom was being tortured for Allah, and that about him was revealed, '*And the most fearfully obedient will be averted from it (the Fire)…*' (Qur'an 96: 18-21) to the end of the *surah*.

Al-Bazzar narrated that 'Abdullah ibn az-Zubayr said: This *ayah*, '*And there is not for anyone with him a benefit to be recompensed*,'[6] (Qur'an 96: 19) was revealed about Abu Bakr as-Siddiq, may Allah be pleased with him.

Al-Bukhari narrated that 'A'ishah, may Allah be pleased with her, said that Abu Bakr never used to break oaths until Allah revealed the atonement for breaking an oath.

Al-Bazzar and Ibn 'Asakir narrated that Usayd ibn Safwan, who enjoyed companionship (of the Prophet, may Allah bless him and grant him peace), said: 'Ali said, '"*And the one who came with the truth (al-haqq)*" (Qur'an 39: 33) is Muhammad "*and he affirmed it*" (Ibid.) refers to Abu Bakr as-Siddiq.' Ibn 'Asakir said: The narration is this way, 'with *al-haqq* (truth)' (rather than *as-sidq* [sincerity or truthfulness] the usual reading in Qur'an) and perhaps it was a variant reading of 'Ali.

Al-Hakim narrated that Ibn 'Abbas spoke about His words, exalted is He, '*And take their counsel in the matter.*' (Qur'an 3: 159) He said, 'It was revealed about Abu Bakr and 'Umar.'

Ibn Abi Hatim narrated that Ibn Shaw'dhab said: '*And for him who fears the standing (before) his Lord there are two gardens*,' (Qur'an 55: 46) was revealed about Abu Bakr, may Allah be pleased with him.

At-Tabarani narrated in *al-Awsat* that Ibn 'Umar and Ibn 'Abbas

---

[6] 'i.e. he does not do good as a recompense for a favour that someone has shown him, rather he does it spontaneously purely for the Face of Allah' *Kitab at-Tashil li 'Ulum at-Tanzil*, Ibn Juzayy.

each said about His words, exalted is He, '*And the right-acting of the believers,*' (Qur'an 66: 4) that they were revealed about Abu Bakr and ʿUmar.

ʿAbdullah ibn Abi Humayd narrated in his *tafsir* that Mujahid said: When '*Truly Allah and His angels send blessings on the Prophet,*' (Qur'an 33: 56) was revealed, Abu Bakr said, 'Messenger of Allah, Allah has not sent down on you good but that we share in it,' and then this *ayah* was revealed, '*He is the One Who sends blessings upon you (the mu'minun) and His angels (send blessings upon you).*' (Qur'an 33: 43)

Ibn ʿAsakir narrated that ʿAli ibn al-Hussein said that this *ayah* was revealed about Abu Bakr, ʿUmar and ʿAli, '*And We wrest away that which is in their breasts of malice, as brothers on couches, facing each other.*' (Qur'an 15: 47)

Ibn ʿAsakir narrated that Ibn ʿAbbas said: There was revealed about Abu Bakr, '*And We have counselled man with good treatment of his parents,*' up to His words, '*the promise of sincerity which they were promised.*' (Qur'an 46: 15-16)

Ibn ʿAsakir narrated that Ibn ʿUyaynah said: Allah reproached all of the Muslims concerning the Messenger of Allah, may Allah bless him and grant him peace, excepting only Abu Bakr alone, for he was definitely excluded from the reproach. Then he recited, '*If you do not help him then Allah has already helped him when the ones who disbelieve expelled him as the second of two, when they two were in the cave.*' (Qur'an 9: 40).

The *hadith* related on his merit coupled with ʿUmar, apart from what has already been mentioned

The two Shaykhs narrated that Abu Hurayrah, may Allah be pleased with him, said: I heard the Messenger of Allah say, may Allah bless him and grant him peace, 'While a shepherd was in the middle of his flock, a wolf rushed upon it and carried off from it a sheep and the shepherd pursued it. The wolf turned to him and said, "Who will look after it on the Day of Rising, the day when there will be no other shepherd than me?" And as a man was driving an ox which he had laden it turned to him and said, "I was not created for this, but I was created for tillage,"' and the people said, 'Glory be to Allah, that an ox should talk?' The Prophet, may Allah bless him and grant him peace, said, 'I believe in that and Abu Bakr and ʿUmar (believe),' and Abu Bakr and ʿUmar weren't there at that time, i.e. they weren't in the gathering. He bore witness to their belief in that, perhaps meaning the perfection of their belief.

At-Tirmidhi narrated that Abu Saʿid al-Khudri said: The Messenger of Allah, may Allah bless him and grant him peace, said, 'There has been no prophet but that he had two deputies from the people of heaven and two deputies from the people of earth. As for my two deputies from the people of heaven, they are Jibril and Mika'il, and as for my two deputies from the people of earth they are Abu Bakr and ʿUmar.'

The authors of the *Sunan* collections and others narrated that Saʿid ibn Zaid said: I heard the Messenger of Allah, may Allah bless him and grant him peace, saying, 'Abu Bakr is in the Garden, ʿUmar is in the Garden, ʿUthman is in the Garden, ʿAli is in the Garden, …' and he mentioned all of the ten (who were promised the Garden).

At-Tirmidhi narrated that Abu Saʿid said: The Messenger of Allah, may Allah bless him and grant him peace, said, 'The ones of the highest ranks, those beneath them will see them as you see the stars rising over the horizon of the sky, and Abu Bakr and ʿUmar are among them.' At-Tabarani also recorded it in *hadith* of Jabir ibn Samurah and Abu Hurayrah.

At-Tirmidhi narrated that Anas said that the Messenger of Allah, may Allah bless him and grant him peace, used to come out to his companions of the *Muhajirun* and the *Ansar* while they were sitting, among them Abu Bakr and ʿUmar, and none of them would lift their eyes to him except for Abu Bakr and ʿUmar. They used to gaze upon him and he would gaze upon them and they would smile at him and he would smile at them.

At-Tirmidhi and al-Hakim narrated that Ibn ʿUmar said that the Messenger of Allah, may Allah bless him and grant him peace, went out one day and entered the mosque, with Abu Bakr and ʿUmar, one on his right hand side and the other on his left hand side, he holding their hands. He said, 'Like this we will be raised up on the Day of Rising.' At-Tabarani also recorded it in *al-Awsat* from Abu Hurayrah.

At-Tirmidhi and al-Hakim narrated that Ibn ʿUmar said: The Messenger of Allah, may Allah bless him and grant him peace, said, 'I will be the first over whom the earth will split open, then Abu Bakr and ʿUmar.'

At-Tirmidhi and al-Hakim, and he declared it *sahih*, narrated that ʿAbdullah ibn Hantab said that the Prophet, may Allah bless him and grant him peace, saw Abu Bakr and ʿUmar and said, 'These two are hearing and sight.' At-Tabarani also recorded it from *hadith* of Ibn ʿUmar and Ibn ʿAmr.

Al-Bazzar and al-Hakim narrated that Abu Arwa ad-Dawsi said: I was with the Prophet, may Allah bless him and grant him peace, (seated) and then Abu Bakr and ʿUmar came up, so he said, 'Praise belongs to Allah Who has helped me through you two.' It has been transmitted also in a *hadith* of al-Bara' ibn ʿAzib, which at-Tabarani recorded in *al-Awsat*.

Abu Yaʿla narrated that ʿAmmar ibn Yasir said: The Messenger of Allah, may Allah bless him and grant him peace, said, 'Jibril came to me previously and I said, "O Jibril, tell me of the merits of ʿUmar ibn al-Khattab." He said, "Even if I were to tell you his merits for the length of time that Nuh remained among his people the merits of ʿUmar would not be exhausted, and truly ʿUmar is one of the good actions of Abu Bakr."'

Ahmad narrated that ʿAbd ar-Rahman ibn Ghanam said that the Messenger of Allah, may Allah bless him and grant him peace, said to Abu Bakr and ʿUmar, 'If you two were to agree on a counsel I would not oppose you.' At-Tabarani also recorded it from a *hadith* of al-Bara' ibn ʿAzib.

Ibn Saʿd narrated that Ibn ʿUmar was asked, 'Who used to give *fatwa* in the time of the Messenger of Allah, may Allah bless him and grant him peace?' He said, 'Abu Bakr and ʿUmar and I know of no others apart from them.' He narrated that al-Qasim ibn Muhammad said: Abu Bakr, ʿUmar, ʿUthman and ʿAli used to give *fatwa* in the time of the Messenger of Allah, may Allah bless him and grant him peace.

At-Tabarani narrated that Ibn Masʿud, may Allah be pleased with him, said that the Messenger of Allah, may Allah bless him and grant him peace, said, 'Truly, every prophet has an elect from his *ummah* and my elect from my *ummah* are Abu Bakr and ʿUmar.'

Ibn ʿAsakir narrated that ʿAli said: The Messenger of Allah, may Allah bless him and grant him peace, said, 'May Allah show mercy to Abu Bakr. He wed me his daughter, and he carried me to the abode of the Hijrah, and he set Bilal free. May Allah show mercy to ʿUmar. He says the truth even if it is bitter. The truth has left him without a friend. May Allah show mercy to ʿUthman. The angels are shy of him. May Allah show mercy to ʿAli. O Allah, make the truth turn with him wherever he turns.'

At-Tabarani narrated that Sahl, may Allah be pleased with him, said: When the Prophet, may Allah bless him and grant him peace, came back from the Farewell Hajj, he ascended the *minbar* and praised Allah, then said, 'People, Abu Bakr has never harmed me, so know that about him. People, I am pleased with him, and with ʿUmar, ʿUthman, ʿAli, Talhah, az-Zubayr, Saʿd, ʿAbd ar-Rahman ibn ʿAwf, and the first emigrants (*muhajirun*), so know that of them.'

ʿAbdullah ibn Ahmad [Ibn Hanbal] narrated in *Zawa'id az-Zuhd* that Ibn Abi Hazim said: A man came to ʿAli ibn al-Hussein and said, 'What was the position of Abu Bakr and ʿUmar with the Messenger of Allah, may Allah bless him and grant him peace?' He said, 'Just like their position with respect to him this very hour.'

(They are buried right beside the Prophet, may Allah bless him and grant him peace).

Ibn Sa'd narrated that Bistam ibn Muslim said: The Messenger of Allah, may Allah bless him and grant him peace, said to Abu Bakr and 'Umar, 'No-one shall have command over you after me.'

Ibn 'Asakir narrated that Anas related, as a *marfu'* hadith, 'Love of Abu Bakr and 'Umar is *iman* (belief) and hatred of them is *kufr* (disbelief).'

He narrated that Ibn Mas'ud said: Love of Abu Bakr and 'Umar and a knowledge of them is (a part) of the *Sunnah*.

And he narrated that Anas related as a *marfu'*, 'I hope for my *ummah* in their love for Abu Bakr and 'Umar what I hope for them in the saying, "No god but Allah."'

The *hadith* related on his merit alone apart from what has already been mentioned

The two Shaykhs narrated that Abu Hurayrah said: I heard the Messenger of Allah saying, 'Whoever spends two of a pair of anything in the way of Allah will be called from one of the doors of the Garden, "Slave of Allah, this is good." Whoever was one of the people of prayer will be called from the door of prayer, whoever was one of the people of *jihad* will be called from the door of *jihad*, whoever was one of the people of *sadaqah* will be called from the door of *sadaqah*, and whoever was one of the people of fasting will be called from the door of fasting.' Abu Bakr said, 'There will not be any need left with one who is called from these doors. Will anyone be called from them all, Messenger of Allah?' He said, 'Yes, and I hope that you are one of them, Abu Bakr.'

Abu Dawud narrated and al-Hakim, and he declared it *sahih*, that Abu Hurayrah, may Allah be pleased with him, said: The Messenger of Allah, may Allah bless him and grant him peace, said, 'As for you, Abu Bakr, you will be the first of my *ummah* to enter the Garden.'

The two Shaykhs narrated that Abu Sa'id, may Allah be pleased with him, said: The Messenger of Allah, may Allah bless him and grant him peace, said, 'Truly, one of the most generous people to me, with his company and his property, is Abu Bakr, and if I were to take an intimate friend apart from my Lord I would have taken Abu Bakr as an intimate friend, but there is the brotherhood of Islam.' This *hadith* has been narrated by transmissions from Ibn ʿAbbas, Ibn az-Zubayr, Ibn Masʿud, Jundub ibn ʿAbdullah, al-Baraʾ, Kaʿb ibn Malik, Jabir ibn ʿAbdullah, Anas, Abu'l-Waqid al-Laythi, Abu'l-Maʿalli, ʿAʾishah, Abu Hurayrah, and Ibn ʿUmar, may Allah be pleased with all of them, and their paths of transmission have been enumerated in *ahadith* which are *mutawatir* (narrated by a number of Companions to large numbers of others).

Al-Bukhari narrated that Abu'd-Dardaʾ said: I was sitting with the Prophet, may Allah bless him and grant him peace, when Abu Bakr came up and greeted and said, 'There was something between me and ʿUmar ibn al-Khattab, and I was hasty with him, then later I regretted and I asked him to forgive me, but he refused, so I have come to you.' He said, 'May Allah forgive you, Abu Bakr,' three times. Later, ʿUmar relented and went to the house of Abu Bakr but did not find him. He came to the Prophet, may Allah bless him and grant him peace. The face of the Prophet, may Allah bless him and grant him peace, became flushed until Abu Bakr grew afraid and fell down on his knees saying, 'Messenger of Allah, by Allah, I was more in the wrong than him,' twice. The Prophet, may Allah bless him and grant him peace, said, 'Truly, Allah sent me to you and you said, "You lie," and Abu Bakr said, "You have told the truth," and he shared himself and his wealth with me. Will you leave me my companion?' saying this last twice. He was not caused any hurt after that. Ibn ʿAdi narrated that Ibn ʿUmar, may Allah be pleased with him, related the like of it, in which he said: Then the Messenger of Allah, may Allah bless him and grant him peace, said, 'Do not cause me hurt in my companion, for Allah sent me with guidance and the life-transaction of the Truth. You said, "You lie!" and Abu Bakr said, "You have told the truth." If it was not that Allah named him a "companion" I would have taken him as an intimate friend. But there is the brotherhood of Islam.'

Ibn ʿAsakir narrated that al-Miqdam said that: ʿAqil ibn Abi Talib and Abu Bakr insulted each other. Abu Bakr was a genealogist, except that he refrained because of his (ʿAqil's) kinship to the Prophet, may Allah bless him and grant him peace, and turned away from him. He complained to the Prophet, may Allah bless him and grant him peace. Then the Prophet, may Allah bless him and grant him peace, stood among the people and said, 'Will you not leave me my companion? What is your business compared to his business? For, by Allah, there is not one man of you but that upon the door of his house there is a darkness, except for the door of Abu Bakr, for upon his door there is light. By Allah, you said, "You lie!" and Abu Bakr said, "You have told the truth!" and you withheld your wealth and he was liberal to me with his wealth, and you abandoned me and he shared with me and followed me.'

Al-Bukhari narrated that Ibn ʿUmar, may Allah be pleased with both of them, said: The Messenger of Allah, may Allah bless him and grant him peace, said, 'Whoever trails his robe haughtily, Allah will not look upon him on the Day of Rising.' So Abu Bakr said, 'One of the two sides of my robe hangs loosely unless I repeatedly correct that.' The Messenger of Allah, may Allah bless him and grant him peace, said, 'You don't do it out of haughtiness.'

Muslim narrated that Abu Hurayrah, may Allah be pleased with him, said: The Messenger of Allah, may Allah bless and grant him and his family peace, said, 'Who of you has started today fasting?' Abu Bakr said, 'I did.' Then he said, 'Who of you has followed a funeral cortege?' Abu Bakr said, 'I have.' He said, 'Who of you has fed a bereft person today?' Abu Bakr said, 'I have.' He said, 'Who of you has visited a sick person today?' Abu Bakr said, 'I have.' The Messenger of Allah, may Allah bless him and grant him peace, said, 'They are not gathered together in a man but that he will enter the Garden.' This *hadith* has been transmitted in narrations of Anas ibn Malik and ʿAbd ar-Rahman ibn Abi Bakr. In the *hadith* of Anas, which al-Bayhaqi narrated in *al-Asl*, at the end of it there is, 'The Garden has become obligatory for you.' In the *hadith* of ʿAbd ar-Rahman, which al-Bazzar narrated, its wording is: The Messenger of Allah, may Allah bless him and grant him peace, performed the dawn prayer, then turned his face to his companions and said, 'Who of you has started today fasting?' So ʿUmar said, 'Messenger of Allah, I did not decide to fast yesterday, so I have not begun today fasting.' Abu Bakr said, 'But I did decide to fast yesterday so I have begun today fasting.' He said, 'Has anyone of you today visited a sick person?' So ʿUmar said, 'Messenger of Allah, we haven't left (the mosque after the dawn prayer) yet. How could we have visited a sick person?' Abu Bakr said, 'It reached me that my brother ʿAbd ar-Rahman ibn ʿAwf is complaining (of an illness) so I made my way to him to see how he is this morning.' He said, 'Has anyone of you fed a bereft person today?' ʿUmar said, 'Messenger of Allah, we haven't left yet.' Abu Bakr said, 'I entered the mosque and there was a beggar, then I found a piece of barley bread in ʿAbd ar-Rahman's (his son's) hand, so I took it and gave it to him.' Then he said, 'You! So rejoice in the Garden.' Then he said a word which pleased ʿUmar, and he (ʿUmar) claimed that he had never meant to do a good action but that Abu Bakr had preceded him to it.

Abu Yaʿla narrated that Ibn Masʿud, may Allah be pleased with him, said: I was in the mosque praying and the Messenger of Allah, may Allah bless him and grant him peace, entered, with him Abu Bakr and ʿUmar. He found me making supplication and said, 'Ask and you will be given it.' Then he said, 'Whoever loves to recite the Qur'an freshly, then let him recite with the recitation of Ibn Umm ʿAbd (an affectionate name for Ibn Masʿud).' I returned to my house and Abu Bakr came to me to give me the good news (of what the Prophet, may Allah bless him and grant him peace, had said). Then ʿUmar came and found Abu Bakr coming out having beaten him to it, so he said, 'Truly, you always outdo with good.'

Ahmad narrated with a good *isnad* that Rabiʿah al-Aslami, may Allah be pleased with him, said: There were some words between me and Abu Bakr, and he said to me something I disliked, and then he regretted it and said to me, 'Rabiʿah repeat the like of it back to me so that it can be retaliation.' I said, 'I will not do it.' Abu Bakr said, 'You must say it or I will appeal to the Messenger of Allah, may Allah bless him and grant him peace, for help against you.' I said, 'I am not going to do it.' So Abu Bakr, may Allah be pleased with him, went off to the Prophet, may Allah bless him and grant him peace, and I went off following him. Some people from Aslam came and said to me, 'May Allah show mercy to Abu Bakr. For what reason is he appealing to the Messenger of Allah, may Allah bless him and grant him peace, for help against you and he was the one who said to you what he said?' So I said, 'Do you grasp who this is? This is Abu Bakr as-Siddiq. This is the *"second of the two"* (Qur'an 9: 40), and this is the white-haired one of the Muslims. Beware that he should turn and see you supporting me against him and so become angry, then come to the Messenger of Allah, may Allah bless him and grant him peace, who will become angry because of his anger, and then Allah will become angry, because of their anger and Rabiʿah will be destroyed.' They said, 'What do you tell us to do?' He said, 'Go back.' Abu Bakr, may Allah be pleased with him, went and I alone followed him, until he came to the Messenger of Allah, may Allah bless him and grant him peace, and told him the story just as it was. He raised his head to me and said, 'Rabiʿah, what is it with you and as-Siddiq?' So I said, 'Messenger of Allah such and such happened, and he said to me a word which I disliked, and then he said to me, "Say as I said so that it will be retaliation," and I refused.' Then the Messenger of Allah, may Allah bless him and grant him peace, 'Right! Do not repeat it back to him, but rather say, "May Allah forgive you,

Abu Bakr.'" So I said to him, 'May Allah forgive you, Abu Bakr.' (Al-Hasan said: So Abu Bakr, may Allah be pleased with him, turned away and he was weeping).

At-Tirmidhi narrated, and he declared it *hasan*, that Ibn ʿUmar, may Allah be pleased with both of them, said that the Messenger of Allah, may Allah bless him and grant him peace, said to Abu Bakr, 'You are my companion at the *hawd* (Pool) and my companion in the cave.' Its *isnad* is good.

ʿAbdullah ibn Ahmad, may Allah be pleased with him, narrated that Ibn ʿAbbas, may Allah be pleased with him, said: The Messenger of Allah, may Allah bless him and grant him peace, said, 'Abu Bakr was my companion and my solace in the cave.'

Al-Bayhaqi narrated that Hudhayfah, may Allah be pleased with him, said: The Messenger of Allah, may Allah bless him and grant him peace, said, 'There are in the Garden birds the likes of Bactrian camels.' Abu Bakr, 'Truly, they must be blessed, Messenger of Allah.' He said, 'More blessed than them is whoever eats them, and you are one of those who will eat them.' This *hadith* has been narrated in a transmission of Anas.

Abu Yaʿla narrated that Abu Hurayrah, may Allah be pleased with him, said: The Messenger of Allah, may Allah bless him and grant him peace, said, 'I was made to ascend to heaven. I did not pass by a heaven but I found in it my name, "Muhammad is the Messenger of Allah and Abu Bakr as-Siddiq is his successor."' Its *isnad* is weak but it has been narrated also in *hadith* of Ibn ʿAbbas, Ibn ʿUmar, Anas, Abu Saʿid, and Abu'd-Dardaʾ, may Allah be pleased with all of them, with weak *isnads*, yet which support and strengthen each other.

Ibn Abi Hatim and Abu Nuʿaym narrated that Saʿid ibn Jubayr,[7] may Allah be pleased with him, said: I recited in the presence of the Prophet, may Allah bless him and grant him peace, '*O you self*

---

[7] Saʿid ibn Jubayr was an eminent Follower and not a Companion. Perhaps the Companion from whom he narrates is missing, or the name is a mistake.

made tranquil!' (Qur'an 89: 28-30) and Abu Bakr said, 'Messenger of Allah, this is beautiful.' So the Messenger of Allah, may Allah bless him and grant him peace, said, 'Certainly the angel will say it to you at the time of death.'

Ibn Abi Hatim narrated that ᶜAmir ibn ᶜAbdullah ibn az-Zubayr, may Allah be pleased with him, said: When, '*And if we had decreed for them, "Kill yourselves!"*' (Qur'an 4: 66) to the end of the *ayah* was revealed, Abu Bakr said, 'Messenger of Allah, if you had ordered me to kill myself I would have done it.' He said, 'You have told the truth.'

Abu'l-Qasim al-Baghawi narrated: Dawud ibn ᶜUmar narrated to us: ᶜAbdu'l-Jabbar ibn al-Ward narrated that Ibn Abi Mulaykah said: The Messenger of Allah, may Allah bless him and grant him peace, and his companions entered a pool and he said, 'Let every man swim to his companion.' He said: So every man swam until there only remained the Messenger of Allah, may Allah bless him and grant him peace, and Abu Bakr. So the Messenger of Allah, may Allah bless him and grant him peace, swam to Abu Bakr until he embraced him, and said, 'If I were to take an intimate friend until I meet Allah I would have taken Abu Bakr as an intimate friend, but he is my companion.' Wakiᶜ concurred with him from ᶜAbdu'l-Jabbar ibn al-Ward. Ibn ᶜAsakir recorded it. ᶜAbdu'l-Jabbar is trustworthy and his shaykh, Ibn Abi Mulaykah is an imam, apart from the fact that it is a *mursal* except that it is very unusual (*ghareeb*). I say: at-Tabarani narrated it in *al-Kabir*, Ibn Shahin in *as-Sunnah* in another way connected back through Ibn ᶜAbbas.

Ibn Abi'd-Dunya narrated in *Makarim al-Akhlaq* and Ibn ᶜAsakir by way of Sadaqah ibn Maimun al-Qurashi that Sulayman ibn Yasar said: The Messenger of Allah, may Allah bless him and grant him peace, said, 'The qualities of good are three hundred and sixty qualities. Whenever Allah wishes good for a slave He puts in him one of those qualities by which he enters the Garden.' Abu Bakr said, 'Messenger of Allah, is there in me anything of them?' He said, 'Yes, a summing of them all.'

Ibn ʿAsakir narrated by another route from Sadaqah al-Qurashi related from a man that he said: The Messenger of Allah, may Allah bless him and grant him peace, said, 'The qualities of good are three hundred and sixty.' So Abu Bakr said, 'Messenger of Allah, do I have anything of them?' He said, 'All of them are in you, so therefore joy to you, Abu Bakr.'

Ibn ʿAsakir narrated by way of Mujammaʿ ibn Yaʿqub al-Ansari from his father that he said: The circle of the Prophet, may Allah bless him and grant him peace, was numerous and tightly gathered together until it became like walls. Abu Bakr's seat would be empty, and none of the people would aspire to it. When Abu Bakr came he would sit in that spot, and the Prophet, may Allah bless him and grant him peace, would turn his face to him, and direct his discourse to him, and people would listen.

Ibn ʿAsakir narrated that Anas, may Allah be pleased with him, said: The Prophet, may Allah bless him and grant him peace, said, 'Love of Abu Bakr and gratitude to him are a duty on everyone of my *ummah*.' He narrated the like of it in a *hadith* of Sahl ibn Saʿd.

He narrated that ʿA'ishah, may Allah be pleased with her, in a *hadith* which is *marfuʿ*, said: All people will be taken to account except for Abu Bakr.

That which has been related from the Companions and the right-acting early generations on his merit

Al-Bukhari narrated that Jabir, may Allah be pleased with him, said: ʿUmar ibn al-Khattab said, 'Abu Bakr is our chief (*Sayyid*).'

Al-Bayhaqi narrated in *Shuʿab al-Iman* that ʿUmar, may Allah be pleased with him, said, 'If the *iman* of Abu Bakr were to be weighed against the *iman* of the inhabitants of the earth, he would outweigh them.'

Ibn Abi Khaythamah and ʿAbdullah ibn Ahmad, in *Zawa'id az-Zuhd*, that ʿUmar, may Allah be pleased with him, said, 'Abu Bakr was a surpassing outstripper.' And ʿUmar said, 'I would that

I were a hair upon the chest of Abu Bakr.' Musaddad narrated it in his *Musnad*. And he said, 'I would love to be in the Garden in such a position that I could see Abu Bakr.' Ibn Abi'd-Dunya and Ibn ᶜAsakir narrated it. And he said, 'Certainly the scent of Abu Bakr was sweeter than the scent of musk.' Abu Nuᶜaym narrated it.

Ibn ᶜAsakir narrated that ᶜAli entered upon Abu Bakr when he was shrouded and said, 'No-one who will meet Allah with his pages (of the records of his deeds) is more beloved to me than this shrouded one.'

Ibn ᶜAsakir narrated that ᶜAbd ar-Rahman ibn Abi Bakr as-Siddiq said: The Prophet, may Allah bless him and grant him peace, said, 'ᶜUmar ibn al-Khattab told me that he never attempted to be before Abu Bakr in a good action but that Abu Bakr was before him in it.'

At-Tabarani narrated in *al-Awsat* that ᶜAli said: By the One in Whose hand is my self, we never strove to be first in a good action but that Abu Bakr was before us in it.

He also narrated in *al-Awsat* from Juhayfah that ᶜAli said: The best of mankind after the Messenger of Allah, may Allah bless him and grant him peace, are Abu Bakr and ᶜUmar. Love of me will never be united with hatred of Abu Bakr and ᶜUmar in the heart of a believer.

He narrated in *al-Kabir* that Ibn ᶜUmar said: Three of Quraysh are the most handsome faced of Quraysh and the best of them in character, and the surest hearted of them. If they were to tell you something they would not lie to you. If you told them something they would not call you a liar; Abu Bakr as-Siddiq, Abu ᶜUbaydah ibn al-Jarrah and ᶜUthman ibn ᶜAffan.

Ibn Saᶜd narrated that Ibrahim an-Nakhaᶜi said: Abu Bakr was named, '*Al-Awwah* – Compassionate (literally: one saying "Ah" and sighing a great deal for pity for people),' because of his pity and his mercy.

Ibn ᶜAsakir narrated that ar-Rabiᶜ ibn Anas said: It is recorded in the First Book, 'The likeness of Abu Bakr as-Siddiq is the likeness of rain, wherever it falls it is of benefit.'

Ibn ʿAsakir narrated that ar-Rabiʿ ibn Anas said: We considered the companions of the prophets and we couldn't find a prophet who had a companion the like of Abu Bakr as-Siddiq. He narrated that az-Zuhri said: One of the merits of Abu Bakr is that he never doubted about Allah for an hour.

He narrated that az-Zubayr ibn Bakkar said: I heard one of the people of knowledge saying, 'The orators (who gave the *khutbah*) among the companions of the Messenger of Allah, may Allah bless him and grant him peace, were Abu Bakr as-Siddiq and ʿAli ibn Abi Talib, may Allah be pleased with both of them.'

He narrated that Abu Husayn said: There was not born to Adam among his descendants anyone better than Abu Bakr, after the prophets and messengers. Abu Bakr took a stand on the Day of *ar-Riddah* (repudiation of Islam by many of the Arab tribes on the death of the Prophet, may Allah bless him and grant him peace) which was like the stand of one of the prophets.

Section

Ad-Dinuri narrated, in *al-Mujalasah*, and Ibn ʿAsakir that ash-Shaʿbi said: Allah singled out Abu Bakr for four qualities with which he did not single out any other person: He named him as-Siddiq and named no-one apart from him as-Siddiq; and he was the Companion of the Cave along with the Messenger of Allah, may Allah bless him and grant him peace; his close companion on the Hijrah; and the Messenger of Allah, may Allah bless him and grant him peace, ordered him to lead the prayer while the Muslims were witnesses to that.

Ibn Abi Dawud narrated in *Kitab al-Masahif* that Jaʿfar said: Abu Bakr used to listen to the intimate conversation of Jibril with the Prophet, may Allah bless him and grant him peace, without seeing him.

Al-Hakim narrated that Ibn al-Musayyab said: Abu Bakr was, in relation to the Prophet, may Allah bless him and grant him peace, in the position of a deputy and he would take his counsel in all his affairs. He was his second in Islam, and his second in the Cave, his second in the shelter on the Day of Badr, and his second in the grave. The Messenger of Allah, may Allah bless him and grant him peace, would not prefer anyone over him.

The *hadith* and *ayat* which indicate his *khilafah*, and the words of the *imams* on that

At-Tirmidhi narrated, and he declared it *hasan*, and al-Hakim, and he declared it *sahih*, that Hudhayfah, may Allah be pleased with him, said: The Messenger of Allah, may Allah bless him and grant him peace, said, 'Follow the lead of the two who come after me, Abu Bakr and ᶜUmar.' At-Tabarani narrated it from a *hadith* of Abu'd-Darda' and al-Hakim in a *hadith* of Ibn Masᶜud, may Allah be pleased with him.

Abu'l-Qasim al-Baghawi narrated with a good *isnad* that ᶜAbdullah ibn ᶜUmar, may Allah be pleased with him, said: I heard the Messenger of Allah, may Allah bless him and grant him peace, saying, 'There will be twelve *khalifahs* after me; Abu Bakr will only last for a little.' There is unanimous agreement on the authenticity of the first part of this *hadith*, as it is narrated by many different paths. Its explanation has been given earlier in the introduction of the book. In the two *sahih* books in the preceding *hadith* there is that he, may Allah bless him and grant him peace, when he gave a *khutbah* close to his death, said, 'There is a slave whom Allah has given a choice …' and in the end of which there is, 'And let not a door remain but that it is closed except for the door of Abu Bakr.' And in a wording of the two of them (al-Bukhari and Muslim), 'Let there not remain in the mosque a passageway except the passageway of Abu Bakr.' The men of knowledge say, 'This is an indication of the *khilafah* because he would go out by it (the door and passageway) to take the lead in the prayer for the Muslims.' This has been narrated of a *hadith* of Anas, may Allah be pleased with him, and its wording is, 'Close these doors which open into the mosque except for the door of Abu Bakr.' It is narrated by Ibn ʿAdi. And it is recorded in *hadith* of ʿA'ishah, may Allah be pleased with her, which at-Tirmidhi and others narrated, and in a *hadith* of Ibn ʿAbbas in *Zawa'id al-Musnad*, and in a *hadith* of Muʿawiyah ibn Abi Sufyan which at-Tabarani narrated, and in a *hadith* of Anas narrated by al-Bazzar.

The two Shaykhs narrated that Jubayr ibn Mutʿim, may Allah be pleased with him, related from his father that he said: A woman came to the Prophet, may Allah bless him and grant him peace, and he told her to come back to him later. She said, 'What do you think if I come and don't find you?' as if she were saying, 'Death.' He said, 'If you don't find me then come to Abu Bakr.'

Al-Hakim narrated, and he declared it *sahih*, that Anas, may Allah be pleased with him, said: Banu Mustaliq sent me to the Messenger of Allah, may Allah bless him and grant him peace, (saying), 'Ask him, "To whom should we pay our *sadaqat* (*zakat*) after you?"' So I came to him and asked him and he said, 'To Abu Bakr.'

Ibn ʿAsakir narrated that Ibn ʿAbbas, may Allah be pleased with both of them, said: A woman came to the Prophet, may Allah bless him and grant him peace, to ask him about something. He said to her, 'Return (another time).' She said, 'Messenger of Allah, if I return and I don't find you?' (referring to his death). He said, 'If you come and don't find me, then come to Abu Bakr, for he is the *khalifah* after me.'

Muslim narrated that ʿA'ishah, may Allah be pleased with her, said: The Messenger of Allah, may Allah bless him and grant him peace, said to her, 'Call your father (Abu Bakr) and your brother so that I can write something, for I fear that some desirous person will covet, and someone will say, "I am more worthy," and Allah and the believers refuse all except Abu Bakr.'

Ahmad and others narrated it by various routes from her in some of which she said: The Prophet, may Allah bless him and grant him peace, said to me in his sickness in which he died, 'Call ʿAbd ar-Rahman ibn Abi Bakr and I will write a testament for Abu Bakr so that no-one will disagree about him after me.' Then later he said, 'Leave it. I seek refuge with Allah that the believers should disagree about Abu Bakr.'

Muslim narrated that ʿA'ishah, may Allah be pleased with her, was asked, 'Who would the Prophet, may Allah bless him and grant him peace, have left as *khalifah* if he had left a *khalifah*?' She said, 'Abu Bakr.' It was said to her, 'Then who after Abu Bakr?' She said, 'ʿUmar.' It was said to her, 'Who after ʿUmar?' She said, 'Abu ʿUbaydah ibn al-Jarrah.'

The two Shaykhs narrated that Abu Musa al-Ashʿari, may Allah be pleased with him, said: The Prophet, may Allah bless him and grant him peace, became ill and his illness became severe. So he said, 'Command Abu Bakr and let him lead the people in prayer.' ʿA'ishah said, 'Messenger of Allah, he is a man who has a tender heart. If he stands in your place he will not be able to lead the people in prayer.' He said, 'Command Abu Bakr and let him lead the people in prayer.' She repeated what she had said and so he said, 'Command Abu Bakr and let him lead the people in prayer; truly you are the female companions of Yusuf.' So the messenger came to him (Abu Bakr) and he led the people in prayer in the lifetime of the Prophet, may Allah bless him and grant him peace. This *hadith* is *mutawatir* and it is also narrated in *hadith* of ʿA'ishah, Ibn Masʿud, Ibn ʿAbbas, Ibn ʿUmar, ʿAbdullah ibn Zamʿah, Abu Saʿid, ʿAli ibn Abi Talib and Hafsah, may Allah be pleased with her, and I have classified their routes of transmission among the *mutawatir hadith*. In some of the versions of the *hadith* of ʿA'ishah, may Allah be pleased with her, she said, 'I persisted in that with the Messenger of Allah, may Allah bless him and grant him peace. All that carried me to do that was that it did not occur to me in my heart that people could ever love a man who stood in his position after him. It was only that I was of the view that never would anyone stand in his position but that people would take a bad omen from it, and so I wished that the Messenger of Allah, may Allah bless him and grant him peace, might turn from Abu Bakr.'

Ibn Zam'ah, may Allah be pleased with him, said that the Prophet, may Allah bless him and grant him peace, ordered them to perform the prayer and Abu Bakr was not there, so that 'Umar stepped forward and he prayed (as *imam*). The Prophet, may Allah bless him and grant him peace, said, 'No! No! No! Allah and the Muslims refuse any but Abu Bakr. Let Abu Bakr lead the people in prayer.'

Ibn 'Umar said: 'Umar said, '*Allahu Akbar.*' The Prophet, may Allah bless him and grant him peace, heard his '*Allahu Akbar*', raised his head in anger and said, 'Where is Ibn Abi Quhafah?'

The men of knowledge say: In this *hadith* there is the clearest of proofs that as-Siddiq was absolutely the best of the Companions, and the one having most right to the *khilafah*, and the most worthy of them for leadership.

Al-Ash'ari said: It is known of necessity that the Prophet, may Allah bless him and grant him peace, ordered as-Siddiq that he should lead the people in prayer in the presence of the *Muhajirun* and the *Ansar*. Along with his saying, 'He must lead the people who is the best read of them in the Book of Allah,' it proves that he (Abu Bakr) was the best read of them, i.e. the most knowledgeable of them in the Qur'an.

The Companions themselves sought to prove by this that he was the one with the most right to the *khilafah*, among them 'Umar – and his words will follow in the section on the act of pledging allegiance – and among them 'Ali.

Ibn 'Asakir narrated that he ['Ali] said: Truly the Prophet ordered Abu Bakr to lead the people in prayer and indeed I was present, and I was not absent and was not ill; and we were pleased for our worldly affairs with the one whom the Prophet, may Allah bless him and grant him peace, was pleased with for our *deen*.

The men of knowledge say that Abu Bakr was recognised for his fitness for the *imamah* during the time of the Prophet, may Allah bless him and grant him peace.

Ahmad, Abu Dawud and others narrated that Sahl ibn Sa'd said: There was fighting among Bani 'Amr ibn 'Awf and it reached the Prophet, may Allah bless him and grant him peace, so he came to them after the midday prayer in order to make peace between them. He said to Bilal, 'If it is the time of the prayer, and I don't come, then order Abu Bakr to lead the people in prayer.' When it was time for the afternoon prayer Bilal announced the prayer (with the *iqamah*) and then ordered Abu Bakr, so he led the prayer.

Abu Bakr ash-Shafi'i narrated, in *al-Ghaylaniyyat*, and Ibn 'Asakir that Hafsah, may Allah be pleased with her, said to the Prophet, may Allah bless him and grant him peace, 'When you were ill you gave precedence to Abu Bakr.' He said, 'I am not the one who gives precedence to him, but it is Allah Who gives him precedence.'

Ad-Daraqutni narrated, in *al-Afrad*, al-Khateeb and Ibn 'Asakir that 'Ali, may Allah be pleased with him, said: The Prophet, may Allah bless him and grant him peace, said to me, 'I asked Allah to give precedence to you three times, but He refused me save to give precedence to Abu Bakr.'

Ibn Sa'd narrated that al-Hasan said: Abu Bakr said, 'Messenger of Allah, I still see myself (in dream) treading in people's courtyards.' He said, 'You will be, among men, on a way (*sabeel*).' He said, 'And I saw on my breast something like two small dark marks.' He said, 'Two years.'

Ibn 'Asakir narrated that Abu Bakrah said: I came to 'Umar, and there were people with him eating. He threw a look among the hindmost of the people to a man and said, 'What do you find in what you read of the books from before you?' He said, 'The *khalifah* of the Prophet, may Allah bless him and grant him peace, is his Siddiq.'

Ibn 'Asakir narrated that Muhammad ibn az-Zubayr said: 'Umar ibn 'Abd al-'Aziz sent me to al-Hasan al-Basri to ask him some things. So I came to him and said, 'Satisfy me regarding that about which people disagree. Did the Prophet, may Allah bless him and grant him peace, appoint Abu Bakr as *khalifah*?' So al-Hasan who was seated drew himself up and said, 'Is it in any doubt? You have no father (a proverbial Arabic expression)! By Allah, the One Whom there is no god but Him, he definitely appointed him as *khalifah*. He was certainly more knowing of Allah, and more fearfully obedient of Him, and more strongly fearful of Him than that he should die upon it without making him take the command.'

Ibn ʿAdi narrated that Abu Bakr ibn ʿAyyash said: Ar-Rashid said to me, 'Abu Bakr, how did the people appoint Abu Bakr as *khalifah*?' I said, '*Amir al-Mu'minin*, Allah was silent, and His Messenger was silent and the *mu'minun* were silent.' He said, 'By Allah, you have only increased me in confusion.' He said, '*Amir al-Mu'minin*, the Prophet, may Allah bless him and grant him peace, was sick for eight days and Bilal entered upon him and said, "Messenger of Allah, who should lead the people in prayer?" He said, "Order Abu Bakr to lead the people in prayer." So Abu Bakr led the people in prayer for eight days while the revelation was still descending. So the Messenger of Allah, may Allah bless him and grant him peace, was silent because of the silence of Allah, and the *mu'minun* were silent because of the silence of the Messenger of Allah, may Allah bless him and grant him peace.' So he (Ibn ʿAyyash) astonished him (ar-Rashid), and he said, 'May Allah bless you.'

A group of the men of knowledge deduced the *khilafah* of as-Siddiq from *ayat* of the Qur'an. Al-Hasan al-Basri said, concerning His words, exalted is He, '*O you who believe, whoever of you reneges on his deen then Allah will bring a people whom He loves and who love Him, ...*' (Qur'an 5: 54) – 'It means Abu Bakr and his companions, for, when the Arabs reneged on their Islam, Abu Bakr and his companions waged *jihad* against them until they made them return to Islam.'

Yunus ibn Bukayr narrated that Qatadah said, 'When the Prophet, may Allah bless him and grant him peace, died, the Arabs reneged (on their Islam).' Then he mentioned Abu Bakr's fighting them until he said, 'We used to say that this *ayah* was revealed about Abu Bakr and his companions, "*Then Allah will bring a people whom He loves and who love Him.*" (Qur'an 5: 54)'

Ibn Abi Hatim narrated that Juwaybir said, concerning His words, exalted is He, '*Say to those who were left behind of the desert Arabs, "You will be called to (fight) a people of great power ..."*' (Qur'an 48: 16), 'They were Banu Hanifah.' Ibn Abi Hatim and Ibn Qutaybah said, 'This *ayah* is a proof of the *khilafah* of as-Siddiq, because he was the one who called people to fight them.'

The Shaykh Abu'l-Hasan al-Ash'ari said: I heard Abu'l-'Abbas ibn Shurayh saying, 'The *khilafah* of as-Siddiq is in the Qur'an in this *ayah* (above).' He said, 'Because the people of knowledge unanimously agree that after its revelation there was not any fight which they were called to except for Abu Bakr's calling them, and the people, to fight those who reneged (on their Islam) and refused the *zakat*.' He said, 'That indicates the necessity of the *khilafah* of Abu Bakr and the obligation of obedience to him, since Allah informs us that the one who turns away from that will be punished painfully.' Ibn Kathir said: And whoever explains the 'people of great power' as being the Persians and the Byzantines then as-Siddiq is the one who equipped and prepared the armies to go against them, and the completion of their affair was left to 'Umar and 'Uthman who are two branches of as-Siddiq. And Allah, exalted is He, says, '*Allah has promised the ones who believe and do right actions that He will definitely appoint them as khulafa' in the land, ...*' (Qur'an 24: 55) up to the conclusion of the *ayah*. This *ayah* fits the *khilafah* of as-Siddiq.

Ibn Abi Hatim narrated in his *tafsir* that 'Abd ar-Rahman ibn 'Abd al-Hamid al-Mahdi said: The granting of authority to Abu Bakr and 'Umar is in the Book of Allah. Allah, exalted is He, says, '*Allah has promised the ones who believe and do right actions that*

He will definitely appoint them as khulafa' in the land, ...' up to the conclusion of the *ayah*.

Al-Khateeb narrated that Abu Bakr ibn 'Ayyash said: Abu Bakr as-Siddiq is the *khalifah* of the Messenger of Allah, may Allah bless him and grant him peace, in the Qur'an, because Allah, exalted is He, says, *'For the poor emigrants who were expelled from their homes and their properties seeking bounty from Allah and contentment, and they help Allah and His Messenger. Those they are the truthful.'* (Qur'an 59: 8). The ones Allah named 'truthful (*siddiqun*)' are not liars, and they said, 'Khalifah of the Messenger of Allah.' Ibn Kathir said: A good deduction.

Al-Bayhaqi narrated from az-Za'farani that ash-Shafi'i said: People are unanimously agreed on the *khilafah* of Abu Bakr as-Siddiq. That is because people were hard pressed after the Messenger of Allah, may Allah bless him and grant him peace, but they did not find under the expanse of the sky one better than Abu Bakr, so they gave him authority over them.

Asad as-Sunnah narrated in his *Fada'il* that Mu'awiyah ibn Qurrah said: The Companions of the Messenger of Allah, may Allah bless him and grant him peace, never doubted that Abu Bakr was the *khalifah* of the Messenger of Allah, may Allah bless him and grant him peace, and they would not call him anything but the *khalifah* of the Messenger of Allah, may Allah bless him and grant him peace, and they never agreed unanimously on a mistake or a misguidance.

Al-Hakim narrated, and he declared it *sahih*, that Ibn Mas'ud, may Allah be pleased with him, said: What the Muslims view as good is with Allah good. And what the Muslims view as bad is with Allah bad. The Companions all held the view that they should appoint Abu Bakr as the *khalifah*.

Al-Hakim narrated, and adh-Dhahabi declared it *sahih*, that Murrah at-Tayyib said: Abu Sufyan ibn Harb came to 'Ali and said, 'What is it with this authority that it is among the very least of

Quraysh and the humblest of them?' meaning Abu Bakr, 'By Allah, if I had wished I would have filled it against him with horses and men.' He said that ʿAli said, 'How long you have been at enmity with Islam and its people, Abu Sufyan, and that did not hurt it at all. We found Abu Bakr worthy of it (the *khilafah*).'

The oath of allegiance to him

The two Shaykhs narrated that ʿUmar ibn al-Khattab, may Allah be pleased with him, addressed the people upon his return from the Hajj and said in his *khutbah*: It has reached me that so-and-so of you said, 'If ʿUmar were to die I would pledge allegiance to so-and-so.' Let no man deceive himself by saying, 'The pledge of allegiance to Abu Bakr was made suddenly and unexpectedly.' It was like that but Allah protected (us) from the evil of it. There is not among you today one behind whom the necks of competitors stop short (an Arabic expression) like Abu Bakr. He was one of the best of us when the Messenger of Allah, may Allah bless him and grant him peace, died. ʿAli and az-Zubayr and those with them stayed back in the house of Fatimah. The *Ansar* all stayed away from us in the roofed gallery of Bani Saʿidah. The *Muhajirun* gathered around Abu Bakr, so I said to him, 'Abu Bakr, let us be off to our brethren, the *Ansar*.' So we went off until two good men met us and mentioned to us what the people had done. They said, 'Where do you intend (going) *Muhajirun*?' I said, 'We want our brethren the *Ansar*.' They said, 'You must not approach them, but decide your own affair, *Muhajirun*.' I said, 'By Allah, we will go to them.' We went on until we came to them in the roofed gallery of Bani Saʿidah and there they were all gathered, and right in the middle of them a man all muffled up. I said, 'Who is this?' They said, 'Saʿd ibn ʿUbadah.' I said, What is wrong with him?' They said, 'He is in pain.' When we sat down, their speaker stood, praised Allah as He is worthy and said, 'And now, we are the *Ansar* of Allah, and the battalion of Islam and you, *Muhajirun*, are a handful of us, and a party of you have come at a leisurely pace wishing to uproot us and exclude us from the command.' When he became silent I wanted to speak. I had prepared a speech that pleased me and which I wanted to deliver in the presence of Abu Bakr. I used to fear in him a lack of incisiveness and he was milder, more forbearing than me and more dignified. Then Abu Bakr said, 'Gently.' I disliked to anger him, and he was more knowledgeable than me. By Allah, he did not leave a word that had pleased me in my prepared speech but that he said it in his spontaneous talk, the like of it and better than it until he was silent. He said, 'Now, as for that good which you have mentioned about yourselves, you are worthy of it, but the Arabs will never recognise this command except among this section of Quraysh. They are the midmost (noblest) of the Arabs by descent and by tribe, and I am contented for you with either of these two men, (so pledge allegiance to) whichever of them you wish.' He took hold of my hand and the hand of Abu ʿUbaydah ibn al-Jarrah (and he was seated between us) and I disliked nothing he had said apart from that. It was, by Allah, such that if I were to be put forward and my head struck off, that not approaching me because of any guilt, it would have been more beloved to me than that I should assume command over a people among whom was Abu Bakr. Then a speaker from them said, 'I am of those by means of whose counsel people seek relief and one having a family that will aid and defend me (literally, 'I am their much-rubbed little rubbing post and their honoured little palm-tree'). Let there be from us an *amir* and from you an *amir*, Quraysh.' Then the confusion increased and voices were raised until I became afraid of dissension, so I said, 'Stretch out your hand, Abu Bakr,' and he stretched out his hand and I swore allegiance to him, the *Muhajirun* swore allegiance to him, then the *Ansar* swore allegiance to him. By Allah, we did not find in that for which we assembled a matter more fitting than the pledge of allegiance to Abu Bakr. We feared that if we separated from the people and there was no pledge of allegiance that they would conclude a pledge of allegiance after we had gone, and we would have to pledge allegiance on a basis with which we were not pleased, or we would have to oppose them so that there would be strife over that.

An-Nasa'i, Abu Ya'la and al-Hakim, who declared it *sahih*, narrated that Ibn Mas'ud said: When the Messenger of Allah, may Allah bless him and grant him peace, was taken, the *Ansar* said, 'Let there be from us an *amir* and from you an *amir*.' 'Umar ibn al-Khattab, may Allah be pleased with him, came to them and said, '*Ansar*, do you not know that the Messenger of Allah, may Allah bless him and grant him peace, ordered Abu Bakr to lead the people (in *salah*)? So which of you would be pleased to give himself precedence over Abu Bakr?' The *Ansar* said, 'We seek refuge with Allah that we should give ourselves precedence over Abu Bakr.'

Ibn Sa'd, al-Hakim and al-Bayhaqi narrated that Abu Sa'id al-Khudri said: The Messenger of Allah, may Allah bless him and grant him peace, died and the people assembled in the house of Sa'd ibn 'Ubadah and among them were Abu Bakr and 'Umar, and the public speakers of the *Ansar* stood up and one of them began to speak, saying, 'You men of the *Muhajirun*, whenever the Messenger of Allah, may Allah bless him and his family and grant them peace, appointed one of you to any position of authority, he paired one of us with him; we think therefore that a man from us and a man from you should be appointed to this command.' The public speakers of the *Ansar* followed each other on that same theme. Then Zaid ibn Thabit stood up and said, 'Do you not know that the Messenger of Allah, may Allah bless him and grant him peace, was one of the *Muhajirun* and his *khalifah* is one of the *Muhajirun* and we were the *Ansar* of the Messenger of Allah and we shall be the *Ansar* of the *khalifah* of the Messenger of Allah just as we were his *Ansar*.' He took the hand of Abu Bakr and said, 'This is your man,' then 'Umar swore allegiance to him and then the *Muhajirun* and the *Ansar*. Abu Bakr ascended the *minbar* and looked at people's faces and did not find az-Zubayr, so he called for az-Zubayr and he came. He (Abu Bakr) said, 'You said, son of the aunt of the Messenger of Allah, may Allah bless him and grant him peace, and his disciple, that you want to break the staff of the Muslims.' So he said, 'There is no blame on you Khalifah of the Messenger of Allah,' and he stood and pledged allegiance to him. Then he looked at the faces of the people and could not see ʿAli so he summoned him and he came. He said, 'You said, son of the uncle of the Messenger of Allah, may Allah bless him and grant him peace, and his relation through marriage to his daughter, that you want to break the staff of the Muslims.' So he said, 'There is no blame on you, Khalifah of the Messenger of Allah,' and he pledged allegiance to him.

Ibn Ishaq said in *as-Sirah*: az-Zuhri narrated to me: Anas ibn Malik narrated to me and he said: When Abu Bakr was pledged allegiance in the assembly hall, then, on the morrow, he sat upon the *minbar* and ʿUmar stood and spoke before Abu Bakr, praised Allah, and said, 'Allah has gathered your authority to the best of you, the Companion of the Messenger of Allah and the "*second of the two when they two were in the cave*" (Qur'an 9: 40), so stand and pledge allegiance to him,' and the people pledged allegiance to Abu Bakr with a general and public allegiance after the allegiance made in the assembly hall. Then Abu Bakr spoke, praised Allah, and said, 'And now, people, I have been put in authority over you and I am not the best of you. So if I do right then help me, and if I do wrong then put me straight. Truthfulness is a sacred trust and lying is a betrayal. The weak one among you is strong as far as I am concerned until I restore to him his right, *insha'Allah*, and the strong one of you is weak until I take what is due from him, *insha'Allah*. No people forsake *jihad* in the way of Allah but that Allah delivers a humiliating blow to them. Nor does indecency ever spread among a people but that Allah envelops them in trials. Obey me as long as I obey Allah and His Messenger, and if I disobey Allah and His Messenger then you do not owe me obedience. Stand up for your prayer, may Allah have mercy upon you.'

Musa ibn ʿUqbah narrated, in his *Maghazi*, and al-Hakim, who declared it *sahih*, that ʿAbd ar-Rahman ibn ʿAwf said: Abu Bakr gave an address (*khutbah*) and said, 'By Allah, I was never eager for a position of command for even as long as a day or a night, and I never desired it, and I have never asked Allah for it in secret nor openly. However, I was afraid of dissension. I will have no rest in command. I have been invested with a mighty matter for which I have not the energy, nor the power, except it be by Allah's strengthening.' ʿAli and az-Zubayr said, 'We were not angry except that we were too late for the counsel, and we see Abu Bakr as the person most fitted for it. He was the Companion of the Cave. We know his honour and his excellence. The Messenger of Allah, may Allah bless him and grant him peace, ordered him to lead the people in prayer while he was yet alive.'

Ibn Saʿd narrated that Ibrahim at-Tamimi said: When the Messenger of Allah, may Allah bless him and his family and grant them peace, died, ʿUmar came to Abu ʿUbaydah ibn al-Jarrah and said, 'Stretch out your hand so that I can pledge allegiance to you. You are the trusted one of this *ummah* according to the tongue of the Prophet, may Allah bless him and grant him peace.' So Abu ʿUbaydah said to ʿUmar, 'I never thought you weak in your mind before this, since I became a Muslim. Would you pledge allegiance to me when among you there is as-Siddiq, the "*second of the two*"?'

Muhammad ibn Abi Bakr said that Abu Bakr said to ʿUmar, 'Stretch out your hand so that I can pledge allegiance to you.' ʿUmar said to him, You are better than me.' Abu Bakr said to him, 'You are stronger than me,' and he repeated it, but ʿUmar said, 'My strength shall be for you along with your merit,' and he swore allegiance to him.

Ahmad narrated that Humayd ibn ʿAbd ar-Rahman ibn ʿAwf said: The Messenger of Allah, may Allah bless him and grant him peace, died while Abu Bakr was with some of the people of

Madinah, so he came and uncovered his face and kissed him and said, 'May my father and mother be your ransom, how sweet you are in life and death. Muhammad has died, by the Lord of the Ka'bah!' and he mentioned the rest of the *hadith* and then he said: Abu Bakr and 'Umar went off in haste until they came to them. Then Abu Bakr spoke and he didn't leave out anything that Allah had revealed about the *Ansar* nor anything that the Messenger of Allah, may Allah bless him and grant him peace, had mentioned about them but that he mentioned it, and he said, 'You know that the Messenger of Allah, may Allah bless him and grant him peace, said, "If mankind were to travel in one valley and the *Ansar* were to travel in another valley, I would travel in the valley of the *Ansar*." You know, Sa'd, that the Messenger of Allah, may Allah bless him and grant him peace, said while you were seated, "Quraysh are the authorities of this matter, and the best of mankind will follow the best of them and the worst of them will follow the worst of them."' So Sa'd said to him, 'You have told the truth. We are the deputies and you are the commanders.'

Ibn 'Asakir narrated that Abu Sa'id al-Khudri said: When Abu Bakr was pledged allegiance, he saw some dejection among people and so he said, 'What is holding you back? Am I not the one with the most right to this command? Am I not the first to accept Islam? Am I not …? Am I not …?' and he mentioned various qualities.

Ahmad narrated that ar-Rafi' at-Ta'i said: Abu Bakr told me about his pledge of allegiance and what the *Ansar* had said, and what 'Umar had said, and he said, 'So they pledged allegiance to me and I accepted it from them. I was afraid that there would be dissension and, after it, reneging (from Islam).' Ibn Ishaq and Ibn 'Abid, in his *Maghazi*, from him that he (ar-Rafi') said to Abu Bakr, 'What made you take upon yourself the governance of the people and you forbade me taking command of (even) two people?' He said, 'I could not find any escape from that. I was afraid of division in the *ummah* of Muhammad, may Allah bless him and grant him peace.'

Ahmad narrated that Qais ibn Abi Hazim said, 'I sat with Abu Bakr as-Siddiq a month after the death of the Messenger of Allah, may Allah bless him and grant him peace,' and he mentioned his story. 'Then the cry went up among people, "The prayer is summoned." People gathered and he ascended the *minbar* then said, "I would love that someone other than me would take care of this authority for me. If you take me to task by the *Sunnah* of your Prophet I am not up to it. He was protected from the *shaytan*, and revelation used to descend upon him from heaven."'

Ibn Sa'd narrated that al-Hasan al-Basri said: When Abu Bakr was pledged allegiance he stood addressing the people and said, 'Now, I have been put in charge of this authority and I dislike it. By Allah, I would love that one of you would take care of it for me. If you charge me with acting among you with the like of the action of the Prophet, may Allah bless him and grant him peace, I cannot undertake that. The Prophet, may Allah bless him and grant him peace, was a slave whom Allah honoured with revelation and protected him by it (from error). I am only human. I am no better than any of you. Take care of me, and if you see me going straight then follow me and if you see me deviating then set me straight. Know that I have a *shaytan* who seizes upon me; when you see me becoming angry then avoid me, so that I do not leave traces and marks on your hairs and your skins.'

Ibn Sa'd narrated, and al-Khateeb, in the narration of Malik, that 'Urwah said: When Abu Bakr was appointed, he addressed people with a *khutbah*. He praised Allah and said, 'Now, I have been appointed in command over you and I am not the best of you. However, the Qur'an was revealed, the Prophet, may Allah bless him and grant him peace, laid down as customary different *sunnahs* and we were taught, so we learnt. So, know, people, that the most acute of sharp intellect is (he who has) the most fearful obedience (*tuqa*); that the most incapable (form) of incapacity is wickedness; that the strongest of you, as far as I am concerned, is the weak one until I take his right for him; and that the weakest of you, as far as I am concerned, is the strong one until I take from him what he is due (to give). People, I am only a follower, I am not an innovator, so that if I do well, help me and if I deviate then put me straight. I say these words of mine and I seek the forgiveness of Allah for me and for you.' Malik said, 'No-one will ever be an *imam* (i.e. *amir*) unless on this condition.'

Al-Hakim narrated in his *Mustadrak* that Abu Hurayrah, may Allah be pleased with him, said: When the Messenger of Allah, may Allah bless him and grant him peace, died, Makkah was shaken with an earthquake and Abu Quhafah heard that and said, 'What is this?' They said, 'The Messenger of Allah, may Allah bless him and grant him peace, has died.' He said, 'A momentous thing. Who has undertaken the command after him?' They said, 'Your son.' He said, 'Are Banu ᶜAbd Manaf and Banu al-Mughirah contented with that?' They said, 'Yes.' He said, 'No-one may put down what they raise up and no-one may raise up what they put down.'

Al-Waqidi narrated in a variety of ways that ᶜA'ishah, Ibn ᶜUmar, Saᶜid ibn al-Musayyab and others relate that Abu Bakr was pledged allegiance on the day that the Messenger of Allah, may Allah bless him and grant him peace, died, on Monday the 12th night of Rabiᶜ al-Awwal in the eleventh year of the Hijrah.

At-Tabarani narrated in *al-Awsat* that Ibn ᶜUmar said: Abu Bakr never sat on that place upon which the Messenger of Allah, may Allah bless him and grant him peace, sat upon the *minbar* until he met Allah. ᶜUmar did not sit on the place Abu Bakr sat until he met Allah and ᶜUthman did not sit in ᶜUmar's place until he met Allah.

That which happened in his *khilafah*

Those weighty matters which happened in his days were the despatch of Usamah's army; fighting against the people who reneged (on Islam) and against those who refused the *zakat*; Musaylimah the Liar; and the collection of the Qur'an.

Al-Isma'ili narrated that 'Umar, may Allah be pleased with him, said: When the Messenger of Allah, may Allah bless him and grant him peace, died there reneged whoever reneged of the Arabs and they said, 'We will pray but we will not produce the *zakat*.' I went to Abu Bakr and said, 'Khalifah of the Messenger of Allah, be conciliatory with the people and be gentle and mild with them, for they are only on the level of wild animals.' He said, 'I hoped for your help and you have come to me holding back your help. Tyrannical in *Jahiliyyah* and granting licence in Islam! With what did you think I should conciliate them? With composed verses and forged magic? Away, away! The Prophet, may Allah bless him and grant him peace, has gone and revelation is cut off. By Allah, I will fight them as long as the sword remains in my hand, even if they refuse me a year's *zakat* (*'iqal*).' 'Umar said: I found him more penetrating on the matter than me, more resolute, and he collected the people together on matters which appeared little and unimportant to many because of their inconvenience to them when I was appointed in command over them.

Abu'l-Qasim al-Baghawi, Abu Bakr ash-Shafi'i, in his *Fawa'id*, and Ibn 'Asakir narrated that 'A'ishah, may Allah be pleased with her, said: When the Messenger of Allah, may Allah bless him and grant him peace, died then hypocrisy raised its head, the Arabs reneged and the *Ansar* secluded themselves. If that which descended on my father had come down on the immovable mountains it would have broken them. They did not disagree on a point but that my father was prompt with its utility and its judgement. They said, 'Where should the Prophet, may Allah bless him and grant him peace, be buried?' We could not find anyone with knowledge of that. Then Abu Bakr said, 'I heard the Messenger of Allah, may Allah bless him and grant him peace, saying, "No Prophet dies but that he is buried beneath the bed upon which he died."' She said: They disagreed about his inheritance and could find no-one with knowledge on that point, then Abu Bakr said, 'I heard the Messenger of Allah, may Allah bless him and grant him peace, saying, "We, the company of the Prophets, we are not inherited from. What we leave is *sadaqah*."'

Some of the men of knowledge said: This was the first disagreement which happened among the Companions, may Allah be pleased with them. Some said, 'We will bury him in Makkah, his city in which he was born', and others said, 'No, in his mosque,' and others said, 'No, in al-Baqi^c, and others said, 'In al-Bait al-Maqdis, the burial ground of the Prophets', until Abu Bakr told them of the knowledge that he had. Ibn Zunjawayh said: This *Sunnah* was one which was uniquely as-Siddiq's among all of the *Muhajirun* and *Ansar* and they had recourse to him for it.

Al-Bayhaqi and Ibn ^cAsakir narrated that Abu Hurayrah, may Allah be pleased with him, said: 'By the One Whom there is no god but Him, if Abu Bakr had not been appointed *khalifah* then Allah would not have been worshipped.' Then he said it a second time and then he said it a third time. Someone said to him, 'How so, Abu Hurayrah?' So he said, 'The Messenger of Allah, may Allah bless him and grant him peace, directed Usamah ibn Zaid, along with seven hundred men, to Syria. When they arrived at Dhu Khushub the Prophet, may Allah bless him and grant him peace, died, the Arabs around Madinah reneged on their Islam and the companions of the Messenger of Allah, may Allah bless him and grant him peace, gathered around him and said, "Bring these back. Do you direct these against the Byzantines while the Arabs around Madinah have reneged?" He said, "By the One Whom there is no god but Him, even if dogs were dragging the wives of the Prophet, may Allah bless him and grant him peace, by their feet I would not return an army which the Messenger of Allah had sent out, nor undo a standard which he had tied!" He sent Usamah, and every tribe he would pass by which was wishing to renege would say (to themselves), "If these (the people of Madinah) did not have power, the like of these (the army) would not have come out from among them, so let us leave them alone until they meet the Byzantines." They met them, defeated them, killed them and returned safely, so that they (the tribes) remained firm in Islam.'

And he narrated that ʿUrwah said: The Messenger of Allah, may Allah bless him and grant him peace, began to say in his illness, 'Despatch the army of Usamah,' so that it travelled until it reached al-Jurf (three miles from Madinah on the road to Syria). His (Usamah's) wife, Fatimah bint Qais, sent a message to him saying, 'Do not hasten, because the Messenger of Allah, may Allah bless him and grant him peace, is heavily afflicted.' He did not proceed until the Messenger of Allah, may Allah bless him and grant him peace, died. When he died, he returned to Abu Bakr and said, 'The Messenger of Allah, may Allah bless him and grant him peace, sent me while we were not in this state of yours. I fear that the Arabs will reject (their Islam), and if they reject, they are the first to be fought. If they do not reject, I will carry on, because with me are the chiefs of the people and the best of them.' Abu Bakr addressed the people and said, 'By Allah, that birds (of prey) were to snatch me away is more beloved to me than that I should give anything precedence over the command of the Messenger of Allah, may Allah bless him and grant him peace.' Then he sent him.

Adh-Dhahabi said: When the death of the Prophet, may Allah bless him and grant him peace, became well known in the districts, many groups of the Arabs reneged on their Islam and refused the *zakat* so Abu Bakr as-Siddiq prepared to fight them. ʿUmar and others counselled him to avoid fighting them, so he said, 'By Allah, if they refused me a year's *zakat* or a young she-goat which they used to pay to the Messenger of Allah, may Allah bless him and grant him peace, I would fight them over its refusal.' ʿUmar said, 'How can you fight people when the Messenger of Allah, may Allah bless him and grant him peace, said, "I have been ordered to fight people until they say: There is no god but Allah, and that Muhammad is the Messenger of Allah, and whoever said it, his property and his blood are safe from me except for its due (punishment for crimes) and his reckoning is up to Allah."?' Abu Bakr said, 'By Allah, I will fight whoever makes a distinction between the prayer and the *zakat*, for the *zakat* is what is due on property, and he said, "Except for its due."' ʿUmar said, 'By Allah, it was only that I saw that Allah had expanded the breast of Abu Bakr to fighting and I knew that it was right.' The two Shaykhs and others narrated it.

ʿUrwah said: Abu Bakr went out with the *Muhajirun* and the *Ansar* until he reached a swamp opposite Najd and the nomadic Arabs fled with their families. The people spoke to Abu Bakr and said, 'Go back to Madinah, to the children and women, and put a man in command of the army,' and they persisted until he returned, putting Khalid ibn al-Walid in command. He said to him, 'If they submit in Islam and pay the *sadaqah* (the *zakat*) then whoever of you wishes to return may return,' and Abu Bakr went back to Madinah.

Ad-Daraqutni narrated that Ibn ʿUmar said: When Abu Bakr set out and was mounted on his camel, ʿAli ibn Abi Talib took hold of its reins and said, 'Where are you going, Khalifah of the Messenger of Allah? I say to you that which the Messenger of Allah, may Allah bless him and grant him peace, said to you on the Day of Uhud, "Sheath your sword, and do not cause us grief and concern for your person," and return to Madinah, for, by Allah, if we are caused to grieve because of you there will not be any order in Islam ever.'

Handhalah ibn ʿAli al-Laythi said that Abu Bakr sent Khalid and ordered him to fight people over five matters, and that whoever abandoned one of them, he was to fight him just as he was to fight whoever abandoned all five: the *shahadah* that there is no god but Allah and that Muhammad is His slave and messenger, the establishment of the prayer, the production of the *zakat*, the fast of Ramadan and the pilgrimage of the House. Khalid and those with him went out in Jumada al-Akhirah and fought Banu Asad and Ghatafan. They killed whomever they killed and captured whomever they captured, and the rest returned to Islam. In this event ʿUkkashah ibn Mihsan and Thabit ibn Aqram were martyred.

In Ramadan of this year, Fatimah, may Allah be pleased with her, the daughter of the Messenger of Allah, may Allah bless him and grant him peace, died, the Mistress (*Sayyidah*) of the world's women, and her age was twenty-four years old. Adh-Dhahabi said: The Messenger of Allah, may Allah bless him and grant him peace, had no descendants but through her, because the issue of his daughter Zaynab became extinct, az-Zubayr ibn Bakkar said. Umm Ayman died a month before her. In Shawwal ʿAbdullah ibn Abi Bakr died. Then Khalid went with his army to al-Yamamah to fight Musaylimah the Liar, towards the end of the year. The two hosts met, the siege lasted some days, and then the Liar was killed, may Allah curse him. Wahshi, the one who killed Hamzah, killed him. A great number of the Companions were martyred there: Abu Hudhayfah ibn ʿUtbah, Salim the freed slave of Abu Hudhayfah, Shujaʿ ibn Wahb, Zaid ibn al-Khattab, ʿAbdullah ibn Sahl, Malik ibn ʿAmr, at-Tufayl ibn ʿAmr ad-Dawsi, Yazid ibn Qais, ʿAmir ibn al-Bukayr, ʿAbdullah ibn Makhramah, as-Sa'ib ibn ʿUthman ibn Madhʿun, ʿAbbad ibn Bishr, Maʿan ibn ʿAdi, Thabit ibn Qais ibn Shamas, Abu Dujanah Simak ibn Harb and a large number totalling seventy (of the Companions). Musaylimah, on the day of his death, was one hundred and fifty years old, his birth having been before the birth of ʿAbdullah, the father of the Prophet, may Allah bless him and grant him peace.

In the twelfth year, as-Siddiq sent al-ʿAla' ibn al-Hadrami to Bahrain who had reneged. So they met at Jawatha and the Muslims were victorious. He sent ʿIkrimah ibn Abi Jahl to Oman who had reneged, and he sent al-Muhajir ibn Abi Umayyah to the people of Nujayr. He sent Ziyad ibn Labid al-Ansari to a group of those who had reneged. In that year Abu'l-ʿAs ibn ar-Rabiʿ died, the husband of Zaynab, the daughter of the Prophet, may Allah bless him and grant him peace, also as-Saʿb ibn Juthamah al-Laythi, and Abu Marthad al-Ghanawi. In that year, after finishing fighting the people who had reneged, as-Siddiq, may Allah be pleased with him, sent Khalid ibn al-Walid to the land of Basra and he raided Ubullah, captured it and took Mada'in Kisra, the one which is in Iraq, partly by treaty and partly by force. In that year Abu Bakr as-Siddiq undertook the Hajj, then returned and sent ʿAmr ibn al-ʿAs and the army to Syria; the battle of Ajnadayn happened in Jumada al-Ula of the thirteenth year, and the Muslims were victorious. Abu Bakr was given the good tidings when he was close to death. ʿIkrimah ibn Abi Jahl was martyred in it and Hisham ibn al-ʿAs among a group of others. In that year there was the battle of Marju's-Suffar, the idolaters were defeated and al-Fadl ibn al-ʿAbbas, among others, was martyred.

The collection of the Qur'an

Al-Bukhari narrated that Zaid ibn Thabit said: Abu Bakr sent for me at the time of the slaughter of people of al-Yamamah and ʿUmar was with him. Abu Bakr said, 'ʿUmar came to me and said, "The slaughter of people was very extensive on the Day of al-Yamamah and I fear the killing will extend to the reciters in these engagements, so that a lot of Qur'an will disappear unless they gather it together. I believe that the Qur'an should be gathered."' Abu Bakr said, 'I said to ʿUmar, "How can I do something that the Messenger of Allah, may Allah bless him and grant him peace, did not do?" ʿUmar said, "It, by Allah! is good," and ʿUmar did not give up returning to the matter until Allah expanded my breast to that, and I came to hold the view that ʿUmar held.' Zaid said: ʿUmar was sitting with him, not talking. Abu Bakr said, 'You are an intelligent young man and we have no doubts of you. You used to write the revelation for the Messenger of Allah, may Allah bless him and grant him peace; search out the Qur'an and collect it together.' By Allah, if he had imposed on me the responsibility of removing one of the mountains it would not have been heavier for me than what they ordered me to do of collecting the Qur'an. I said, 'How can the two of you do something which the Prophet, may Allah bless him and grant him peace, did not do?' So Abu Bakr said, 'It, by Allah! is good,' and he continued insisting on it until Allah expanded my breast to that which he had expanded the breasts of Abu Bakr and ʿUmar. I searched out the Qur'an to collect it all together, from scraps (of paper), shoulder blade bones, palm branches and from the breasts of men, until I found two *ayat* from Surah at-Tawbah (The Surah of Repentance) along with Khuzaymah ibn Thabit which I found with no-one else, '*There has come to you a messenger from among yourselves …*' (Qur'an 9: 128-129) to the end of the *surah*.

The pages upon which the Qur'an was collected were with Abu Bakr until Allah took him, then they were with ʿUmar until Allah took him, then they were with Hafsah the daughter of ʿUmar, may Allah be pleased with her.

Abu Yaʿla narrated that ʿAli said: The one with the greatest reward for the written copies of the Qur'an is Abu Bakr. Abu Bakr was the first to gather the Qur'an between two boards.

The things in which he was first

He was the first to accept Islam, the first to collect the Qur'an together, the first to name it a *mushaf* (written copy) – the proof of that has already been mentioned – and he was the first to be named "*khalifah*".

Ahmad narrated that Abu Bakr ibn Abi Mulaykah said: It was said to Abu Bakr, 'Khalifah of Allah!' He said, 'I am the Khalifah of the Prophet, may Allah bless him and grant him peace, and I am content with that.'

He was the first to rule the *khilafah* while his father was alive.

He was the first *khalifah* whose subjects allocated him a sum.

Al-Bukhari narrated that ʿA'ishah, may Allah be pleased with her, said: When Abu Bakr was appointed *khalifah* he said, 'My people know that my profession is not incapable of providing for my family, and I have become occupied with the command and the affairs of the Muslims so the family of Abu Bakr will eat from this property while he works professionally for the Muslims.'

Ibn Sa'd narrated that 'Ata' ibn as-Sa'ib said: When Abu Bakr was pledged allegiance he arose in the morning and upon his forearm there were some garments and he was going to the market place. 'Umar said, 'Where are you going?' He said, 'To the market place.' He said, 'What are you going to do, when you have been put in charge of the affairs of the Muslims?' He said, 'What am I going to do to feed my family?' He said, 'Let us go. Abu 'Ubaydah will allocate a sum for you.' So they went to Abu 'Ubaydah and he said, 'I allocate you the supplies of a man among the *Muhajirun*, not the best of them nor the least of them, and the clothing of winter and summer. If you wear out something, return and take something in its place.' The two of them allocated him half a sheep everyday and what would clothe his head and his person.

Ibn Sa'd narrated that Maymun said: When Abu Bakr was appointed *khalifah* they allocated him two thousand, so he said, 'Increase me, for I have dependants and you have kept me busy so that I cannot engage in trade,' so they increased him five hundred.

At-Tabarani narrated in his *Musnad* that al-Hasan ibn 'Ali ibn Abi Talib said: When Abu Bakr was near to death, he said, ''A'ishah, look to the milch camel whose milk we used to drink, the bowl in which we used to prepare food, and the outer garments we used to wear, for we used to benefit from that when we were in charge of the command of the Muslims. When I die, return them to 'Umar.' When Abu Bakr died she sent them to 'Umar. 'Umar said, 'May Allah show mercy to you, Abu Bakr! You have exhausted the one who comes after you.'

Ibn Abi'd-Dunya narrated that Abu Bakr ibn Hafs said: When he was close to death, Abu Bakr said to 'A'ishah, may Allah be pleased with her, 'My little daughter, we were put in charge of the affairs of the Muslims, and we didn't take for ourselves a dinar nor a dirham, but we ate of the coarse flour of their food in our bellies, and we dressed with their rough clothing upon our backs.

Nothing remains with us of the booty of the Muslims, neither a little nor a lot, but for this Abyssinian slave, this camel for drawing water, and this threadbare worn-out outer garment. When I die, send them to 'Umar.'

He was the first one to make a *bait al-mal* (a building in which *zakat* and other revenues were stored while they were being distributed).

Ibn Sa'd narrated that Sahl ibn Abi Khaythamah and others said that Abu Bakr had a *bait al-mal* at as-Sunh which no-one guarded. Someone said to him, 'Will you not put someone in charge of it to guard it?' He said, 'There is a lock on it,' and he used to give away what was in it until it was empty. When it was moved to Madinah, he changed it and put it in his house. Property came to him and he used to divide it up among the poorest of the people and he would divide it equally among them. He would buy camels, horses and weapons and put them there to be used in the way of Allah. He would buy outer garments which came from the outlying desert tracts and distribute them among the widows of Madinah. When Abu Bakr died and was buried, 'Umar summoned the trustees, amongst them 'Abd ar-Rahman ibn 'Awf and 'Uthman ibn 'Affan, and with them entered the *bait al-mal* of Abu Bakr. They opened the *bait al-mal* and found nothing in it, neither a dinar nor a dirham.

I say that this tradition refutes the words of al-'Askari in *al-Awa'il* (Firsts), 'The first to take a *bait al-mal* was 'Umar. The Prophet, may Allah bless him and grant him peace, had no *bait al-mal* nor had Abu Bakr, may Allah be pleased with him.' I had refuted this in my book which I composed on 'firsts', then later I saw that al-'Askari alluded to this in another part of his book saying, 'The first to take charge of a *bait al-mal* was Abu 'Ubaydah ibn al-Jarrah on behalf of Abu Bakr.'

Al-Hakim said: The first affectionate nickname in Islam was the nickname of Abu Bakr, may Allah be pleased with him, 'Ateeq.'

Section

The two Shaykhs narrated that Jabir, may Allah be pleased with him, said: The Prophet, may Allah bless him and grant him peace, said, 'If the wealth of Bahrain were to come, I would give you so much and so much.' So when the wealth of Bahrain came after the death of the Prophet, may Allah bless him and grant him peace, Abu Bakr said, 'Whoever was owed anything by the Prophet, may Allah bless him and grant him peace, let him come to us.' I came and told him. He said, 'Take.' I took and found it to be five hundred. Then he gave me one thousand and five hundred.

Some examples of his forbearance and humility

Ibn ʿAsakir narrated that Anisah said: Abu Bakr was settled among us for three years before he was appointed *khalifah* and a year afterwards, and the servant girls of the quarter would come to him with their flocks and he would milk them for them.

Ahmad narratd in *az-Zuhd* that Maymun ibn Mihran said: A man came to Abu Bakr and said, 'Peace be upon you (*as-salamu alaika* –the singular form of address) Khalifah of the Messenger of Allah.' And he said, 'In among all of these.' (The man had greeted him exclusively of those present).

Abu Salih al-Ghifari said that ʿUmar ibn al-Khattab used to take care of an elderly blind woman in one of the outskirts of Madinah at night. He would draw water for her to drink, and would undertake her business. Sometimes when he came to her he would find that someone else had already beaten him to her and done what she wanted. He came to her more than one time so that the other might not beat him to her. ʿUmar lay in wait for him, and it was Abu Bakr who had come to her, and he was at that time *khalifah*. ʿUmar said, 'You are he, by my life!'

Abu Nuʿaym and others narrated that ʿAbd ar-Rahman al-Asbahani said: Al-Hasan ibn ʿAli came to Abu Bakr when he was upon the *minbar* of the Prophet, may Allah bless him and grant him peace, and said, 'Come down from my father's seat.' He said, 'You have told the truth, it is your father's seat,' and he placed him in his lap and wept. ⁽Ali said, 'By Allah, this was not from my command.' He said, 'You have told the truth. By Allah, I did not suspect you.'

Section

Ibn Sa⁽d narrated that Ibn ⁽Umar said: The Messenger of Allah, may Allah bless him and grant him peace, appointed Abu Bakr to lead the Hajj in the first Hajj of Islam, then the Messenger of Allah, may Allah bless him and grant him peace, performed the Hajj the following year. When the Messenger of Allah, may Allah bless him and grant him peace, died and Abu Bakr was appointed *khalifah*, he put ⁽Umar in charge of leading the Hajj, then Abu Bakr performed the Hajj the following year. When Abu Bakr died and ⁽Umar was appointed *khalifah*, he put ⁽Abd ar-Rahman ibn ⁽Awf in charge of the Hajj, then ⁽Umar continued to perform the Hajj every year until he died. ⁽Uthman was then appointed *khalifah*, and he put ⁽Abd ar-Rahman ibn ⁽Awf in charge of the Hajj.

His final illness, his death, his last testament and his appointment of ⁽Umar as *khalifah*

Saif and al-Hakim narrated that Ibn ⁽Umar said: The cause of Abu Bakr's death was the passing away of the Messenger of Allah, may Allah bless him and grant him peace. He was distressed and his body continued to waste away until he died.

Ibn Sa⁽d and al-Hakim narrated with a *sahih isnad* that Ibn Shihab related that Abu Bakr and al-Harith ibn Kaladah were eating a broth which Abu Bakr had been given. Al-Harith said to Abu Bakr, 'Lift your hand (from the dish) Khalifah of the Messenger of Allah. By Allah, in it there is a year's poison. I and you will die on the same day.' He took his hand away from it. Both of them became increasingly sick until they died on the same day at the end of the year.

Al-Hakim narrated that ash-Sha'bi said: What can we expect from this awful world when the Messenger of Allah, may Allah bless him and grant him peace, was poisoned and Abu Bakr was poisoned?

Al-Waqidi and al-Hakim narrated that 'A'ishah, may Allah be pleased with her, said: The beginning of Abu Bakr's illness was that he performed a *ghusl* on Monday the seventh of Jumada al-Akhirah which was a cold day. He had a fever for fifteen days and did not go out to the prayer. He died on the night of Tuesday eight days before the end of Jumada al-Akhirah in 13 AH, when he was sixty-three years old.

Ibn Sa'd and Ibn Abi'd-Dunya narrated that Abu's-Safar said: They entered upon Abu Bakr during his illness and said, 'Khalifah of the Messenger of Allah, shall we not call a doctor for you who will take a look at you?' He said, 'He has already taken a look at me.' They said, 'What did he say?' He said, 'Truly, I do what I will.' (*see* Qur'an 11: 108; 85: 16)

Al-Waqidi narrated by various routes that when Abu Bakr became seriously ill, he called for 'Abd ar-Rahman ibn 'Awf and said, 'Tell me about 'Umar ibn al-Khattab.' He said, 'You do not ask me about any matter but that you are more knowledgeable of it than me.' So Abu Bakr said, 'And even if …?' 'Abd ar-Rahman ibn 'Awf said, 'He, by Allah, is better than your view of him.' Then he summoned 'Uthman ibn 'Affan and said, 'Tell me about 'Umar.' He said, 'You of all of us know best about him.' He said, 'Tell me that,' so he said, "O Allah, my knowledge of him is that his inward is better than his exterior and that there is no-one like him among us.' He included in his counsel, along with the two of them, Sa'id ibn Zaid, Usayd ibn al-Hudayr and others of the *Muhajirun* and *Ansar*. Usayd said, 'O Allah, I know him to be the best after you. He is pleased for the good pleasure (of Allah), and displeased for the displeasure (of Allah). What he conceals is better than what he makes public. No-one stronger for this command than him will ever have authority over it.'

Some of the Companions entered upon him and one said to him, 'What will you say to your Lord when He asks you about your appointing ʿUmar as *khalifah* over us when you have seen his toughness?' Abu Bakr said, 'By Allah, are you trying to frighten me? I will say, "O Allah, I have appointed as *khalifah* over them the best of Your people." Convey from me what I said to those behind you.' Then he called ʿUthman and said, 'Write, "In the name of Allah, the Merciful, the Compassionate. This is the testament of Abu Bakr ibn Abi Quhafah at the end of his time in the world, as he was leaving it, and at the beginning of his time in the *Akhirah*, as he was entering it, where the disbeliever will believe, the wicked will be certain, and the liar will tell the truth. I have appointed after me as *khalifah* over you ʿUmar ibn al-Khattab, so listen to him and obey him. I have not fallen short in my duty to Allah and His Messenger and His *deen* and to myself and you. If he is just, then that is my opinion of him and my knowledge of him. If he changes things, then every man has that which he earned. I intended good, and I do not know the hidden things, '... *and the ones who do wrong shall know what place of transformation they will be transferred to.*' (Qur'an 26: 227) Peace be upon you and the mercy of Allah and His blessings."' He asked for the writing and sealed it. Then he ordered ʿUthman, and he went out with the letter thus sealed, and people pledged allegiance and were pleased with it. Abu Bakr summoned ʿUmar in private and advised him whatever he advised him. Then he left him and Abu Bakr raised his hands and said, 'O Allah, I only meant by that their good and feared dissension for them, and I have done for them what You know best, and I have exerted my intellect for them in arriving at a decision, and have appointed the best of them over them, and the strongest of them, and the most eager of them for that which would guide them. And there has come to me of Your command what has come to me (death), so put another in my place over them, for they are Your slaves, their forelocks are in Your hand. O Allah, put right their rulers, and make him one of Your *khalifahs* who take the right way, and put right his subjects for him.'

Ibn Sa'd and al-Hakim narrated that Ibn Mas'ud said: The most farsighted of people were three: Abu Bakr when he appointed 'Umar as *khalifah*, the woman companion of Musa when she said, '*Hire him!*' (Qur'an 28: 26), and the chief minister (of Fir'awn) when he said to his wife, '*Honour his (Yusuf's) dwelling place.*' (Qur'an 12: 21).

Ibn 'Asakir narrated that Yasar ibn Hamzah said: When Abu Bakr's illness grew serious he stood and looked over the people from a small window and said, 'I have made a covenant, so will you be contented with it?' So the people said, 'We will be content with it, Khalifah of the Messenger of Allah.' Then 'Ali stood and said, 'We will not be content unless it is 'Umar.' He said, 'It is 'Umar.'

Ahmad narrated that 'A'ishah, may Allah be pleased with her, said: When death came to Abu Bakr, he said, 'What day is this?' They said, 'Monday.' He said, 'If I die tonight do not wait until tomorrow (to bury me), because the most beloved of days and nights to me is the closest to the Messenger of Allah, may Allah bless him and grant him peace.'

Malik narrated that 'A'ishah, may Allah be pleased with her, said that Abu Bakr made a present to her of the fruit-cuttings of palm trees, twenty camel loads, from al-Ghabah. When death came to him he said, 'My little daughter, by Allah, there is no human being that I would more love to see wealthy than you, and there is no-one whose poverty after me is more grievous to me than you. I had given you as a gift twenty camel loads of fruit-cuttings of palm trees; if you had cut them and taken them they would have been yours, however today they are only the property of the ones who inherit, who are your two brothers and your two sisters, so divide them up by the Book of Allah.' She said, 'Father, even if it had been so much and so much I would have given it up. There is only Asma' (her sister), who is the other (sister)?' He said, 'The child who is in the womb of Kharijah's daughter; I think it is a girl.' Ibn Sa'd narrated it. In a version he said, 'The child who is in the womb of Kharijah's daughter; it occurs to me that it is a girl, so make her your concern.' Then she gave birth to Umm Kulthum.

Ibn Sa'd narrated that 'Urwah said that Abu Bakr bequeathed one fifth of his property (the rest being divided according to the *shari'ah*), and said, 'I take from my wealth what Allah takes from the booty of the Muslims.' He also narrated that he (Abu Bakr) said, 'That I should bequeath a fifth is preferable to me than that I should bequeath a quarter, and that I should bequeath a quarter would be preferable to me than bequeathing a third. Whoever bequeathed a third leaves nothing.'

Sa'id ibn Mansur narrated that ad-Dahhak said that Abu Bakr and 'Ali both bequeathed a fifth of their properties to those who were not entitled to inherit from them of their close relatives.

'Abdullah ibn Ahmad narrated in *Zawa'id az-Zuhd* that 'A'ishah, may Allah be pleased with her, said: By Allah, Abu Bakr left neither a dinar nor a dirham of which Allah had struck the die.

Ibn Sa'd and others narrated that 'A'ishah, may Allah be pleased with her, said: When Abu Bakr became grievously ill I quoted this verse:

'By your life! Wealth does not avail the man,
 When one day it (the spirit) rattles in the throat and the breast becomes constricted by it,'

and he uncovered his face and said, 'It is not like that. Rather say,

"And the agony of death comes in truth. That is what you used to turn away from." (Qur'an 50: 19)

'Look out my two cloths and wash them, then bury me in them. The living has more need of the new than the dead.'

Abu Ya'la narrated that 'A'ishah, may Allah be pleased with her, said: I entered upon Abu Bakr when he was on the point of death and I said:

'Whoever's tears are ceaseless in sufficiency,
   in bitterness they will be poured out.'

So he said, 'Do not say this; rather say,

"And the agony of death comes in truth. That is what you used to turn away from."'

Then he said, 'On what day did the Messenger of Allah, may Allah bless him and grant him peace, die?' I said, 'Monday.' He said, 'I hope that it is between now and the night,' and he died on the night before Tuesday, and was buried before the morning.

ʿAbdullah ibn Ahmad narrated in *Zawa'id az-Zuhd* that Bakr ibn ʿAbdullah al-Mazani said: When death came to Abu Bakr, ʿA'ishah, may Allah be pleased with her, sat at his head and said:

'Every owner of camels must one day take them to drink,
   and every possessor of plunder must be despoiled.'

Abu Bakr understood it and said, 'It is not like that, my daughter, rather it is as Allah said:

"And the agony of death comes in truth. That is what you used to turn away from."'

Ahmad narrated that ʿA'ishah, may Allah be pleased with her, also said that she quoted this verse while Abu Bakr was dying:

'And a pure one, free from faults,
   from whose face the clouds draw drinking water,

Orphans love (him), a protection for the widows.'

Abu Bakr said, 'That was the Messenger of Allah, may Allah bless him and grant him peace.'

ʿAbdullah ibn Ahmad narrated in *Zawa'id az-Zuhd* that ʿUbadah ibn Qais said: When death came to Abu Bakr he said to ʿA'ishah,

'Wash these two cloths of mine and wrap me in them, for your father is one of two men: either dressed in the best way or stripped in the worst way.'

Ibn Abi'd-Dunya narrated that Ibn Abi Mulaykah said that Abu Bakr left as his last wish that his wife, Asma' bint ʿUmays, should wash his body and that ʿAbd ar-Rahman ibn Abi Bakr should help her.

Ibn Saʿd narrated that Saʿid ibn al-Musayyab said that ʿUmar, may Allah be pleased with him, prayed over Abu Bakr between the grave (of the Prophet, may Allah bless him and grant him peace) and the *minbar*, and said four *takbirs* over him.

He narrated that ʿUrwah and al-Qasim ibn Muhammad said that Abu Bakr left as his last wish to ʿA'ishah that he should be buried by the side of the Messenger of Allah, may Allah bless him and grant him peace. When he died, they dug a grave for him and put his head at the shoulder of the Messenger, may Allah bless him and grant him peace, and the niche (wherein the body was laid) touched the grave of the Messenger, may Allah bless him and grant him peace.

He narrated that Ibn ʿUmar said: ʿUmar, Talhah, ʿUthman and ʿAbd ar-Rahman ibn Abi Bakr got down into Abu Bakr's grave (to place the body in the niche). He narrated by many different routes that he was buried at night.

He narrated that Ibn al-Musayyab said that when Abu Bakr died, Makkah was shaken by an earthquake, and so Abu Quhafah said, 'What is this?' They said, 'Your son has died.' He said, 'A great misfortune! Who has undertaken the command after him?' They said, 'ʿUmar.' He said, 'His companion.'

He narrated that Mujahid said that Abu Quhafah returned the inheritance he received from Abu Bakr to the son of Abu Bakr and that Abu Quhafah only lived six months and some days after Abu Bakr. He died in Muharram of 14 AH when he was ninety-seven years of age.

The men of knowledge said: No-one took the *khilafah* during the life of his father except for Abu Bakr, and no father inherited from a *khalifah* except for Abu Bakr's.

Al-Hakim narrated that Ibn ʿUmar said: Abu Bakr ruled for two years and seven months.

There is in the *Tarikh* of Ibn ʿAsakir with its *isnad* that Asmaʿi said: Khufaf ibn Nudbah as-Salami said, mourning Abu Bakr:

'No living thing, tell it! has permanence, and all of the world, its business is annihilation.

And property with the people is a deposit loaned and the condition on it is repayment.

Man works and there is one lying in wait for him; the eye mourns him, and the fire (excessive grief) of the brain.

He becomes decrepit or he is slain or there overcomes him a sickness which afflicts him and for which there is no cure.

Truly, Abu Bakr he is the succour (the rain) if Orion did not make vegetables to grow with water.

By Allah, the young wearer of a lower garment (common people) nor the wearer of an upper garment (the élite) does not reach his days.

Whoever works to reach his days, exerting himself, will isolate himself in an empty land.

What *hadith* with chains of transmission have been related from him

An-Nawawi said in his *Tahdhib*: As-Siddiq related of the Messenger of Allah, may Allah bless him and grant him peace, one hundred and forty-two *hadith*. The reason for the small number of his narrations given the precedence of his companionship and his staying close to the Prophet, may Allah bless him and grant him peace, was that his death came before the spread of *hadith* and the concern of the Followers for listening to them, acquiring them and memorising them.

I say: ʿUmar, may Allah be pleased with him, mentioned in the previous *hadith* on the oath of allegiance that Abu Bakr left nothing which had been revealed about the *Ansar* or which the Messenger of Allah, may Allah bless him and grant him peace, had said about them but that he mentioned it. This is the best proof of the great amount of material he had memorised of the *Sunnah* and the vastness of his knowledge of the Qur'an. ʿUmar ibn al-Khattab transmitted from him, as did ʿUthman ibn ʿAffan, ʿAli, Ibn ʿAwf, Ibn Masʿud, Hudhayfah, Ibn ʿUmar, Ibn az-Zubayr, Ibn ʿAmr, Ibn ʿAbbas, Anas, Zaid ibn Thabit, al-Bara' ibn ʿAzib, Abu Hurayrah, ʿUqbah ibn al-Harith, his son ʿAbd ar-Rahman, Zaid ibn Arqam, ʿAbdullah ibn Mughaffal, ʿUqbah ibn ʿAmir al-Juhani, ʿImran ibn Husayn, Abu'l-Barzah al-Aslami, Abu Saʿid al-Khudri, Abu Musa al-Ashʿari, Abu't-Tufayl al-Laythi, Jabir ibn ʿAbdullah, Bilal, ʿA'ishah his daughter, Asma' his daughter, and of the Followers: Aslam the freed slave of ʿUmar, Wasit al-Bajili and a number of others.

I have decided to enumerate his *hadith* here concisely, explaining after each *hadith* who made it public. I will treat each of them singly in their different paths of transmission in a *musnad* work devoted to that, *insha'Allah*.

1. The *hadith* of the Hijrah (the two Shaykhs [Al-Bukhari and Muslim] and others).
2. The *hadith* of the sea, 'It is completely pure, its water (for purification and cleansing), permitted are its dead (to eat).' (Ad-Daraqutni).
3. 'The *siwak* (toothstick) cleans the mouth and pleases the Lord.' (Ahmad).
4. 'That the Messenger of Allah, may Allah bless him and grant him peace, ate (meat of a) shoulder then later prayed and did not

perform *wudu'* (washing to prepare for the prayer).' (Al-Bazzar and Abu Ya'la).

5. 'Let none of you make *wudu'* because of the taste of his food which is permitted for him to eat.' (Al-Bazzar).

6. 'The Messenger of Allah, may Allah bless him and grant him peace, forbade striking people at prayer.' (Abu Ya'la and al-Bazzar).

7. 'The last prayer which the Prophet, may Allah bless him and grant him peace, prayed was behind me in a single garment.' (Abu Ya'la).

8. 'Whoever it would please to recite the Qur'an freshly as it was revealed, then let him recite with the recitation of Ibn Umm 'Abd (i.e. Ibn Mas'ud).' (Ahmad).

9. He said to the Messenger of Allah, may Allah bless him and grant him peace, 'Teach me a prayer with which I can supplicate in my *salah*.' He said, 'Say, "O Allah I have wronged myself with a great wrong and none forgives wrong actions but You, so forgive me with a forgiveness from You and show mercy to me. Truly, You are the All-Forgiving, the Compassionate."' (Al-Bukhari and Muslim).

10. 'Whoever prayed the dawn prayer then he is in a covenant with Allah, so do not betray Allah with respect to His covenant. Whoever kills him, Allah will seek him out until He throws him in the Fire upon his face.' (Ibn Majah).

11. 'No Prophet has ever died until a man of his *ummah* led him in prayer.' (Al-Bazzar).

12. 'No man makes a wrong action then performs *wudu'* and does his *wudu'* well, then performs two *raka'at* and seeks Allah's forgiveness but that He will forgive him.' (Ahmad, the authors of the four *Sunan*, and Ibn Hibban).

13. 'Allah has not made a prophet die but in the place in which he would love to be buried.' (At-Tirmidhi).

14. 'May Allah curse the Jews and the Christians; they took the graves of their prophets as places of prostration.' (Abu Ya'la).

15. 'The dead person has boiling water sprinkled on him for the tears of the living (i.e. the tears of wailing and mourning, particularly

ritualised or professional mourning. The tradition is held not to refer to tears of sadness and sorrow).' (Abu Ya'la).

16. 'Protect yourselves from the Fire even if it were with (giving) the half of a date, because it straightens that which is crooked, repels an evil death, and it stands with the hungry one in its stead with the satiated one.' (Abu Ya'la).

17. The *hadith* of the obligations of *sadaqat* in its full length. (Al-Bukhari and others).

18. From Ibn Abi Mulaykah that he said: The reins fell from the hands of Abu Bakr as-Siddiq and he struck upon the foreleg of his camel and made it kneel down. They said to him, 'Why did you not tell us to give it back to you?' He said, 'My beloved, the Messenger of Allah, may Allah bless him and grant him peace, told me that I was not to ask people for anything.' (Ahmad).

19. 'The Messenger of Allah, may Allah bless him and grant him peace, told Asma' bint 'Umays when she brought forth Muhammad ibn Abi Bakr to bathe herself and to enter *ihram* (for the Hajj, as she gave birth on the way to Makkah).' (Al-Bazzar and at-Tabarani).

20. The Messenger of Allah, may Allah bless him and grant him peace, was asked, 'Which part of Hajj is best?' He said, 'The raising of the voice (with *talbiyah*) and the shedding of blood (of animals brought to sacrifice).' (At-Tirmidhi and Ibn Majah).

21. That he kissed the (Black) Stone and said, 'If I had not seen the Messenger of Allah, may Allah bless him and grant him peace, kiss you I would not have kissed you.' (Ad-Daraqutni).

22. That the Messenger of Allah, may Allah bless him and grant him peace, sent an immunity to the people of Makkah, 'Let not an idolater perform Hajj after this year, nor let a naked person go around the House.' (Ahmad).

23. 'That which is between my house and my *minbar* is one of the meadows of the Garden, and my *minbar* is upon one of the fountains of the Garden.' (Abu Ya'la).

24. The full *hadith* of his going, may Allah bless him and grant him

peace, to the home of Abu'l-Haytham ibn at-Tayyihan.' (Abu Ya'la).

25. 'Gold for gold, like for like. And silver for silver, like for like. The one who gives increase or seeks increase is in the Fire.' (Abu Ya'la and al-Bazzar).

26. 'Cursed is whoever harms a believer or plots against him.' (At-Tirmidhi).

27. 'A mean person will not enter the Garden, nor a deceiver, nor a treacherous one, nor one of evil character. The first to enter the Garden is the slave when he obeys Allah and obeys his master.' (Ahmad).

28. 'The clientage (of a slave which includes inheriting from him as a relative) is for the one who sets free.' (Ad-Diya' al-Maqdisi in *al-Mukhtarah*).

29. 'We (prophets) are not inherited from; that which we leave is a *sadaqah*.' (Al-Bukhari).

30. 'When Allah grants a prophet a means of subsistence (such as land yielding an income) and then later makes him die, He will appoint it for the one who undertakes it (the *khilafah*) after him.' (Abu Dawud).

31. 'He is ungrateful (*kafara*) to Allah who declares himself free of his lineage, even though it be in a minute way.' (Al-Bazzar).

32. 'You and that which is yours are for your father.' Abu Bakr said, 'He only meant by that maintenance.' (Al-Bayhaqi).

33. 'Whoever's two feet become dusty in the way of Allah, Allah will forbid them from (entering) the Fire.' (Al-Bazzar).

34. 'I have been ordered to fight men until ...' (The two Shaykhs and others).

35. 'How excellent a slave of Allah and brother to his kinsfolk is Khalid ibn al-Walid, and (he is) one of the swords of Allah, may Allah draw him against the disbelievers and hypocrites.' (Ahmad).

36. 'The sun has not risen over a man better than 'Umar.' (At-Tirmidhi).

37. 'Whoever is put in charge of any affair of the Muslims and he

appoints in command over them anyone out of favouritism, then there is the curse of Allah upon him, and Allah will not accept from him either repentance nor a ransom until He enters him into *Jahannam*. Whoever gives anyone the sanctuary of Allah, and he violates the sanctuary of Allah in any way without right then may the curse of Allah be upon him.' (Ahmad).

38. The *hadith* of Maʿiz and his stoning. (Ahmad).

39. 'He is not persistent (in wrong action) who seeks forgiveness, even if he repeats it seventy times a day.' (At-Tirmidhi).

40. 'That he, may Allah bless him and grant him peace, took counsel on the command of war.' (At-Tabarani).

41. The *hadith* 'When "*Whoever does evil will be recompensed it ...*" (Qur'an 4: 123) was revealed ...' (At-Tirmidhi, Ibn Hibban and others).

42. 'You recite this *ayah*, "*O you who believe, you are responsible for your own selves ...*" (Qur'an 5: 105).' (Ahmad, the four authors of books called *Sunan* and Ibn Hibban).

43. 'What do you think of two of whom Allah is the third?' (The two Shaykhs).

44. 'O Allah, by spear-thrusts and by plague.' (Abu Yaʿla).

45. '(Surah) Hud made me grey ...' (Ad-Daraqutni in *al-ʿIlal*).

46. 'Associating partners (with Allah) among my *ummah* is more hidden than the creeping of ants ...' (Abu Yaʿla and others).

47. 'Messenger of Allah, teach me something I can say in the morning and the evening ...' (Al-Haytham ibn Kulayb in his *Musnad*, and At-Tirmidhi and others have it among those ascribed to Abu Hurayrah).

48. 'Take hold of "No god but Allah" and seeking forgiveness, because Iblis said, "I destroyed people with wrong actions and they destroyed me with 'No god but Allah' and seeking forgiveness. When I saw that, I destroyed them with whims so that they think they are guided aright."' (Abu Yaʿla).

49. 'When, "*Do not raise your voices above the voice of the Prophet!*" (Qur'an 49: 2) was revealed, I said, "Messenger of Allah, I will not speak to you except as the decrepit do."' (Al-Bazzar).

50. 'Each one is eased to that for which he is created.' (Ahmad).

51. 'Whoever forges a lie against me intentionally or rejects something I have ordered, then let him take up his abode in *Jahannam*.' (Abu Ya'la).

52. 'What is the salvation of this matter ... in "No god but Allah".' (Ahmad and others).

53. '"Go out and announce among people that whoever witnesses that there is no god but Allah, the Garden becomes a must for him." So I went out and 'Umar met me ...' (Abu Ya'la. It is recorded from a *hadith* of Abu Hurayrah and is most unusual as a *hadith* of Abu Bakr).

54. 'There are two types from my *ummah* who will not enter the Garden, al-Murji'ah and al-Qadariyyah.' (Ad-Daraqutni in *Al-'Ilal*).

55. 'Ask Allah for health and safety.' (Ahmad, an-Nasa'i and Ibn Majah who has it by many different chains of transmission).

56. 'The Messenger of Allah, may Allah bless him and grant him peace, when he wanted some matter, used to say, "O Allah, do good to me and choose for me."' (At-Tirmidhi).

57. 'The supplication of debt is, "O Allah, the dispeller of worry ..."' (Al-Bazzar and al-Hakim).

58. 'Every body which has grown from (the nourishment of) usury, the Fire is more appropriate for it,' and in another wording, 'A body nourished on what is forbidden will not enter the Garden.' (Abu Ya'la).

59. 'There is nothing in the body which does not complain of the sharpness of the tongue.' (Abu Ya'la).

60. 'Allah descends on the midmost night of Sha'ban and in it forgives every human apart from a *kafir* or a man in whose heart there is a grudge.' (Ad-Daraqutni).

61. 'The Dajjal will emerge in the east from a land known as Khurasan, and peoples will follow him whose faces are as if they are shields formed of two hides, one sewn upon the other.' (At-Tirmidhi and Ibn Majah).

62. 'I have been given seventy thousand who will enter the Garden without any reckoning.' (Ahmad).

63. The Hadith of Intercession in its full length with people's going back and forward between prophet after prophet. (Ahmad).

64. 'Even if mankind were to travel in a valley and the *Ansar* were to travel in another valley, I would travel in the valley of the *Ansar*.' (Ahmad).

65. 'Quraysh are the masters of this authority, the best of them following the best of them and the worst of them following the worst of them.' (Ahmad).

66. The *hadith* that he, may Allah bless him and grant him peace, made a last testament about the *Ansar* at his death and said, 'Accept from their one who behaves excellently well and overlook (the behaviour of) their evildoer.' (Al-Bazzar and at-Tabarani).

67. 'I know a land which is called Oman whose shores the sea sprinkles, and in which there is a tribe of the Arabs. If my messenger were to come to them they would not shoot him either with arrows or stones.' (Ahmad and Abu Ya'la).

68. The *hadith* that Abu Bakr passed by al-Hasan while he was playing with some boys and he put him upon his neck and said, 'My father! A resemblance with the Prophet and no resemblance to 'Ali.' Ibn Kathir said: This is as if it were a *hadith* connected to the Prophet, because it has the strength of him saying, 'Truly the Prophet, may Allah bless him and grant him peace, used to resemble al-Hasan.'

69. The *hadith* that 'The Prophet, may Allah bless him and grant him peace, used to visit Umm Ayman.' (Muslim).

70. The *hadith* on the killing of the thief for the fifth theft. (Abu Ya'la and ad-Daylami).

71. The *hadith* of the story of Uhud. (At-Tayalisi and at-Tabarani).

72. 'While I was with the Messenger of Allah, may Allah bless him and grant him peace, I saw him pushing something away from himself but I did not see anything, so I said, "Messenger of Allah,

may Allah bless him and grant him peace, what are you pushing away?" He said, "The world. It extended itself towards me, so I said, 'Get away from me!' So it said to me, 'Why! You will not grasp me!?'" (Al-Bazzar).

This is what Ibn Kathir narrated in *Musnad as-Siddiq* of the *hadith* which are connected back to the Prophet, may Allah bless him and grant him peace, but there escaped him other *hadith* which we will follow on with in order to complete the number which an-Nawawi mentioned.

73. 'Kill the individual[8] whatever he may be among men.' (At-Tabarani in *al-Awsat*).

74. 'Look to whose houses you frequent, whose land you inhabit and in whose path you walk.' (Ad-Daylami).

75. 'Increase in sending blessings upon me, for Allah has appointed an angel for my grave, so that when a man of my *ummah* sends blessings, that angel will say to me, "So-and-so the son of so-and-so has this very hour sent blessings upon you."' (Ad-Daylami).

76. 'The *Jumuʿah* (Friday prayer) to the *Jumuʿah* is an expiation for what is between them, and the *ghusl* (complete washing of the entire body) on the day of the *Jumuʿah* is an expiation.' (A *hadith* of al-ʿAqili in *ad-Duʿafa* [weak traditions]).

77. 'The heat of *Jahannam* will only be for my *ummah* like the heat of the hot baths.' (At-Tabarani).

78. 'Beware of lying, for lying is remote from *iman*.' (Ibn Lal in *Makarim al-Akhlaq*).

---

8 The edition from which I worked had *qurd* which I translated as "tick (bloodsucker)" and that agreed with the existing 19th century translation. But further investigation shows that most editions of the *Tarikh* as well as of the *Awsat* from which as-Suyuti cites the hadith have *fard* "individual". This is understood to be the individual who stands against the ruler in such a fashion as to divide the Muslims. However, because the hadith has only one narrator at one point in the *isnad* and is transmitted through no other channels, it is not itself the basis for a legal judgement.

62. 'I have been given seventy thousand who will enter the Garden without any reckoning.' (Ahmad).

63. The Hadith of Intercession in its full length with people's going back and forward between prophet after prophet. (Ahmad).

64. 'Even if mankind were to travel in a valley and the *Ansar* were to travel in another valley, I would travel in the valley of the *Ansar*.' (Ahmad).

65. 'Quraysh are the masters of this authority, the best of them following the best of them and the worst of them following the worst of them.' (Ahmad).

66. The *hadith* that he, may Allah bless him and grant him peace, made a last testament about the *Ansar* at his death and said, 'Accept from their one who behaves excellently well and overlook (the behaviour of) their evildoer.' (Al-Bazzar and at-Tabarani).

67. 'I know a land which is called Oman whose shores the sea sprinkles, and in which there is a tribe of the Arabs. If my messenger were to come to them they would not shoot him either with arrows or stones.' (Ahmad and Abu Yaʿla).

68. The *hadith* that Abu Bakr passed by al-Hasan while he was playing with some boys and he put him upon his neck and said, 'My father! A resemblance with the Prophet and no resemblance to ʿAli.' Ibn Kathir said: This is as if it were a *hadith* connected to the Prophet, because it has the strength of him saying, 'Truly the Prophet, may Allah bless him and grant him peace, used to resemble al-Hasan.'

69. The *hadith* that 'The Prophet, may Allah bless him and grant him peace, used to visit Umm Ayman.' (Muslim).

70. The *hadith* on the killing of the thief for the fifth theft. (Abu Yaʿla and ad-Daylami).

71. The *hadith* of the story of Uhud. (At-Tayalisi and at-Tabarani).

72. 'While I was with the Messenger of Allah, may Allah bless him and grant him peace, I saw him pushing something away from himself but I did not see anything, so I said, "Messenger of Allah,

may Allah bless him and grant him peace, what are you pushing away?" He said, "The world. It extended itself towards me, so I said, 'Get away from me!' So it said to me, 'Why! You will not grasp me!?'" (Al-Bazzar).

This is what Ibn Kathir narrated in *Musnad as-Siddiq* of the *hadith* which are connected back to the Prophet, may Allah bless him and grant him peace, but there escaped him other *hadith* which we will follow on with in order to complete the number which an-Nawawi mentioned.

73. 'Kill the individual[8] whatever he may be among men.' (At-Tabarani in *al-Awsat*).

74. 'Look to whose houses you frequent, whose land you inhabit and in whose path you walk.' (Ad-Daylami).

75. 'Increase in sending blessings upon me, for Allah has appointed an angel for my grave, so that when a man of my *ummah* sends blessings, that angel will say to me, "So-and-so the son of so-and-so has this very hour sent blessings upon you."' (Ad-Daylami).

76. 'The *Jumuʿah* (Friday prayer) to the *Jumuʿah* is an expiation for what is between them, and the *ghusl* (complete washing of the entire body) on the day of the *Jumuʿah* is an expiation.' (A *hadith* of al-ʿAqili in *ad-Duʿafa* [weak traditions]).

77. 'The heat of *Jahannam* will only be for my *ummah* like the heat of the hot baths.' (At-Tabarani).

78. 'Beware of lying, for lying is remote from *iman*.' (Ibn Lal in *Makarim al-Akhlaq*).

---

8   The edition from which I worked had *qurd* which I translated as "tick (bloodsucker)" and that agreed with the existing 19th century translation. But further investigation shows that most editions of the *Tarikh* as well as of the *Awsat* from which as-Suyuti cites the hadith have *fard* "individual". This is understood to be the individual who stands against the ruler in such a fashion as to divide the Muslims. However, because the hadith has only one narrator at one point in the *isnad* and is transmitted through no other channels, it is not itself the basis for a legal judgement.

79. 'Give the good news of the Garden to whoever took part in Badr.' (Ad-Daraqutni in *al-Afrad*).
80. 'The *deen* is Allah's weighty banner. Who is able to carry it?' (Ad-Daylami).
81. 'Surah Yasin is called the one which encompasses people generally in its goodness, which feeds and provides the means of living.' (Ad-Daylami, and al-Bayhaqi in *Shuʿab al-Iman*).
82. 'The humble and just ruler (*sultan*) is the shade of Allah and His spear in the land. There will be raised up for him (in the record of his actions) every day and night the actions of sixty siddiqs.' (Abu'sh-Shaykh and al-ʿAqili in *ad-Duʿafa*, and Ibn Hibban in *Kitab ath-Thawab*).
83. 'Musa said to his Lord, "What is the recompense for whoever consoles a mother bereaved of her child?" He said, "I will shade him in My shade."' (Ibn Shahin in *at-Targheeb*, and ad-Daylami).
84. 'O Allah, strengthen Islam with ʿUmar ibn al-Khattab.' (At-Tabarani in *al-Awsat*).
85. 'Game is not caught, nor a thorny tree lopped, nor the root of a tree cut except through insufficient glorification (of Allah).' (Ibn Rahwayh in his *Musnad*).
86. 'If I had not been sent among you, ʿUmar would have been sent.' (Ad-Daylami).
87. 'If the people of the Garden had traded, they would have traded in cloth.' (Abu Yaʿla).
88. 'Whoever rebels, inviting (allegiance) to himself or to another, while there is an *imam* (*amir* or *khalifah*) over people, then the curse of Allah, the angels and all men is upon him, so kill him.' (Ad-Daylami in *at-Tarikh*).
89. 'Whoever records some knowledge or a *hadith* from me, reward will not cease being recorded for him as long as that knowledge or *hadith* remains.' (Al-Hakim in *at-Tarikh*).
90. 'Whoever walks barefoot in obedience of Allah, then Allah will not ask him on the Day of Resurrection about what He made

obligatory upon him.' (At-Tabarani in *al-Awsat*).

91. 'Whoever it would please that Allah should shade him from the boiling of *Jahannam*, and that He should place him in His shade, then let him not be tough on the *mu'minun*, and let him be compassionate to them.' (Ibn Lal in *Makarim al-Akhlaq*, Abu'sh-Shaykh, and Ibn Hibban in *ath-Thawab*).

92. 'Whoever rises in the morning intending obedience towards Allah, Allah will record for him the reward of his day even if he disobeys Him.' (Ad-Daylami).

93. 'A people do not abandon *jihad* but that Allah will envelop them in punishment.' (At-Tabarani in *al-Awsat*).

94. 'One who forges a lie will not enter the Garden.' (Ad-Daylami without an *isnad*).

95. 'Do not despise any one of the Muslims because the small one of the Muslims is, with Allah, great.' (Ad-Daylami).

96. 'Allah says, "If you wish for My mercy then show mercy to My creation."' (Abu'sh-Shaykh, Ibn Hibban and ad-Daylami).

97. 'I asked the Prophet, may Allah bless him and grant him peace, about the lower garment and he took hold of the calf muscle. I said, "Messenger of Allah, increase me!" He took hold of the forepart of the muscle. I said, "Increase me," and he said, "There is no good in what is lower than that." I said, "We are destroyed, Messenger of Allah!" He said, "Abu Bakr, aim for and take a middle course and you will be safe."' (Abu Nu'aym in *Hilyat al-Awliya'*).

98. 'My palm and the palm of 'Ali are equal in justice.' (Ad-Daylami and Ibn 'Asakir).

99. 'Do not neglect to seek refuge from the *shaytan*, for if you do not see him, he is not unaware of you.' (Ad-Daylami who did not quote a chain of transmission).

100. 'Whoever builds a mosque for Allah, then Allah will build a house for him in the Garden.' (At-Tabarani in *al-Awsat*).

101. 'Whoever has eaten of this foul-smelling herb (garlic) then let

him not approach our mosque.' (At-Tabarani in *al-Awsat*).
102. The *hadith* of the raising of the hands in the opening, the bowing, the prostration and the rising. (Al-Bayhaqi in *as-Sunan*).
103. 'That he, may Allah bless him and grant him peace, gave a camel as a gift to Abu Jahl.' (Al-Isma'ili in his *Mu'jam*).
104. 'Looking at 'Ali is an act of worship.'[9] (Ibn 'Asakir).

That which is narrated from as-Siddiq in commentary on the Qur'an

Abu'l-Qasim al-Baghawi narrated that Ibn Abi Mulaykah said: Abu Bakr was asked about an *ayah* and he said, 'What land would hold me or what sky would shade me if I were to say about an *ayah* of the Book of Allah that which Allah did not wish?'

Abu 'Ubaydah narrated that Ibrahim at-Taymi said: Abu Bakr was asked about His words, exalted is He, '*And fruits and herbage,*' (Qur'an 80: 31) and he said, 'Which sky would shade me and what land would sustain me if I were to say about the Book of Allah that which I do not know?'

Al-Bayhaqi and others narrated that Abu Bakr was asked about *al-Kalalah* and he said, 'I will say my view on it and if it is correct it is from Allah, and if it is wrong it is from me and from *shaytan*. I think that it is the one who has no child nor parent (surviving to inherit from him).' When 'Umar was appointed *khalifah* he said, 'I am shy of rejecting something which Abu Bakr said.'

Abu Nu'aym narrated in *al-Hilyah* that al-Aswad ibn Hilal said: Abu Bakr said to his companions, 'What do you say about these two *ayat*, "*Truly, the ones who say, 'Our Lord is Allah', and then go straight, …*" (Qur'an 41: 30) and "*And the ones who believe and do not clothe their belief in wrongdoing …*"? (Qur'an 6: 82).' They said, 'Then they go straight and do not do wrong actions and do not clothe their belief in error.' He said, 'You have made it to carry

---

[9] Since the intelligent understand the greatness of the Creator from the glance at the creation. And Allah knows best.

a meaning which it cannot carry.' Then he said, 'They say, "Our Lord is Allah," and then they go straight, so they do not incline towards a god other than Him and do not clothe their belief in *shirk* (associating others as partners with Him)."

Ibn Jarir narrated that ʿAmir ibn Saʿd al-Bajili related from Abu Bakr as-Siddiq about His words, exalted is He, '*For the ones who do excellently well there is the very best and more,*' (Qur'an 10: 26) that he said, 'Gazing on the face of Allah, exalted is He.'

Ibn Jarir narrated that Abu Bakr said about His words, exalted is He, 'Truly the ones who say, "*Our Lord is Allah," and then go straight, …*' (Qur'an 41: 30), that he said, 'People have said it. So whoever dies upon that is of those who go straight.'

What is narrated from as-Siddiq of traditions which stop short at him, sayings, judgements, *khutbahs*, and prayers

Al-Lalika'i narrated in *as-Sunnah* that Ibn ʿUmar said: A man came to Abu Bakr and said, 'Do you see adultery as a decree (of Allah)?' He said, 'Yes.' He said, 'So Allah has decreed it for me and then later He will punish me for it?' He said, 'Yes, son of the uncircumcised woman. By Allah, if there were anybody with me, I would order him to cut off your nose.'

Ibn Abi Shaybah narrated in his *Musannaf* that az-Zubayr narrated that Abu Bakr said, while he was delivering the *khutbah* to people, 'People, be shy and modest before Allah. By the One in Whose hand my self is, I shade myself when I go to the toilet in the open spaces, covering my head out of modesty towards Allah.'

ʿAbd ar-Razzaq narrated in his *Musannaf* that ʿAmr ibn Dinar said: Abu Bakr said, 'Be shy before Allah. By Allah, I enter the toilet and I lean my back against the wall out of modesty before Allah.'

Abu Dawud narrated in his *Sunan* that Abu ʿAbdullah as-Sunabihi related that he once prayed the prayer after sunset behind Abu Bakr as-Siddiq and he recited in the first two sets of bowing and prostration the Fatihah and a *surah* from among the small *surahs* (at the end of the Qur'an) and that he recited in the third, '*Our Lord, do not cause our hearts to deviate after You have guided us.*' (Qur'an 3: 8)

Ibn Abi Khaythamah and Ibn ʿAsakir narrated that Ibn ʿUyaynah said: Abu Bakr used to say, when he was consoling a man for a bereavement, 'There is no harm in patience, and no benefit in impatience, and death is less serious than what comes before it and more severe than what comes after it. Remember the loss of the Prophet, may Allah bless him and grant him peace, and your affliction will seem little to you, and Allah will magnify your reward.'

Ibn Abi Shaybah and ad-Daraqutni narrated that Salim ibn ʿUbayd, and he was a Companion, said: Abu Bakr as-Siddiq used to say to me, 'Stand between me and the dawn so that I can take the pre-dawn meal (preparatory to fasting).'

And he narrated that Abu Qilabah and Abu's-Safar both said: Abu Bakr as-Siddiq used to say, 'Shut the door until we have eaten the pre-dawn meal.'

Al-Bayhaqi and Abu Bakr ibn Ziyad an-Naysaburi, in *Kitab az-Ziyadat*, narrated that Hudhayfah ibn Usayd said: I observed Abu Bakr and ʿUmar and what they would make apparent (of their actions), wishing to set sunnahs.

Abu Dawud narrated that Ibn ʿAbbas said: I bear witness that Abu Bakr as-Siddiq said, 'Eat the fish which float (on the surface, i.e. which have died naturally, as it is permitted to eat them).'

Ash-Shafiʿi narrated in *al-Umm* that Abu Bakr as-Siddiq disliked trading meat for live animals.

Al-Bukhari narrated that he placed the grandfather in the same standing as the father, meaning in inheritance.

Ibn Abi Shaybah narrated in his *Musannaf* that ʿAta' narrated from Abu Bakr that he said: The grandfather has the same degree as the father as long as there is no father but him, and the son of the son is in the place of the son as long as there is no son apart from him.

He narrated that al-Qasim narrated that Abu Bakr was brought a man who had denied his father and so Abu Bakr said, 'Hit the head for the *shaytan* is in the head.'

He narrated that Ibn Abi Malik said: Abu Bakr, when he prayed over the dead, used to say, 'O Allah, [he is] Your slave, whose family, property and relatives have forsaken him; the wrong action is great, and You are all-forgiving, compassionate.'

Sa'id ibn Mansur narrated in his *Sunan* that 'Umar narrated that Abu Bakr gave judgement that 'Asim ibn 'Umar ibn al-Khattab should go to Umm 'Asim ('Umar's ex-wife), and that he said (to 'Umar), 'Her scent, her odour and her gentleness are better for him than you are.'

Al-Bayhaqi narrated that Qais ibn Abi Hazim said: A man came to Abu Bakr and said, 'My father wants to take my property, all of it and he will make an end of it.' Abu Bakr said to his father, 'You can only have of his property that which will be sufficient for you.' He (the father) said, 'Khalifah of the Messenger of Allah, did the Messenger of Allah, may Allah bless him and grant him peace, not say, "You and your property belong to your father"?' So he said, 'Yes, and by that he only meant expenditure on maintenance.'

Ahmad narrated that 'Amr ibn Shu'ayb narrated from his father from his grandfather that Abu Bakr and 'Umar would not kill a freeman (in retaliation) for (the killing of) a slave.

Al-Bukhari narrated that Ibn Abi Mulaykah narrated from his grandfather that a man bit the hand of a man and so caused his (own) incisor to fall out, and Abu Bakr declared that there was no retaliation for it.

Ibn Abi Shaybah and al-Bayhaqi narrated that 'Ikrimah said that Abu Bakr gave judgement that there were fifteen camels for (cutting off or mutilating) an ear, and said, 'The hair and the turban will conceal its disfigurement.'

Al-Bayhaqi and others narrated that Abu 'Imran al-Juni said that Abu Bakr sent troops to Syria and put in command over them Yazid ibn Abi Sufyan and said, 'I counsel you with ten qualities:

do not kill a woman, nor a child, nor a feeble old man; do not cut down a fruitful tree; do not ruin cultivated land; do not slaughter a camel or a sheep except for its owner; do not destroy the date-palm, nor burn it; do not conceal plunder; and do not be cowardly.'

Ahmad, Abu Dawud and an-Nasa'i narrated that Abu Barzah al-Aslami said: Abu Bakr was angry with a man and his anger became very severe indeed, so I said, 'Khalifah of the Messenger of Allah, strike off his head!' He said, 'Woe to you! That belongs to no-one after the Messenger of Allah, may Allah bless him and grant him peace.'

Saif narrated in the *Kitab al-Futuh* from his shaykhs that al-Muhajir ibn Abi Umayyah, who was the Amir of al-Yamamah, had two women singers brought before him, one of whom had sung abuse of the Prophet, may Allah bless him and grant him peace, so he cut off her hand and pulled out her teeth; and the other had sung ridicule of the Muslims, so he cut off her hand, and pulled out her teeth. Abu Bakr wrote to him, 'It has reached me that which you have done with the woman who sang abusing the Prophet, may Allah bless him and grant him peace, and if it were not that you had preceded me I would have told you to kill her, because the *hadd* punishment for the prophets does not resemble other *hadd* punishments. Whoever of the Muslims dares to do that is a renegade, and if he is a non-Muslim who has a covenant with the Muslims then he is a treacherous and hostile enemy. As for the one who sang ridiculing the Muslims; if she was one of those who claim to be Muslims, then she should be taught manners and punished but not mutilated. If she was one of the people of the *dhimmah* (People of the Book living under the governance of the Muslims), then, by my life, that *shirk* which you have turned away from is greater (as a crime than ridicule of the Muslims). If I had previously commanded you in a case the like of this (and then later you had done what you did) you would have reached affliction, so accept that I will let things be, and beware of mutilating people, because it is a crime and must be avoided except in retaliation (for a similar crime of mutilation).'

Malik and ad-Daraqutni narrated that Safiyyah bint Abi ᶜUbayd narrated that a man had sexual intercourse with a virgin slave girl and confessed it, so he ordered that he should be whipped and then he exiled him to Fadak.

Abu Yaᶜla narrated that Muhammad ibn Hatib said: A man who had stolen was brought to Abu Bakr and already all his hands and feet had been cut off (for thefts), so Abu Bakr said, 'I cannot find anything for you except what the Messenger of Allah, may Allah bless him and grant him peace, decided about you on the day he ordered that you be killed, and he certainly knew better about you,' and he ordered that he be killed.

Malik narrated that al-Qasim ibn Muhammad said that a man from Yemen, who had a hand and a foot cut off, came and stayed with Abu Bakr. He complained to him that the governor of the Yemen had wronged him, and he used to pray at night. So Abu Bakr would say, 'By your father, your night is not the night of a thief.' Then later they missed some jewellery belonging to Asma' bint ᶜUmays, Abu Bakr's wife. He began to go around with them saying, 'Allah, You must take [to task] whoever plotted against the people of this righteous house.' Then they found the jewellery with a jeweller who claimed that the man whose limbs were amputated had brought it, and he confessed or someone witnessed against him. Abu Bakr gave the command and his left hand was cut off. Abu Bakr said, 'By Allah, his supplication against himself, for me is stronger and more severe against him than his theft.'

Ad-Daraqutni narrated that Anas said that Abu Bakr would cut (off the hand) for a shield whose value was five dirhams.

Abu Nuᶜaym narrated in *al-Hilyah* that Abu Salih said: When the people of the Yemen came in the time of Abu Bakr and they heard the Qur'an, they began to weep. Abu Bakr said, 'Just like this we used to be, then the hearts became hard.' Abu Nuᶜaym said, 'i.e. they became strong and tranquil with the *maʿrifah* (gnosis) of Allah, exalted is He.'

Al-Bukhari narrated that Ibn ʿUmar said: Abu Bakr said, 'Be regardful of Muhammad, may Allah bless him and grant him peace, in the people of his house.'

Abu ʿUbayd narrated in *al-Ghareeb* that Abu Bakr said, 'Fragrant good fortune to whoever dies in the time of weakness,' i.e. in the very beginning of Islam before the stirrings of dissensions.

The Four and Malik narrated that Qabisah said: A grandmother came to Abu Bakr as-Siddiq asking him for her inheritance and he said, 'There is nothing for you in the Book of Allah and I have not learnt that there is anything for you in the *Sunnah* of the Prophet of Allah, may Allah bless him and grant him peace, so go back until I ask people.' He asked people and al-Mughirah ibn Shuʿbah said, 'I attended the Messenger of Allah who gave her (a grandmother) a sixth.' Abu Bakr said, 'Is there anyone else with you?' Muhammad ibn Maslamah arose and said the like of what al-Mughirah had said. So Abu Bakr allocated her that.

Malik and ad-Daraqutni narrated that al-Qasim ibn Muhammad said that two grandmothers came to Abu Bakr seeking their inheritances, the mother of a mother and the mother of a father, and so he gave the inheritance to the mother of the mother. ʿAbd ar-Rahman ibn Sahl al-Ansari, who was one of those who had been present at Badr and was a member of Bani Harithah, said to him, 'Khalifah of the Messenger of Allah, you have given to the one from whom he would not have inherited if she had died!' And so he divided it between the two of them.

ʿAbd ar-Razzaq narrated in his *Musannaf* that ʿA'ishah, may Allah be pleased with her, narrated the *hadith* of the wife of Rifaʿah who was divorced from him and married ʿAbd ar-Rahman ibn az-Zubayr after him but he was unable to consummate the marriage, and so she wanted to return to Rifaʿah. The Messenger of Allah, may Allah bless him and grant him peace, said to her, 'No, not until you taste the sweetness of intercourse with him and he tastes the sweetness of intercourse with you.' This much is in the *Sahih*. ʿAbd ar-Razzaq added: She remained for a while and then she came to him and informed him that he had touched her. He forbade her to return to her first husband and said, 'O Allah, if it was more expansive for her that she should return to Rifaʿah, then her marriage to him would not be completed for her another time.' Then later she came to Abu Bakr and ʿUmar in their *khilafahs* and they both forbade her.

Al-Bayhaqi narrated that ʿUqbah ibn ʿAmir said that ʿAmr ibn al-ʿAs and Shurahbil ibn Hasanah both sent him as a messenger to Abu Bakr with the head of Bannan, the Byzantine general of Syria. When he came to Abu Bakr, he disapproved of that strongly and so ʿUqbah said to him, 'Khalifah of the Messenger of Allah, they (the Byzantines) do that with us.' He said, 'Are they following the *Sunnah* of the Persians and the Byzantines? Don't carry the head to me; a letter and news are enough.'

Al-Bukhari narrated that Qais ibn Abi Hazim said: Abu Bakr went into a woman of Ahmas called Zaynab, and he saw her not talking and he said, 'What is wrong with her that she does not talk?' They said, 'She performed the Hajj in silence.' He said to her, 'Speak, because this is not permitted. This is one of the acts of *Jahiliyyah*.' So she spoke and said, 'Who are you?' He said, 'I am a man of the *Muhajirun*.' She said, 'Which of the *Muhajirun*?' He said, 'From Quraysh.' She said, 'From which group of Quraysh?' He said, 'You are a real questioner – I am Abu Bakr.' She said, 'How long will we remain on this right matter which Allah has brought us after ignorance?' He said, 'Your remaining upon it will be as long as your *imams* stay upstanding.' She said, 'Who are the *imams*?' He said, 'Do your people not have leaders and nobles who order them and they obey them?' She said, 'Of course.' He said, 'They are those people.'

Al-Bukhari narrated that ʿAʾishah, may Allah be pleased with her, said: Abu Bakr had a slave who used to pay him his revenue. One day he brought him something and Abu Bakr ate of it. The slave said to him, 'Do you know what this is?' Abu Bakr said, 'What is it?' He said, 'I used to act as a foreteller of the future for a man in the *Jahiliyyah* and how good was the foretelling, except that I deceived. Then he met me and gave me that which you have eaten from.' So Abu Bakr thrust his hand in his mouth and vomited everything in his stomach. Ahmad narrated in *az-Zuhd* that Ibn Sirin said, 'I know of no-one who made himself vomit food which he had eaten except for Abu Bakr,' and he told the same story.

An-Nasa'i narrated that Aslam said that ʿUmar discovered Abu Bakr grasping his tongue, saying, 'This is the one which has brought me to so many places.'

Abu ʿUbayd narrated in *al-Ghareeb* that Abu Bakr passed by ʿAbd ar-Rahman ibn ʿAwf while he was quarrelling with his neighbour and he said, 'Do not quarrel with your neighbour for he will remain when people have left you.'

Ibn ʿAsakir narrated that Musa ibn ʿUqbah related that Abu Bakr as-Siddiq used to deliver the *khutbah* saying, 'Praise belongs to Allah, the Lord of the creatures, I praise Him and seek His aid, and We ask Him for generosity for that which is after death, because my term and yours have drawn near. And I witness that there is no god but Allah alone, no partner with Him and that Muhammad is His slave and messenger whom He sent with the Truth, as a bringer of good news and a warner and an illuminating lamp so that he might warn whoever is alive and that the word would be realised on the disbelievers. Whoever obeys Allah and His Messenger is truly guided, and whoever disobeys them has gone astray into clear error. I counsel you to have fearful obedience of Allah, and to cling strongly to the command of Allah which He has laid down for you and by which He has guided you, because the comprehensive summation of the guidance of Islam after the word of sincerity (the *shahadah*) is 'hearing and obedience' to whomever Allah has given authority over your affairs, for whoever obeys Allah and those who order the well-recognised virtues and forbid what is rejected, has succeeded and prospered, and discharged that duty with which he is obliged. Beware of following the whim of passion, for he is successful and prospers who is protected from the whim of passion, greed, ambition, and anger. Beware of boasting, for what boast can he have who is created from dust, and then will later return to dust, then later maggots will eat him, and he is today alive and tomorrow dead? So know a day by a day (the Last Day) and an hour by an hour (the Hour of the end). Protect yourselves from the supplication of the wronged one, and count yourselves among the dead, and be patient, for all action is by patience, and be on your guard, for watchfulness is useful. And act, and action will be accepted. Guard yourselves from that which Allah cautioned you about of His torment, and hasten to that which Allah promised you of His mercy. Understand and you will be understood, have fearful obedience (*taqwa*; literally – self-protecting) and you will be guarded, for Allah has made clear to you that for which He destroyed those who were before you, and that for which He saved whomever He saved before you. He has made clear to you in His book His *halal* and His *haram*, and which actions He loves and which He deplores. I will not neglect you and myself, and Allah is the One from Whom aid is sought. And there is no power (to prevent evil) and strength (to do right) but by Allah. Know that as long as you are sincere towards your Lord in your actions then you have obeyed your Lord and you have protected and guarded your portion, and you will be in a state of wellbeing. And that which you offer voluntarily for your *deen*, then make it a free-will offering (which you send) before you and you will receive full payment for your loan, and you will be given your permanent daily allowance of food during your poverty and in your (time of) need of it. Then reflect, slaves of Allah, on your brethren and your companions who have passed away. They have come to that which they sent before them and they are established upon that, and they are alone in the grief and the happiness in that which is after death. Allah has no partner, and there is no relationship between Him and any one of His creatures by which He will give him good or avert evil, excepting by obedience to Him and following His command. Truly, there is no good in a good after which comes the Fire, nor any evil in an evil after which comes the Garden. I say this word of mine and I seek the forgiveness of Allah, for me and for you. Send blessings on your Prophet, may Allah bless him and grant him peace, and peace be on him, the mercy of Allah and His blessings.'

Al-Hakim and al-Bayhaqi narrated that ʿAbdullah ibn Hakim said: Abu Bakr as-Siddiq addressed a *khutbah* to us and in it he praised Allah as He is worthy and then said, 'I counsel you with fearful obedience of Allah, that you praise Him as He is worthy, and that you mix longing with fear, because Allah, exalted is He, praised Zakariyya and the people of his family saying, "*They used to hasten competitively in doing good actions, and they would supplicate Us, full of longing and fear, and they were humble to Us.*" (Qur'an 21: 90). Then know, slaves of Allah, that Allah has taken, by His right, your selves as a pledge, and He has taken on that basis your covenants, and He has bought from you the transient little with the everlasting much. This Book of Allah is among you; its light does not become snuffed out and its wonders never end, so take illumination from its light, accept the sincere advice of His Book, and seek light from it for the Day of darkness; for He has only created you for His worship and service, and He has entrusted over you noble scribes who know what you are doing. Then know, slaves of Allah, that you go out in the mornings and come back in the evenings for a period of time (the life-span) the knowledge of which He has concealed from you; so if you are able that your life-spans should come to an end while you are on the work of Allah, then do so, and you will only be able to by the permission of Allah. Race in your life-spans before they pass away and return you to the worst of your actions, for some people have given their lives to others and forgotten themselves and I forbid you to be like them. Make haste! Make haste! Be quick! Be quick! For behind you there is a nimble pursuer whose command is very fast.'

Ibn Abi'd-Dunya, Ahmad in *az-Zuhd*, and Abu Nu'aym in *al-Hilyah* narrated that Yahya ibn Abi Kathir narrated that Abu Bakr used to say in his *khutbah*, 'Where are the handsome fair of face, conceited with their youth? Where are the kings who built the cities and fortified them? Where are those who used to be given conquests in battles? Their strongest were humbled when time betrayed them and they awoke in the darknesses of the graves. Make haste! Make haste! Be quick! Be quick!'

Ahmad narrated in *az-Zuhd* that Salman said: I came to Abu Bakr and said, 'Counsel me!' He said, 'Salman, have fearful obedience of Allah, and know that there will be conquests, but I do not know what your portion of them will be, that which you put in your belly or throw upon your back (clothing). Know that whoever prays the five prayers enters the morning in a covenant with Allah, exalted is He, and enters the evening in a covenant with Allah, exalted is He. Do not kill anyone of the people who is in a covenant with Allah and thus behave treacherously towards Allah concerning His covenant, for then Allah will throw you down in the Fire upon your face.'

He narrated that Abu Bakr, may Allah be pleased with him, also said, 'The right-acting people will be taken away, the foremost and then the next foremost until there only remain chaff, husks and dregs of people like those left over from dates and barley, for whom Allah will not be concerned or care.'

Sa'id ibn Mansur narrated in his *Sunan* that Mu'awiyah ibn Qurrah narrated that Abu Bakr as-Siddiq, may Allah be pleased with him, used to say in his supplication, 'O Allah, make the best of my life the last of it, and the best of my action its seals and the best of my days the day I meet You.'

Ahmad narrated in *az-Zuhd* that al-Hasan said: It has reached me that Abu Bakr used to say in his supplication, 'O Allah, I ask You that which is best for me at the end of the affair. O Allah, make the last that You give me of good Your good pleasure and the highest ranks in the Gardens of Bliss.'

He narrated that ʿArfajah said: Abu Bakr, may Allah be pleased with him, said, 'Whoever is able to weep let him weep, and if not let him endeavour to weep.'

He narrated that ʿAzrah narrated: Abu Bakr, may Allah be pleased with him, said, 'Two reds have destroyed them (women): gold and saffron.'

He narrated that Muslim ibn Yasar narrated that Abu Bakr said, 'The Muslim is rewarded for everything, even a hurt (in the foot) caused by a stone, the breaking of his sandal's thong, or some article in his sleeve which he misses and fears for, then finds it in the fold (of his garment).'

He narrated that Maymun ibn Mihran said: Abu Bakr was brought a crow with large wings and he turned it over and said, 'No game is caught nor tree lopped but because of the glorification it neglected.'

Al-Bukhari narrated in *al-Adab*, and ʿAbdullah ibn Ahmad in the *Zawa'id az-Zuhd* that as-Sunabihi narrated that he heard Abu Bakr saying, 'The supplication of the brother for his brother for the sake of Allah is expected to be answered.'

ʿAbdullah ibn Ahmad in the *Zawa'id az-Zuhd* narrated from ʿUbayd ibn ʿUmayr that Labid the poet said that he came to Abu Bakr and said, 'Every thing apart from Allah is false.' Abu Bakr said, 'You have told the truth.' He said, 'And every bliss inevitably fades away.' He (Abu Bakr) said, 'You lie! With Allah there is a bliss that does not pass away.' When he turned away Abu Bakr said, 'Perhaps the poet said the word from wisdom.'

His words indicative of the strength of his fear of his Lord

Abu Ahmad al-Hakim narrated that Muʿadh ibn Jabal said: Abu Bakr entered a walled garden and there was a species of pigeon in the shade of a tree, so he sighed and then said, 'Fragrant good fortune to you, bird! You eat of the trees, you find shade in the trees, and you fly off without reckoning. Would that Abu Bakr was like you.'

Ibn ʿAsakir narrated that al-Asmaʿi said: When Abu Bakr was praised he used to say, 'O Allah, You know my self better than I do, and I know my self better than they do. O Allah, make me better than what they think, and forgive me for what they don't know, and don't take me to task for what they say.'

Ahmad narrated in *az-Zuhd* that Abu ʿImran al-Juni said: Abu Bakr said, 'I would love to be a hair in the side of a believing slave.'

Ahmad narrated in *az-Zuhd* that Mujahid said: Ibn az-Zubayr used to be like a piece of wood, when he stood in prayer, out of fearful humility and he said, 'I have been told that Abu Bakr was like that.'

He narrated that al-Hasan said: Abu Bakr said, 'By Allah, I wish that I was this tree which is eaten (from) and chopped down.'

He narrated that Qatadah said: It has reached me that Abu Bakr said, 'I wish that I was herbage which cattle eat.'

He narrated that Damrah ibn Habib said: Death came to a son of Abu Bakr as-Siddiq. The young man began to glance towards a mattress. When he died they said to Abu Bakr, 'We saw your son glancing towards the mattress.' They removed him from the mattress and found underneath it five or six dinars. Abu Bakr struck his hand upon the other repeatedly saying, '*Truly, we belong to Allah and truly we are returning to Him.* So and so, I don't think your skin would be ample enough for it.'

He narrated that Thabit al-Banani narrated that Abu Bakr used to quote this poem as a proverb:

'You will continue lamenting the death of a beloved until you are him,
  and the youth hopes a hope which he dies short of (attaining).'

Ibn Saʿd narrated that Ibn Sirin said: No-one after the Prophet, may Allah bless him and grant him peace, was as much in awe of what he did not know as Abu Bakr. No-one after Abu Bakr was as much in awe of what he did not know as ʿUmar. Sometimes a case would come before Abu Bakr for which he could find no source in the Book of Allah nor any trace or tradition in the *Sunnah* and so he would say, 'I will exert myself to arrive at my own conclusion. If it is right then it is from Allah. If it is wrong it is from me and I seek forgiveness of Allah.'

That which is narrated from him in interpretation of dreams

Saʿid ibn Mansur narrated that Saʿid ibn al-Musayyab said: ʿA'ishah, may Allah be pleased with her, saw in a dream as if three moons fell in her room. She told it to Abu Bakr – he was one of the best of men in interpretation – and he said, 'If your dream is true, then three of the best people on the earth will be buried in your room.' When the Prophet, may Allah bless him and grant him peace, died, he said, 'ʿA'ishah, this is the best of your moons.'

He also narrated that ʿUmar ibn Shurahbil said: The Messenger of Allah, may Allah bless him and grant him peace, said, 'I saw myself herding black sheep, then herding white sheep after them, until the black could not be seen among them.' Abu Bakr said, 'Messenger of Allah, as for the black sheep, they are the Arabs who will become Muslims in great numbers. The white sheep are the non-Arabs who will become Muslims until the Arabs cannot be seen among them because of their huge numbers.' The Messenger of Allah, may Allah bless him and grant him peace, said, 'In exactly the same way, the angel interpreted it before dawn.'

He has also narrated that Ibn Abi Layla said: The Messenger of Allah, may Allah bless him and grant him peace, said, 'I saw myself at a well drawing water from it, and black sheep came to me to drink, then later dusty white coloured sheep.' Abu Bakr said, 'Let me interpret it,' and he mentioned the like of the previous *hadith*.

Ibn Saʿd narrated that Muhammad ibn Sirin said: The most skilled in interpretation of dreams of this *ummah* after its Prophet was Abu Bakr.

Ibn Saʿd narrated that Ibn Shihab said: The Messenger of Allah, may Allah bless him and grant him peace, saw a dream and told it to Abu Bakr. He said, 'I saw as if I hastened to be first, I and you, up a ladder and that I beat you by two and a half steps.' He said, 'Messenger of Allah, Allah will take you to His forgiveness and mercy and I will live after you for two and a half years.'

ʿAbd ar-Razzaq narrated in his *Musannaf* that Abu Qilabah narrated that a man said to Abu Bakr as-Siddiq, 'I saw in sleep that I was urinating blood.' He said, 'You are a man who comes to his wife (in intercourse) while she is menstruating, so ask forgiveness of Allah and don't do it again.'

A point of interest

Al-Bayhaqi narrated in *ad-Dala'il* that ʿAbdullah ibn Buraydah said: The Messenger of Allah, may Allah bless him and grant him peace, sent ʿAmr ibn al-ʿAs in a raiding party in which were Abu Bakr and ʿUmar. When they reached the place of the war, ʿAmr told them not to light a fire. ʿUmar became angry, and he wanted to come to him, but Abu Bakr forbade him. He told him that the Messenger of Allah, may Allah bless him and grant him peace, only appointed him because of his knowledge of war. So he (ʿUmar) became calm.

Al-Bayhaqi narrated that Abu Maʿshar narrated from one of his shaykhs that the Messenger of Allah, may Allah bless him and grant him peace, said, 'I put a man in charge of a people, among whom there is one who is better than him, because he is more alert of the eye and more perceptive about war.'

Section

Khalifah ibn Khayyat, Ahmad ibn Hanbal and Ibn ʿAsakir narrated that Yazid ibn al-Asamm narrated that: The Prophet, may Allah bless him and grant him peace, said to Abu Bakr, 'Am I older (*akbar* also: greater) or you?' He said, 'You are greater and more noble and I have more years than you.' This is a *mursal* and very unusual tradition. If it is authentic this answer is counted as evidence of the high degree of his intelligence and courtesy. But it is well known that this reply was made by al-ʿAbbas, and that similarly it happened for Saʿid ibn Yarbuʿ in this wording: That the Messenger of Allah, may Allah bless him and grant him peace, said to him, 'Which of us is older (*akbar*)?' He said, 'You are greater and better than me and I am older.'

Abu Nuʿaym narrated that it was said to Abu Bakr, 'Khalifah of the Messenger of Allah, will you not confer authority on the people of Badr?' He said, 'I know their rank, but I dislike to sully them with the world.'

Ahmad narrated in *az-Zuhd* from Ismaʿil ibn Muhammad that Abu Bakr divided up some property equally among the people. ʿUmar said to him, 'Do you make the companions of Badr and other people equal?' Abu Bakr said to him, 'The world is only a sufficiency and the best sufficiency is the vastest. Their merit is only in their wages.'

Section

Ahmad narrated in *az-Zuhd* that Abu Bakr ibn Hafs said: It has reached me that Abu Bakr used to fast in summertime and break his fast in wintertime.

Ibn Saʿd narrated that Hayan as-Saʾigh said: The engraving on the signet ring of Abu Bakr was, 'Blessed as the One Who Decrees is Allah.'

Note: At-Tabarani narrated that Musa ibn ʿUqbah said, 'We don't know of four who reached the Prophet, may Allah bless him and grant him peace, and their sons as well, except for these four: Abu Quhafah, his son Abu Bakr as-Siddiq, his son ʿAbd ar-Rahman and Abu ʿAteeq ibn ʿAbd ar-Rahman whose name was Muhammad.

Ibn Mandah and Ibn ʿAsakir narrated that ʿAʾishah, may Allah be pleased with her, said: None of the *Muhajirun*'s fathers became Muslims except for Abu Bakr's.

Note: Ibn Saʿd and al-Bazzar narrated with a good *isnad* that Anas said: The oldest of the companions of the Messenger of Allah, may

Allah bless him and grant him peace, were Abu Bakr as-Siddiq and Suhayl ibn ʿAmr ibn Bayda'.

Note: Al-Bayhaqi narrated in *ad-Dala'il* that Asma' bint Abi Bakr said: When it was the year of the Opening (of Makkah to Islam) a daughter of Abu Quhafah went out and the cavalry met her. She was wearing a neck-ring of silver around her neck, and a man tore it off her neck. When the Prophet, may Allah bless him and grant him peace, entered the mosque, Abu Bakr stood and said, 'I adjure you (the Muslims) by Allah and Islam, (to return) my sister's neck-ring.' By Allah, no-one answered him. He said it a second time and no-one answered him. Then he said, 'Sister, hope for a recompense (from Allah) for your neck-ring, for, by Allah, trustworthiness this day among people is very scarce.'

Note: I have seen in the handwriting of al-Hafidh adh-Dhahabi:

Those who were unique in their ages for their skills were: Abu Bakr as-Siddiq in genealogy, ʿUmar ibn al-Khattab in strength in the command of Allah, ʿUthman ibn ʿAffan in modesty, ʿAli in judgement, Ubayy ibn Kaʿb in recitation, Zaid ibn Thabit in the laws of inheritance, Abu ʿUbaydah ibn al-Jarrah in trustworthiness, Ibn ʿAbbas in commentary (on Qur'an), Abu Dharr in truthfulness, Khalid ibn al-Walid in bravery, al-Hasan al-Basri in reminding, Wahb ibn Munabbih in stories, Ibn Sirin in interpretation (of dreams), Nafiʿ in recitation, Abu Hanifah in *fiqh*, Ibn Ishaq in [history of] the battles, Muqatil in allegorical interpretation, al-Kalbi in the stories of the Qur'an, al-Khalil in the measures and metres of poetry, Fudayl ibn ʿIyad in worship, Sibawih in grammar, Malik in knowledge, Yahya ibn Maʿin in knowledge of men (i.e. the transmitters of knowledge and *hadith*), Abu Tammam in poetry, Ahmad ibn Hanbal in *Sunnah*, Al-Bukhari in criticism of the *hadith*, al-Junayd in *at-Tasawwuf*, Muhammad ibn Nasr al-Marwazi in those matters of *fiqh* on which there is disagreement, al-Jabani on al-Ashʿari *iʿtizal* in theology, Muhammad ibn Zakariyya ar-Razi in medicine, Abu Maʿshar in astrology, Ibrahim al-Karmani in interpretation (of dreams), Ibn Nabatah in *khutbahs*, Abu'l-Farj al-Asbahani in public speaking, Abu'l-Qasim at-Tabarani in adjustments in cases of inheritance, Ibn Hazm in the apparent meanings (adh-Dhahir), Abu'l-Hasan al-Bakri in lies, al-Hariri in his *al-Maqamat*, Ibn Mandah in the breadth of his travelling, al-Mutanabbi in poetry, al-Mawsili in singing, as-Suli in chess, al-Khatib al-Baghdadi in swiftness of reading, ʿAli ibn Hilal in calligraphy, ʿAta' as-Sulaymi in fear, the *Qadi* al-Fadil in composition, al-Asmaʿi in anecdotes, Ashʿab in ambition, Muʿabbad in singing and Ibn Sina' in philosophy.

ʿUmar ibn al-Khattab
may Allah be pleased with him

ʿUmar ibn al-Khattab ibn Nufayl ibn ʿAbdu'l-ʿUzza ibn Riyah ibn Qart ibn Razah ibn ʿAdi ibn Kaʿb ibn Luʾayy, *Amir al-Muʾminin*, Abu Hafs, al-Qurashi, al-ʿAdawi, al-Faruq.

He accepted Islam in the sixth year of prophecy when he was twenty-seven years old, says adh-Dhahabi.

An-Nawawi says: ʿUmar was born thirteen years after the Elephant, he was one of the nobility of Quraysh, and he had the role of ambassador in the *Jahiliyyah*; Quraysh, whenever war broke out among them or between them and others, would send him as an ambassador, i.e. a messenger, and when someone called them to judgement – often over a matter of standing or lineage – then they sent him as a response to that.

He accepted Islam very early on, after forty other men and eleven women. Some say that it was after thirty-nine men and twenty-three women, and some say, after forty-five men and eleven women. But it was only after he accepted Islam that Islam was shown openly in Makkah and the Muslims rejoiced in him.

He said: He was one of the outstripping first ones, one of the ten for whom it was witnessed that they were for the Garden, one of the *khulafaʾ* who took the right way, one of the in-laws of the Prophet, may Allah bless him and grant him peace, one of the great men of knowledge of the Companions and one of their abstinent people.

There are related from him five hundred and thirty-nine *hadith* from the Prophet, may Allah bless him and grant him peace.

ʿUthman ibn ʿAffan narrated from him, ʿAli (ibn Abi Talib), Talhah (ibn ʿUbaydullah), Saʿd (ibn Abi Waqqas), ʿAbd ar-Rahman ibn ʿAwf, Ibn Masʿud, Abu Dharr, ʿAmr ibn ʿAbasah and his son ʿAbdullah, Ibn ʿAbbas, Ibn az-Zubayr, Anas, Abu Hurayrah, ʿAmr ibn al-ʿAs, Abu Musa al-Ashʿari, al-Baraʾ ibn ʿAzib, Abu Saʿid al-Khudri, and a great number of the Companions and others, may Allah be pleased with them.

I say: I attach here some sections in which there are some collections of interest connected to his biography.

The reports on his acceptance of Islam

At-Tirmidhi narrated that Ibn ʿUmar narrated that: The Prophet, may Allah bless him and grant him peace, said, 'O Allah, strengthen Islam with whoever is more beloved to You of these two men: ʿUmar ibn al-Khattab or Abu Jahl ibn Hisham.' At-Tabarani narrated this from *hadith* of Ibn Masʿud and Anas, may Allah be pleased with them.

Al-Hakim narrated that Ibn ʿAbbas related that the Prophet, may Allah bless him and grant him peace, said, 'O Allah, strengthen Islam by ʿUmar ibn al-Khattab especially.' At-Tabarani narrated this in the *Awsat* from a *hadith* of Abu Bakr as-Siddiq and in the *Kabir* from *hadith* of Thawban.

Ahmad narrated that ʿUmar said: I went out to confront the Messenger of Allah, may Allah bless him and grant him peace, and found that he had preceded me to the mosque (of Makkah). I stood behind him and he began by reciting Suratu'l-Haqqah. I was astonished by the composition of the Qur'an, so I said, 'By Allah, this is a poet as Quraysh say.' Then he recited, '*It is truly the saying of a noble messenger, and it is not the saying of a poet, how little you believe...*' (Qur'an 69: 40) to the end of the *ayah*, and Islam came about in my heart.

Ibn Abi Jabir narrated that Jabir said: The beginning of ʿUmar's Islam was that ʿUmar said, 'My sister's time to give birth came to her at night so I went out of the house, and entered the precincts of the Ka'bah. Then the Prophet, may Allah bless him and grant him peace, came and entered the *Hijr* (the low-walled, semi-circular area to one end of the Ka'bah) and on him there were two rough cloths. He prayed to Allah as much as Allah willed, then he turned away and I heard something the like of which I had not heard. He went out and I followed him and he said, "Who is this?" I said, "'Umar." He said, "'Umar, will you not leave me alone, either by night or by day?" I became afraid that he might supplicate against me, so I said, "I witness that there is no god but Allah and that you are the Messenger of Allah." He said, "'Umar, keep it secret." I said, "No, by the One Who sent you with the truth, I will openly declare it just as I openly declared idolatry."'

Ibn Sa'd, Abu Ya'la, al-Hakim, and al-Bayhaqi in *ad-Dala'il*, narrated that Anas, may Allah be pleased with him, said: 'Umar went out wearing his sword, and a man from Bani Zuhrah met him and said, 'Where do you intend going, 'Umar?' He said, 'I want to kill Muhammad.' He said, 'How will you be safe from Bani Hashim and Bani Zuhrah if you have killed Muhammad?' He said, 'I can only believe that you have converted.' He said, 'Shall I show you something astonishing; your brother-in-law and your sister have converted and abandoned your *deen*.' 'Umar walked on and came to the two of them while Khabbab was with them. When he heard the sound of 'Umar he hid in the house, and then he ('Umar) entered and said, 'What is this murmur of lowered voices?' They had been reciting Taha. They said, 'Nothing but some conversation which we were holding.' He said, 'Perhaps you two have converted?' His brother-in-law said to him, ''Umar, what if the truth were outside of your *deen*?' So 'Umar leapt upon him and struck him severely. His sister came to push him away from her husband and he struck her a blow with his hand so that her face bled. Then she said, and she was angry, 'And if the truth were outside of your *deen*? I witness that there is no god but Allah and that Muhammad is His slave and

His Messenger.' ʿUmar said, 'Give me the writing which you have and I will read it,' – and ʿUmar used to read. His sister said to him, 'You are dirty, and no-one reads it but the purified (so stand and bathe yourself or perform *wudu*').' He stood and performed *wudu*', then he took the writing and read Taha until it came to, *'Truly I, I am Allah there is no god except Me, so worship Me and establish the prayer for My remembrance.'* (Qur'an 20: 14). ʿUmar said, 'Show me the way to Muhammad.' When Khabbab heard the words of ʿUmar he came out and said, 'Rejoice, ʿUmar! Because I hope that you are the (answer to the) supplication which the Messenger of Allah made for you on the night of Thursday, "O Allah, strengthen Islam with ʿUmar ibn al-Khattab or with ʿAmr ibn Hisham."' The Messenger of Allah, may Allah bless him and grant him peace, was in the lower part of the house which was at the foot of Safa and ʿUmar went off until he came to the house, at the door of which were Hamzah, Talhah and others. Hamzah said, 'This is ʿUmar; If Allah wants good for him he will become a Muslim; and if He wishes other than that, then killing him will be a little thing for us.' He said: And the Prophet, may Allah bless him and grant him peace, was inside receiving revelation. He came out when ʿUmar arrived, took hold of the folds of his clothes and the straps of his sword, and said, 'You won't give up, ʿUmar, until Allah visits you with disgrace and punishment like he did al-Walid ibn al-Mughirah.' ʿUmar said, 'I witness that there is no god but Allah and that you are the slave of Allah and His Messenger.'

Al-Bazzar, at-Tabarani, Abu Nuʿaym in *al-Hilyah*, and al-Bayhaqi in *ad-Dala'il* narrated that Aslam said: ʿUmar said to us, 'I was the most severe of people against the Messenger of Allah, may Allah bless him and grant him peace. Then one hot day at midday I was in one of the pathways of Makkah, and a man met me and said, "I am amazed at you, Ibn al-Khattab. You claim that you are like this and like this, and this matter has entered your own house." I said, "What is that?" He said, "Your sister has become a Muslim." So I went back in a fury and struck the door. Someone said, "Who is it?" I said, "ʿUmar." They hurried and hid from me. They had been reciting a page which they had and they abandoned it and forgot it. My sister got up to open the door, and I said to her, "Enemy of her own self, have you converted?" I struck her upon the head with something that I had in my hand so that the blood flowed and she cried. She said, "Ibn al-Khattab, whatever you are going to do, then do it, for I have converted." I entered and sat down on the couch. Then I glanced at the page and said, "What is this? Give it to me." She said, "You are not one of its people, you don't clean yourself after intercourse, and this is a writing which none touches except for those who have purified themselves." But I wouldn't give up until she gave it to me. I opened it and there in it was, "*In the name of Allah, the Merciful, the Compassionate.*" When I passed by one of the names of Allah, exalted is He, I became afraid of it and I put down the page. Then I came back to myself and picked up the page and there in it was, "*There glorifies Allah that which is in the heavens and the earth,*" and I became afraid. I read up until, "*believe in Allah and His messenger!*" (Qur'an 57: 1-7) and so I said, "I witness that there is no god but Allah," and so they all came out to me hastily, saying, "*Allahu Akbar!*" and said, "Rejoice! Because the Messenger of Allah, may Allah bless him and grant him peace, supplicated on Monday and said, 'O Allah strengthen Your *deen* with whoever is the more beloved of the two men to You, either Abu Jahl ibn Hisham or ʿUmar.'" They directed me to the Prophet, may Allah bless him and grant him peace, in a house at the foot of as-Safa, and I went to it and knocked on the door. They said, "Who is it?" I said, "Ibn al-Khattab." They knew my severity against the Messenger of Allah, may Allah bless him and grant him peace, so nobody moved to open the door until he said, may Allah bless him and grant him peace, "Open it for him." They opened it for me, two men grabbed hold of me by the upper arms and brought me to the Prophet, may Allah bless him and grant him peace, who said, "Leave him alone." Then he grabbed me by my shirt and dragged me forcibly towards him and said, "Accept Islam, Ibn al-Khattab. O Allah guide him," and I bore witness and the Muslims said, "*Allahu Akbar*!" so loudly that it was heard in the valleys of Makkah.

'They had been concealing themselves. I did not wish to see a man striking and being struck but that I experienced it myself and none of that touched me. I went to my uncle Abu Jahl ibn Hisham, who was one of the nobility, and knocked on his door. He said, "Who is it?" I said, "Ibn al-Khattab, and I have converted." He said, "Don't do it," and slammed the door on me. I said, "This isn't anything," and went to one of the great ones of Quraysh, called out to him and he came out to me. I said to him the same as I had said to my uncle, he said to me the same as my uncle had said to me, went in and slammed the door on me. I said, "This isn't anything, the Muslims are being struck and I am not being struck." A man said to me, "Would you like your acceptance of Islam to be known?" I said, "Yes." He said, "When people are seated in the *Hijr* go to so-and-so, a man who cannot possibly conceal a secret, and say to him, just between yourself and him, 'I have converted,' for it is very rare that he has ever concealed a secret." I went and people had already gathered in the *Hijr*. I said, just between me and him, "I have converted." He said, "Did you really do that?" I said, "Yes." He cried at the top of his voice, "Ibn al-Khattab has converted." They ran up to me; I was hitting them, they were hitting me and people gathered around me. Then my uncle said, "What is this group?" Someone said, "ᶜUmar has converted." He stood upon the *Hijr* and indicated with the palm of his hand, "I have helped the son of my sister." They dispersed from around me. I did not want to have seen any of the Muslims being struck and striking without seeing it myself, so I said, "This which has happened to me is nothing." I went to my uncle and said, "Your help is returned to you," and I continued to hit and be hit until Allah strengthened Islam.'

Abu Nu'aym narrated in *ad-Dala'il* and Ibn 'Asakir that Ibn 'Abbas, may Allah be pleased with both of them, said: I asked 'Umar, may Allah be pleased with him, 'For what reason were you called Al-Faruq?' He said, 'Hamzah accepted Islam three days before me. I went to the mosque, and Abu Jahl hurried up to abuse the Prophet, may Allah bless him and grant him peace, and Hamzah was told about it. He took his bow and came to the mosque up to the circle of Quraysh in which Abu Jahl was. He leant upon his bow facing Abu Jahl and looked at him, and Abu Jahl recognised the mischief in his face, and said, "What is wrong with you, Abu 'Umarah?" He raised his bow and with it struck one of the veins in his neck, cutting it so that blood flowed. Quraysh rectified that from fear of mischief and trouble.' He said, 'The Messenger of Allah, may Allah bless him and grant him peace, was concealed in the house of al-Arqam al-Makhzumi so Hamzah went off and accepted Islam. I went out three days after him and there was so-and-so son of so-and-so al-Makhzumi, and I said to him, "Do you yearn to get out of the *deen* of your ancestors and follow the *deen* of Muhammad?" He said, "If I did, then one who has much greater right upon you has also done it." I said, "Who is he?" He said, "Your sister and your brother in-law." I went off, found the door locked and heard the murmur of lowered voices. Then the door was opened for me. I entered and said, "What is this I hear with you?" They said, "You didn't hear anything," and the conversation continued between us until I took hold of my brother in-law's head and hit him, making him bleed. My sister stood up to me and took hold of my head and said, "That has happened despite you." I was ashamed when I saw the blood, so I sat down and said, "Show me this writing." My sister said, "No-one touches it except for the purified. If you are truthful then get up and bathe yourself." I got up and bathed myself, then I returned and sat down. They brought me a page in which was, "*In the name of Allah, the Merciful, the Compassionate.*" I said, "Wholesome and pure names!" "*Taha. We have not revealed* the Qur'an to you for you to grieve, ..." up to His words, "... *His are the most beautiful names.*" (Qur'an 20: 1-8). It became a great matter in my heart and I said, "From this Quraysh have fled!" I accepted Islam and said, "Where is the Messenger of Allah, may Allah bless him and grant him peace?" She said, "He is in the house of al-Arqam." I went to the house and knocked on the door. The people gathered and Hamzah said to them, "What is wrong with you." They said, "ᶜUmar." He said, "And if it is ᶜUmar? Open the door for him. If he has accepted, then we will accept that from him, and if he turns his back, we will kill him." The Messenger of Allah, may Allah bless him and grant him peace, heard that and came out. I pronounced the *shahadah* and the people of the house said, "*Allahu Akbar!*" in such a way that the people of Makkah heard it. I said, "Messenger of Allah, are we not upon the truth?" He said, "Of course." I said, "Why do we conceal it?" We went out in two ranks, in one of which I was and in the other Hamzah, until we entered the mosque, and Quraysh looked at me and at Hamzah. There came upon them gloom and depression the like of which had never before come upon them. The Messenger of Allah, may Allah bless him and grant him peace, named me on that day "al-Faruq" because Islam had been shown openly and a separation made between the truth and falsehood.'

Ibn Saᶜd narrated that Dhakwan said: I said to ᶜA'ishah, 'Who named ᶜUmar "*al-Faruq*"?' She said, 'The Prophet, may Allah bless him and grant him peace.'

Ibn Majah and al-Hakim narrated that Ibn ᶜAbbas, may Allah be pleased with them both, said: When ᶜUmar accepted Islam, then Jibril descended and said, 'Muhammad, the inhabitants of heaven rejoice in ᶜUmar's acceptance of Islam.'"

Al-Bazzar and al-Hakim, who declared it *sahih*, narrated that Ibn ᶜAbbas, may Allah be pleased with them both, said: When ᶜUmar accepted Islam, the idolaters said, 'The people have been split in half from us today,' and Allah revealed, '*O Prophet, Allah is enough for you; and whoever follows you of the believers.'* (Qur'an 8: 64).

Al-Bukhari narrated that Ibn Masᶜud, may Allah be pleased with him, said: We continued to become mighty after the acceptance of Islam by ᶜUmar.

Ibn Saᶜd and at-Tabarani narrated that Ibn Masᶜud, may Allah be pleased with him, said: The Islam of ᶜUmar was an opening, his emigration was a help and his imamate was a mercy. I saw us unable to pray towards the House until ᶜUmar accepted Islam. When ᶜUmar accepted Islam, he fought them until they left us alone and we prayed.

Ibn Saᶜd and al-Hakim narrated that Hudhayfah said: When ᶜUmar accepted Islam, Islam was like the man advancing towards you, only increasing in nearness. When ᶜUmar was killed, Islam was like the man backing away from you, only increasing in distance.

At-Tabarani narrated that Ibn ᶜAbbas, may Allah be pleased with them both, said: The first man to be open about Islam was ᶜUmar ibn al-Khattab.

Ibn Saᶜd narrated that Suhayb said: When ᶜUmar, may Allah be pleased with him, accepted Islam, he was open about it, invited people to it openly; we sat around the House in circles, we made circuits around the House, we took our rights from whoever was tough with us, and we retaliated against him for some of what he brought us.

Ibn Saᶜd narrated that Aslam the freed slave of ᶜUmar said: ᶜUmar accepted Islam in Dhu'l-Hijjah of the sixth year of prophethood while he was twenty-six years old.

His emigration

Ibn ᶜAsakir narrated that ᶜAli said: I don't know of anyone who didn't emigrate in secret except for ᶜUmar ibn al-Khattab; because when he wanted to emigrate he strapped on his sword, put his bow over his shoulder, carried his arrows in his hand, and came to the Kaᶜbah where the nobles of Quraysh were in the courtyard.

He performed seven circuits, and then prayed two *raka'at* at the Station (of Ibrahim). Then he approached their circle one step at a time and said, "What ugly faces! Whoever wishes to bereave his mother, orphan his children and widow his wife then let him meet me behind this valley." Not one of them followed him.

He narrated that al-Bara', may Allah be pleased with him, said: The first of the *Muhajirun* who came to us was Mus'ab ibn 'Umayr, then Ibn Umm Maktum, then 'Umar ibn al-Khattab mounted among twenty others. We said, 'What has the Messenger of Allah, may Allah bless him and grant him peace, done?' He said, 'He is right behind me.' Then later, the Prophet, may Allah bless him and grant him peace, came and Abu Bakr, may Allah be pleased with him, along with him.

An-Nawawi said: 'Umar attended, along with the Messenger of Allah, may Allah bless him and grant him peace, all of the battles, and he was one of those who stood firm beside him on the Day of Uhud.

The *hadith* on his merit, other than those already quoted in the chapter on as-Siddiq

The two Shaykhs narrated that Abu Hurayrah, may Allah be pleased with him, said: The Prophet, may Allah bless him and grant him peace, said, 'While I was asleep I saw myself in the Garden, and there was a woman performing *wudu'* beside a palace. I said, "Whose is this palace?" They said, "It belongs to 'Umar." Then I remembered your jealousy and turned away.' 'Umar wept and said, 'Could I be jealous of you, Messenger of Allah?'

The two Shaykhs narrated that Ibn 'Umar narrated that the Messenger of Allah, may Allah bless him and grant him peace, said, 'While I was asleep I drank – meaning milk – until I saw satiation flowing in my nails, and then I passed it to 'Umar.' They said, 'How did you interpret it, Messenger of Allah?' He said, 'Knowledge.'

The two Shaykhs narrated that Abu Sa'id al-Khudri, may Allah be pleased with him, said: I heard the Prophet, may Allah bless him and grant him peace, saying, 'While I was sleeping I saw people being shown to me and they had shirts on. Some of them reached to the breast, and some of them reached lower than that. ʿUmar was shown to me and he had on a shirt which he was dragging along.' They said, 'How did you interpret it, Messenger of Allah?' He said, 'The *deen*.'

The two Shaykhs narrated that Saʿd ibn Abi Waqqas said: The Prophet, may Allah bless him and grant him peace, said, 'Ibn al-Khattab, by Him in Whose hand is my self, the *shaytan* never met you travelling on a road but that he would travel on a road other than your road.'

Al-Bukhari narrated that Abu Hurayrah said: The Prophet, may Allah bless him and grant him peace, said, 'There were in the nations before you people who were inspired, and if there is one in my *ummah* it is ʿUmar.'

At-Tirmidhi narrated from Ibn ʿUmar that the Prophet, may Allah bless him and grant him peace, said, 'Allah has put the truth upon ʿUmar's tongue and (in) his heart.' Ibn ʿUmar said: No affair ever happened among people and they spoke about it and ʿUmar spoke about it but that the Qur'an was revealed confirming what ʿUmar said.

At-Tirmidhi narrated, as did al-Hakim who declared it *sahih*, that ʿUqbah ibn ʿAmir said: The Prophet, may Allah bless him and his family and grant them peace, said, 'If there were to be a prophet after me it would be ʿUmar ibn al-Khattab.' At-Tabarani narrated it from Abu Saʿid al-Khudri and ʿIsmah ibn Malik and Ibn ʿAsakir narrated it from Ibn ʿUmar.

At-Tirmidhi narrated that ʿA'ishah, may Allah be pleased with her, said: The Prophet, may Allah bless him and grant him peace, said, 'I am looking at the *shaytans* of the *jinn* and men who have fled from ʿUmar.'

Ibn Majah and al-Hakim narrated that Ubayy ibn Kaʿb said: The

Prophet, may Allah bless him and grant him peace, said, 'The first one whom the Truth will shake hands with is ʿUmar, the first He will greet (with the greeting of peace), and the first He will take by the hand and enter into the Garden.'

Ibn Majah and al-Hakim narrated that Abu Dharr said: The Prophet, may Allah bless him and grant him peace, said, 'Truly Allah has placed the truth upon the tongue of ʿUmar, it speaks by him (or he speaks by it).'

Ahmad and al-Bazzar narrated that Abu Hurayrah said: The Prophet, may Allah bless him and grant him peace, said, 'Truly Allah has placed the truth on the tongue of ʿUmar and (in) his heart.' At-Tabarani narrated this *hadith* from ʿUmar ibn al-Khattab, Bilal, Muʿawiyah ibn Abi Sufyan and ʿA'ishah, may Allah be pleased with them, and Ibn ʿAsakir narrated it from a *hadith* of Ibn ʿUmar,

Ibn Maniʿ narrated in his *Musnad* that ʿAli, may Allah be pleased with him, said: We, the Companions of Muhammad, used not to doubt that the *sakinah* (tranquillity or Divine presence) spoke by the tongue of ʿUmar.

Al-Bazzar narrated that Ibn ʿUmar said: The Prophet, may Allah bless him and grant him peace, said, 'ʿUmar is the lamp of the people of the Garden.' This *hadith* was narrated by Abu Hurayrah and as-Saʿb ibn Juththamah.

Al-Bazzar narrated from Qudamah ibn Madhʿun that his paternal uncle ʿUthman ibn Madhʿun said: The Prophet, may Allah bless him and grant him peace, said, 'This one is the lock upon the *fitnah* (sedition and trials),' and he indicated ʿUmar with his hand. 'There will remain a door strongly locked between you and the *fitnah* as long as this one lives among you.'

At-Tabarani narrated in *al-Awsat* that Ibn ʿAbbas, may Allah be pleased with both him and his father, said: Jibril came to the Prophet, may Allah bless him and grant him peace, and said, 'Greet ʿUmar with the greeting of peace and inform him that his anger is might and his good pleasure is judgement.'

Ibn 'Asakir narrated that 'A'ishah, may Allah be pleased with her, said that the Prophet, may Allah bless him and grant him peace, said, 'The *shaytan* is afraid of 'Umar.'

Ahmad narrated by way of Buraydah that the Prophet, may Allah bless him and grant him peace, said, 'The *shaytan* is afraid of you, 'Umar.'

Ibn 'Asakir narrated that Ibn 'Abbas, may Allah be pleased with both of them, said: The Prophet, may Allah bless him and grant him peace, said, 'There is no angel in the heaven that does not respect 'Umar, and no *shaytan* on the earth but that is afraid of 'Umar.'

At-Tabarani narrated in *al-Awsat* that Abu Hurayrah, may Allah be pleased with him, said: The Prophet, may Allah bless him and grant him peace, said, 'Allah glories in the people of 'Arafah generally and He glories in 'Umar particularly.' He narrated the same in *al-Kabir* in a *hadith* of Ibn 'Abbas, may Allah be pleased with them both.

At-Tabarani and ad-Daylami narrated that al-Fadl ibn 'Abbas said: The Prophet, may Allah bless him and grant him peace, said, 'The truth, after me, is with 'Umar wherever he is.'

The two Shaykhs narrated that Ibn 'Umar and Abu Hurayrah, may Allah be pleased with both of them, said: The Prophet, may Allah bless him and grant him peace, said, 'While I was asleep I saw myself at a well upon which was a bucket, so I drew from it as long as Allah willed. Then later Abu Bakr took it and drew a full bucket or two, and in his drawing there was some weakness, and Allah will forgive him. Then 'Umar ibn al-Khattab came and drew water and it became transformed in his hand into a large bucket, and I have not seen a chief of the people do wonderful deeds such as he did, until the people had satisfied their thirst and settled down (there by the water).'

An-Nawawi said in his *Tahdhib*: The men of knowledge say, 'This points to the *khilafahs* of Abu Bakr and 'Umar, and to the great number of conquests and the victory of Islam in the time of 'Umar.'

At-Tabarani narrated that Sadisah said: The Prophet, may Allah bless him and grant him peace, said, 'The *shaytan* has not met ʿUmar since he accepted Islam but that he fell upon his face.' Ad-Daraqutni narrated this *hadith* in *al-Afrad* by way of Sadisah from Hafsah.

At-Tabarani narrated that Ubayy ibn Kaʿb said: The Prophet, may Allah bless him and grant him peace, said, 'Jibril said to me, "Let Islam weep over the death of ʿUmar."'

At-Tabarani narrated in *al-Awsat* that Abu Saʿid al-Khudri said: The Prophet, may Allah bless him and grant him peace, said, 'Whoever is angry with ʿUmar is angry with me. Whoever loves ʿUmar loves me. Allah glories in the people on the evening of ʿArafah generally, and He glories in ʿUmar particularly. Allah has not sent a prophet except that he put among his *ummah* an inspired man and if there is one such in my *ummah* then it is ʿUmar.' They said, 'Prophet of Allah, how inspired?' He said, 'The angels speak by his tongue.' Its *isnad* is *hasan* (good).

Sayings of the Companions and first generations on him
Abu Bakr as-Siddiq, may Allah be pleased with him, said: There is not on the face of the earth a man more beloved to me than ʿUmar. Ibn ʿAsakir narrated it.

Someone said to Abu Bakr during his (last) illness, 'What will you say to your Lord, when you have appointed ʿUmar?' He said, 'I will say to Him, "I have appointed over them the best of them."' Ibn Saʿd narrated it.

ʿAli, may Allah be pleased with him, said: When the right-acting are mentioned then begin with ʿUmar. We did not think it unlikely that *as-Sakinah* (the Divine Presence) spoke with the tongue of ʿUmar. At-Tabarani narrated it in *al-Awsat*.

Ibn ʿUmar, may Allah be pleased with him, said: I have never seen anyone after the Prophet, may Allah bless him and grant him peace, from the time he died, more perceptive and more liberally generous than ʿUmar. Ibn Saʿd narrated it.

Ibn Mas'ud, may Allah be pleased with him, said: Even if the knowledge of 'Umar were to be put in one scale of a balance and the knowledge of every living being on the earth were put in the other scale, the knowledge of 'Umar would outweigh their knowledge. They used to hold the view that he had gone (i.e. died) with nine-tenths of knowledge. At-Tabarani narrated it in *al-Kabir*, and al-Hakim narrated it.

Hudhayfah, may Allah be pleased with him, said: It is as if the knowledge of mankind was concealed in the understanding of 'Umar.

Hudhayfah, may Allah be pleased with him, said: By Allah, I do not know a man whom the blame of the one who blames, for the sake of Allah, does not overcome, except for 'Umar.

'A'ishah, may Allah be pleased with her, said – and she mentioned 'Umar – 'He was, by Allah! skilful in managing affairs, absolutely unique.'

Mu'awiyah, may Allah be pleased with him, said: As for Abu Bakr, he did not want the world and it did not want him. As for 'Umar, the world wanted him but he did not want it. As for us, we have rolled over in it (like an animal in the dust). Az-Zubayr ibn Bakkar narrated it in *al-Muwaffaqiyat*.

Jabir, may Allah be pleased with him, said: 'Ali entered upon 'Umar – and he was shrouded – and said, 'The mercy of Allah upon you! There is no-one I would prefer to meet Allah with that which is in his page (the record of his actions), after the companionship of the Prophet, may Allah bless him and grant him peace, than this shrouded one.' Al-Hakim narrated it.

Ibn Mas'ud, may Allah be pleased with him, said: When the right-acting ones are remembered, then begin with 'Umar. Truly 'Umar was the most knowledgeable of us of the Book of Allah, and the most understanding (literally: having the most *fiqh*) of us of the *deen* of Allah, exalted is He. At-Tabarani and al-Hakim narrated it.

Ibn 'Abbas was asked about Abu Bakr and he said, 'He was the good, all of it.' He was asked about 'Umar and said, 'He was like the apprehensive bird which thinks that on every path there is a snare to catch it.' He was asked about ʿAli and he said, 'He was full of resolve, sound judgement, knowledge and valour.' He narrated it in *at-Tuyuriyyat*.

At-Tabarani narrated from ʿUmayr ibn Rabiʿah that ʿUmar ibn al-Khattab said to Kaʿb al-Ahbar, 'How do you find my description?' He said, 'I find your description to be a horn of iron.' He asked, 'What is a horn of iron?' He said, 'A strong commander who, for the sake of Allah, the censure of the one who blames does not overcome.' He said, 'Then what?' He said, 'There will be after you a *khalifah* whom a wrongdoing group will kill.' He said, 'Then what?' He said, 'Then there will be the trial (affliction).'

Ahmad, al-Bazzar and at-Tabarani narrated that Ibn Masʿud, may Allah be pleased with him, said: ʿUmar ibn al-Khattab excelled people in four: the affair of the prisoners on the Day of Badr, he ordered that they should be killed and Allah revealed, *'If it were not for a decree of Allah which had preceded ...'* (Qurʾan 8: 68) to the end of the *ayah*; and in the matter of the *hijab*, he ordered the women of the Prophet, may Allah bless him and grant him peace, to veil themselves, so Zaynab said to him, 'And really you are responsible over us Ibn al-Khattab, and the revelation descends upon us in our houses?' So Allah revealed, *'Then if you ask them for some item ...'* (Qurʾan 33: 53) to the end of the *ayah*; and by the supplication of the Prophet, may Allah bless him and grant him peace, 'O Allah, help Islam with ʿUmar'; and in his view of Abu Bakr, for he was the first one to pledge allegiance to him.

Ibn ʿAsakir narrated that Mujahid said: We used to say that the *shaytans* were chained and shackled during the amirate of ʿUmar, then when he was struck they spread abroad.

He narrated that Salim ibn ʿAbdullah said: News of ʿUmar was slow in reaching Abu Musa so he went to a woman who had a *shaytan* in her, and asked her about him. She said, 'Wait until my *shaytan* comes to me.' Then he came and she asked him about him.

He said, 'I left him dressed with a piece of cloth as a waistwrapper, smearing the camels of the *sadaqah* (the *zakat*) with tar (against the mange or scab). And that is a man whom a *shaytan* does not see but that he falls flat on his nostrils; the angel is between his two eyes and the *Ruh al-Quds* (Jibril) speaks with his tongue.'

Section

Sufyan ath-Thawri said: Whoever claimed that ʿAli had more right to authority than Abu Bakr and ʿUmar has made a mistake and has accused Abu Bakr, ʿUmar and all the *Muhajirun* and the *Ansar* of making a mistake.

Sharik said: No-one in whom there is any good advances ʿAli before Abu Bakr and ʿUmar.

Abu Usamah said: Do you grasp who Abu Bakr and ʿUmar were? They were the father and mother of Islam.

Jaʿfar as-Sadiq said: I am quit of whoever mentions Abu Bakr and ʿUmar with anything but good.

The agreements of (the views of) ʿUmar
(with subsequent confirmatory revelations of Qur'an)

Some of them make them amount to more than twenty.

Ibn Mardawayh narrated that Mujahid said: ʿUmar used to hold a view and Qur'an would be revealed with (confirmation of) it.

Ibn ʿAsakir narrated that ʿAli said: In the Qur'an there are some of the views of ʿUmar.

He narrated from Ibn ʿUmar as a *marfuʿ* [*hadith*]: When people said one thing and ʿUmar said another, the Qur'an would be revealed with the like of what ʿUmar said.

The two Shaykhs narrated that ʿUmar said: I agreed with my Lord in three things; I said, 'Messenger of Allah, if only we were to take the Station of Ibrahim as a place of prayer,' and there was revealed, '… *and take the Station of Ibrahim as a place of prayer.*' (Qur'an 2: 125). I said, 'Messenger of Allah, both good and bad people come to visit your wives; if only you would order them to wear *hijabs*,' and the *ayah* of the *hijab* was revealed. The wives of the Prophet, may Allah bless him and grant him peace, united in jealousy, and so I said, '*Perhaps his Lord, if he divorces you, will give him in exchange wives better than you, …*' and it was revealed just like that (with exactly the same words, see Qur'an 66: 5).

Muslim narrated that ʿUmar said, 'I agreed with my Lord in three things: in the *hijab*, in the prisoners at Badr, and in the Station of Ibrahim.' In this *hadith* is a fourth instance.

In *at-Tahdhib* of an-Nawawi, 'The Qur'an was revealed in agreement with him on the prisoners at Badr, on the *hijab*, on the Station of Ibrahim and on the prohibition of wine.' He added a fifth instance and its *hadith* is in the *Sunan* and the *Mustadrak* of al-Hakim that he said, 'O Allah, make clear to us about wine with an explanation which relieves us from all doubt.' Then Allah revealed its prohibition.

Ibn Abi Hatim narrated in his *tafsir* that Anas said: ʿUmar said, 'I was in agreement with my Lord in four things: this *ayah* was revealed, "*And certainly We have created man from an extraction of clay,*" (Qur'an 23: 12) and when it was revealed I said, "So blessed be Allah the best of creators," and then it was revealed, "*So blessed be Allah the best of creators.*"' (Qur'an 95: 8). Here he mentioned a sixth instance. The *hadith* has another chain of transmission from Ibn ʿAbbas which I have narrated in *at-Tafsir al-Musnad*.

Then I saw in the book *Fada'il al-Imamayn* of Abu ʿAbdullah ash-Shaybani that he said, 'ʿUmar agreed with his Lord in twenty-one situations,' and he mentioned these six (aforementioned). He augmented as a seventh the story of ʿAbdullah ibn Ubayy. I say: Its *hadith* is in the *sahih* traditions from him (ʿUmar). He said, 'When ʿAbdullah ibn Ubayy died, the Messenger of Allah, may Allah bless him and his family and grant them peace, was invited to perform the funeral prayer over him so he stood up for that. I rose up until I stood up close to his chest and said, "Messenger of Allah, is it over the enemy of Allah, Ibn Ubayy, who said one day such-and-such?" Then, by Allah, it wasn't very long until it was revealed, "*And do not pray over one of them ever ...*" (Qur'an 9: 84) to the conclusion of the *ayah*.'

8. '*They ask you about wine ...*' (Qur'an 2: 219) to the end of the *ayah*.

9. '*O you who believe, do not approach the prayer ...*' (Qur'an 4: 43) to the end of the *ayah*. I say that the two of them, along with the *ayah* from Al-Ma'idah, are one instance, and the three are in the preceding *hadith*.

10. When the Messenger of Allah, may Allah bless him and grant him peace, increased in seeking forgiveness for a people, ʿUmar said, 'It is equal to them.' Then Allah revealed, '*It is equal to them whether you seek forgiveness for them ...*' (Qur'an 63: 2) to the end of the *ayah*. I say that this *hadith* has been narrated by at-Tabarani from Ibn ʿAbbas.

11. When he, may Allah bless him and grant him peace, sought the advice of the Companions about the expedition to Badr, ʿUmar was in favour of the expedition and so it was revealed, '*Just as your Lord brought you out of your house by the truth ...*' (Qur'an 8: 5) to the end of the *ayah*.

12. When he, may Allah bless him and grant him peace, sought the advice of the Companions with respect to the story of the slander (of ʿA'ishah) ʿUmar said, 'Who married you to her, Messenger of Allah?' He said, 'Allah.' He said, 'Do you think that your Lord would conceal a defect of hers from you? *Glory be to You, this is huge slander!*' (Qur'an 24: 16). Then the revelation came down just like that.

13. His story in the fast when he made love to his wife after waking from sleep (before the pre-dawn meal) – and that was forbidden in the beginning of Islam – and so it was revealed, '*It is permitted to you on the night of the fast ...*' (Qur'an 2: 187) to the end of the *ayah*. I say that Ahmad narrated it in his *Musnad*.

14. His words, Exalted is He, '*Whoever is an enemy to Jibril …*' (Qur'an 2: 97) to the end of the *ayah*. I say that Ibn Jarir and others narrated it from many different narrators the best of which is from ᶜAbd ar-Rahman ibn Abi Layla that: A Jew met ᶜUmar and said, 'Jibril, whom your companion mentions, is an enemy to us.' So ᶜUmar said, '*Whoever is an enemy to Allah and His angels and His messengers and Jibril and Mika'il, then truly Allah is an enemy to the disbelievers.*' So it was revealed on the tongue of ᶜUmar.

15. His words, Exalted is He, '*Then no! By your Lord, they do not believe …*' (Qur'an 4: 65) to the end of the *ayah*. I say that its story has been narrated by Ibn Abi Hatim and Ibn Mardawayh from Abu'l-Aswad. He said: Two men brought a dispute to the Prophet, may Allah bless him and his family and grant them peace, and he gave judgement between them. The one who had judgement given against him said, 'Let us go to ᶜUmar ibn al-Khattab,' and so the two of them went to him. The man said, 'The Messenger of Allah, may Allah bless him and grant him peace, gave judgement in my favour against this man and he said, "Let us go to ᶜUmar."' ᶜUmar said, 'Is it like that?' He said, 'Yes.' So ᶜUmar said, 'Stay where you are until I come out to you.' Then he came out to them wrapping his sword in his garment and struck the one who had said, 'Let us go to ᶜUmar,' and killed him. The other returned and said, 'Messenger of Allah, ᶜUmar killed – by Allah! – my companion.' So he said, 'I wouldn't have thought that ᶜUmar would have ventured to kill a believer.' Then Allah revealed, '*Then no! By your Lord they do not believe …*' to the end of the *ayah*. He declared, there was to be no retaliation or compensation for the blood of the man and declared ᶜUmar free from any wrong in his killing. There is another connected text that supports this story which I have related in *at-Tafsir al-Musnad*.

16. Seeking permission to enter. That was because his servant entered his room when he was sleeping and he said, 'O Allah, forbid entrance.' Then the *ayah* of seeking permission to enter was revealed.

17. His saying about the Jews, 'They are a confounded people.'

18. His words, exalted is He, *'Many of the first ones and many of the latter ones.'* (Qur'an 56: 39-40). I say that Ibn ʿAsakir narrated it in his *Tarikh* from Jabir ibn ʿAbdullah and that it is in the *Asbab an-Nuzul*.

19. The lifting (abrogation) of the recitation of, *'The older man and the older woman when they commit adultery …'* to the end of the *ayah*.⁹

20. His words on the Day of Uhud when Abu Sufyan said, 'Is so-and-so among the people?" (ʿUmar said) "We will not answer him,' and the Prophet, may Allah bless him and grant him peace, agreed with him. I say that Ahmad narrated its story in his *Musnad*.

He said: And one joins to this what ʿUthman ibn Saʿid ad-Darimi narrated in his book *ar-Radd ʿala'l-Jahmiyah* by way of Ibn Shihab from Salim ibn ʿAbdullah that Kaʿb al-Ahbar said, 'Woe to the king of the earth from the King of heaven.' Then ʿUmar said, 'Except for whoever takes himself to account.' Kaʿb said, 'By the One in Whose hand is my soul it is in the Tawrah. You have carried it on (the words of the verse) consecutively.' Then ʿUmar fell prostrate.

Then I have seen in *al-Kamil* of Ibn ʿAdi by the route of ʿAbdullah ibn Nafiʿ – and he is weak – from his father from ʿUmar that Bilal used to say, when he called the *adhan*, 'I witness that there is no god but Allah. Come to prayer.' Then ʿUmar said to him, 'Say after it, "I witness that Muhammad is the Messenger of Allah."' The Prophet, may Allah bless him and grant him peace, said, 'Say as ʿUmar said.'

His miracles

Al-Bayhaqi and Abu Nuʿaym narrated, both of them in [books that they each called] *Dala'il an-Nubuwwah,* and al-Lalka'i in *Sharh as-Sunnah,* ad-Dayrʿaquli in his *Fawa'id,* Ibn al-Aʿrabi in his *Karamat al-Awliya* and al-Khateeb in *Ruwat Malik ʿan Nafiʿ ʿan Ibn ʿUmar*

---

⁹ An *ayah* whose judgement remains valid although it is not in the *mushaf* and is not recited.

that Ibn ʿUmar said: ʿUmar sent an army and he put at the head of them a man called Sariyah. While ʿUmar was delivering the *khutbah* he began to cry out, 'Sariyah, the mountain!' three times. Then later the messenger of the army came and he told ʿUmar, '*Amir al-Mu'minin*, we were being defeated and in that situation we heard a voice crying out, "Sariyah, the mountain!" three times. We put the mountain to our rear, and then Allah defeated them.' Someone said to ʿUmar, 'You cried out with those words.' That mountain, where Sariyah was, is close to Nahawand in the land of the non-Arabs (Persian Iraq). Ibn Hajar said in *al-Isabah*: Its *isnad* is good.

Ibn Mardawayh narrated by way of Maymun ibn Mihran that Ibn ʿUmar said: ʿUmar was delivering the *khutbah* on the day of *Jumuʿah* and then he turned aside during his *khutbah* and said, 'Sariyah, the mountain! He who asks the wolf to be a shepherd will be wronged.' People looked about, one to another. Then ʿAli said to them, 'Let him explain what he meant.' When he had finished they asked him and he said, 'It occurred to me in my mind that the idolaters were defeating our brothers who were passing by a mountain, and that if they were to turn towards it, they would fight on one front only, but if they passed by it they would be destroyed. So there came out of me that which you claim you heard.' He said: The messenger came a month later and mentioned that they had heard the voice of ʿUmar on that day, and he said, 'We turned towards the mountain, and Allah gave us victory.'

Abu Nuʿaym said in *ad-Dala'il* that ʿAmr ibn al-Harith said: While ʿUmar (ibn al-Khattab) was upon the *minbar* delivering the *khutbah* on the day of *Jumuʿah* suddenly he left off the *khutbah* and said, 'Sariyah, the mountain!' two or three times. Some of those present said, 'He has gone mad, he is insane.' ʿAbd ar-Rahman ibn ʿAwf went in to see him – and he had confidence in him – and he said, 'You give them room to talk against you. While you were giving the *khutbah*, suddenly you cried out, "Sariyah, the mountain!" What sort of thing is this?' He said, 'By Allah, I could not control it. I saw them fighting near a mountain and they were being attacked from in front of them and from behind them. I could not stop myself from saying, "Sariyah, the mountain!" so that they would reach the mountain.' Then they waited some time until Sariyah's messenger came with his letter, 'The people met us (in battle) on the day of *Jumuʿah*, and we fought them until, when it was time for *Jumuʿah*, we heard someone cry out, "Sariyah, the mountain!" twice, so we reached the mountain. We continued victorious over our enemy until Allah defeated them and killed them.' Then those people who had accused him said, 'Leave this man alone, because he is in collusion with him.'

Abu'l-Qasim ibn Bishran narrated in his *Fawa'id* by way of Musa ibn ʿUqbah from Nafiʿ that Ibn ʿUmar said: ʿUmar ibn al-Khattab said to a man, 'What is your name?' He said, 'Jamrah (a live coal).' He asked, 'Whose son?' He said, 'The son of Shihab (flame).' He asked, 'From what tribe?' He said, 'From al-Hurqah (a state of burning).' He asked, 'Where is your dwelling?' He said, 'At al-Harrah ("the volcanic tract" from *al-harr* – the heat).' He asked, 'In which of them?' He said, 'Dhat Ladha (the blazing one).' ʿUmar said, 'Go to your family for they have been burnt.' The man returned to his family and found that they had been burnt. Malik narrated the like of it in the *Muwatta* from Yahya ibn Saʿid, Ibn Durayd in *al-Akhbar al-Manthurah,* Ibn al-Kalbi in *al-Jamiʿ* and others narrated it.

Abu'sh-Shaykh narrated in *Kitab al-ʿAdhamah*: Abu't-Tib narrated to us: ʿAli ibn Dawud narrated to us: ʿAbd al-Fattah ibn Salih narrated to us: ʿAbdullah ibn Salih narrated to us: Ibn Lahiʿah narrated to us from Qais ibn al-Hajjaj, from someone he related from, said: When Egypt was conquered, its people came to ʿAmr ibn al-ʿAs, when the first day of one of their months arrived, and they said to him, 'Amir, this Nile of ours has a custom (*sunnah*) without which it does not flow.' He asked, 'And what is that?' They said, 'When eleven nights have elapsed of this month we seek a young virgin from her parents, we obtain the consent of the parents, then we dress her in the best possible clothing and ornaments, and then we throw her in this Nile.' So ʿAmr said to them, 'This will never be in Islam. Islam demolishes what precedes it.' They left, and neither did the Nile flow a little nor a lot, so much so that they intended to emigrate. When ʿAmr saw that, he wrote to ʿUmar ibn al-Khattab about it. He wrote back to him, 'You were right in what you said. Truly, Islam demolishes what precedes it.' He sent a slip of paper inside his letter and wrote to ʿAmr, 'I have sent you a slip of paper inside my letter, so throw it in the Nile.' When ʿUmar's letter reached ʿAmr ibn al-ʿAs, he took the slip and opened it, and there was in it, 'From the slave of Allah ʿUmar ibn al-Khattab *Amir al-Mu'minin* to the Nile of Egypt. Now, if *you* used to flow before, then don't flow! If it was Allah who made you flow, then I ask the Overwhelming One to make you flow.' He threw the slip into the Nile a day before (the Festival of) the Cross. They woke up in the morning, and Allah, Exalted is He, had made it flow (and it rose) sixteen cubits in one night. Allah cut off this *sunnah* (custom) of the people of Egypt right up to this day.

Ibn ʿAsakir narrated that Tariq ibn Shihab said: A man was in conversation with ʿUmar ibn al-Khattab and told him a lie, and he would say, 'Withhold this.' Then later he told him something else and he said, 'Withhold this.' He said to him, 'Everything I told you was true except for what you told me to withhold.'

He narrated that al-Hasan said: If there was anyone who recognised a lie when he was told it, it was ʿUmar ibn al-Khattab.

Al-Bayhaqi narrated in *ad-Dala'il* that Abu Hudbah al-Himsi said: ʿUmar was told that the people of Iraq had pelted their *amir* with pebbles and he went out angry. He performed the prayer but was forgetful in his prayer. When he had completed the prayer, he said, 'O Allah, they have made me confused, so make them confused, and hasten with the youth of (the tribe of) Thaqif who will pass judgement among them with the judgement of *Jahiliyyah*, who will not accept from their good-doers and he will not pass over their wrongdoers with pardon.' I say that this indicates al-Hajjaj. Ibn Lahi'ah said, 'Al-Hajjaj was not yet born at that time.'

Some particulars of his biography

Ibn Sa'd narrated that al-Ahnaf ibn Qays said: We were sitting at 'Umar's door and a slave girl passed by, and they said, 'The concubine of the *Amir al-Mu'minin*.' He said, 'She is not the concubine of the *Amir al-Mu'minin*, and she is not permitted to him. She is of the property of Allah.' So we said, 'Then what is permitted to him of the property of Allah, exalted is He?' He said, 'There is only permitted to 'Umar of the property of Allah two garments, a garment for the winter and a garment for the summer, that with which I can perform the Hajj and the *Umrah* (i.e. an *ihram*), my sustenance and the sustenance of my family, as a man of Quraysh who is not the wealthiest of them nor the poorest, then I am, after that, a man among the Muslims.'

Khuzaymah ibn Thabit said, 'Whenever 'Umar appointed a governor, he wrote to him and made a condition on him that he should not ride a *birdhaun* (a large heavy non-Arabian horse from Asia Minor or Greece), nor eat delicacies, nor dress in finery, nor lock his door against the needy. If he did that, it would be permitted to punish him.'

'Ikrimah ibn Khalid and others said: Hafsah, 'Abdullah and others spoke to 'Umar and said, 'If only you were to eat wholesome food it would strengthen you upon the truth.' He asked, 'Are you all of this view?' They said, 'Yes.' He said, 'I have learnt what your sincere advice is. However, I have left my two companions on a highway, and if I abandon their highway I will not reach them in the house.' He ('Ikrimah) said: An affliction befell the people one year, and that year he did not eat clarified butter nor fat.

Ibn Mulaykah said: 'Utbah ibn Farqad spoke to 'Umar about his food and he said, 'Mercy on you! Should I eat up my wholesome sweet things in my worldly life and seek to enjoy myself with them?'

Al-Hasan said: ʿUmar entered in upon his son ʿAsim when he was eating meat and he said, 'What is this?' He said, 'We had a craving for it.' He said, 'Every time you crave something, do you eat it? It is sufficient wasteful extravagance for a man that he eats everything for which he has an appetite.'

Aslam said: ʿUmar said, 'There occurred to my heart a desire for fresh fish.' He (Aslam) said: Yarfa' mounted his camel and rode four miles there, four miles back, buying a basketful and bringing it back. Then he went to his camel, washed it, and went to ʿUmar. He said, 'Let us go and I will look at the camel.' He said, 'Did you forget to wash this sweat beneath its ears? Have you tormented an animal for the appetite of ʿUmar? No! by Allah! ʿUmar will not taste of your basket.'

Qatadah said: ʿUmar used to dress, while he was *khalifah*, with a garment of wool patched in parts with leather, and he would go around in the markets with a whip over his shoulder with which he would correct people. He would pass bits of rags and pieces of date-stones, which he would stumble on unexpectedly, and he would throw them into people's houses for them to use.

Anas said: I saw between ʿUmar's shoulder-blades, four patches in his shirt. Abu ʿUthman an-Nahdi said: I saw ʿUmar wearing a waistwrapper patched with leather. ʿAbdullah ibn ʿAmir ibn Rabiʿah said: I performed the Hajj with ʿUmar and he did not pitch a tent of goat's hair nor of wool. He used to throw the upper part of his *ihram* and his leather mat over a bush and seek shelter underneath it. ʿAbdullah ibn ʿIsa said: There were two dark furrows in ʿUmar's face from his weeping. Al-Hasan said: ʿUmar used to pass by an *ayah* in his *wird* (daily portion set aside to recite) and he would fall down (in a faint) until he revived after some days. Anas said: I entered a walled garden and heard ʿUmar saying, while there was a wall between us, 'ʿUmar ibn al-Khattab, *Amir al-Mu'minin*. Well done! Well done! By Allah, you will fear Allah, Ibn al-Khattab or Allah will punish you.' ᶜAbdullah ibn ᶜAmir ibn Rabiᶜah said: I saw ᶜUmar take up a straw from the ground and say, 'I wish I was this straw. I wish I was nothing. I wish that my mother had not given birth to me.' ᶜAbdullah ibn ᶜUmar ibn Hafs said: ᶜUmar carried a skin full of water upon his neck. Someone spoke to him about that and he said, 'My self was filling me with conceit and I wished to humble it.' Muhammad ibn Sirin said: An in-law of ᶜUmar's came to see him and asked him to give him something from the *bait al-mal* and ᶜUmar refused him and said, 'Do you want me to meet Allah as a treacherous King?' Then he gave him from his own property ten thousand dirhams. An-Nakhaᶜi said: ᶜUmar used to trade while he was *khalifah*. Anas said: ᶜUmar's stomach rumbled from eating olive oil the year of the drought – he had forbidden himself clarified butter – and he tapped on his stomach with his finger and said, 'There is nothing else for us, until the people have the means of living.' Sufyan ibn ᶜUyaynah said: ᶜUmar ibn al-Khattab said, 'The person I like most is the one who points out to me my defects.' Aslam said: I saw ᶜUmar ibn al-Khattab taking hold of the ear of the horse, taking hold of his own ear with the other hand, and leaping up on the back of the horse. Ibn ᶜUmar said: I never saw ᶜUmar become angry, and then Allah was mentioned in his presence or he was made to fear, or a person would recite an *ayah* from the Qur'an in his presence, but that he stopped short of what he meant to do. Bilal said to Aslam, 'How do you find ᶜUmar?' He said, 'The best of people, except that when he becomes angry it is a mighty matter.' Bilal said, 'If I was with him when he became angry, I would recite Qur'an to him until his anger went.' Al-Ahwas ibn Hakim said, narrating from his father: ᶜUmar was brought meat dressed with clarified butter and he refused to eat the two of them. He said, 'Both of them are seasonings.' All of the foregoing traditions are from Ibn Saᶜd.

Ibn Saᶜd narrated that al-Hasan said: ᶜUmar said, 'It is an easy thing by which I put right a people, that I exchange them an *amir* in place of an *amir*."

His description

Ibn Sa'd and al-Hakim narrated that Zirr said: I went out with the people of Madinah on the day of *Eid* and I saw 'Umar walking barefoot, an old man, balding, of a tawny colour, left-handed, tall, towering over people as if he were on a riding beast. Al-Waqidi said: It is not known among us that 'Umar was tawny, unless he saw him in the year of the drought, because his colour changed when he ate olive oil.

Ibn Sa'd narrated that Ibn 'Umar described 'Umar and said: A man of fair complexion, with a ruddy tint prevailing, tall, balding and grey-haired.

He narrated that 'Ubaydah ibn 'Umayr said: 'Umar used to overtop people in height.

He narrated that Salamah ibn al-Akwa' said: 'Umar was left and right-handed, meaning that he used both hands together.

Ibn 'Asakir narrated that Abu Raja' al-'Utaridi said: 'Umar was a tall stout man, extremely bald, fair but extremely ruddy, in the two sides of his beard a lightness, his moustache was large and at its extremities there was a redness at the roots of which there was black.

In the *Tarikh* of Ibn 'Asakir by various routes there is that the mother of 'Umar ibn al-Khattab was Hantamah the daughter of Hisham ibn al-Mughirah and she was the sister of Abu Jahl ibn Hisham, so that Abu Jahl was his maternal uncle.

His *khilafah*

He took on the *khilafah* through the covenant of Abu Bakr in Jumada al-Akhirah in the year 13 AH.

Az-Zuhri said, "'Umar was appointed *khalifah* on the day that Abu Bakr died which was Tuesday eight days before the end of Jumada al-Akhirah.' Al-Hakim narrated it. He undertook the command most fully, and there were very many openings in his days.

In the year 14 AH, Damascus was opened [to Islam] partly both by treaty and force, and Homs (ancient Emessa) and Baalbek by treaty, and Basra and Ubullah by force.

'In that year ʿUmar united people in one *jamaʿah* in *salat at-tarawih* (the optional prayers said at night in Ramadan),' said al-ʿAskari in *Al-Awa'il* (Firsts).

In the year 15 AH, all of Jordan was opened [to Islam] by force except for Tiberias which was by treaty. In this year there were the battles of Yarmuk and Qadisiyyah.

Ibn Jarir said: In it Saʿd founded Kufa, and ʿUmar instituted regular wages (for the fighting men), registers, and gave allowances according to priority.

In the year 16 AH, Ahwaz and Mada'in were opened, and in the latter Saʿd established the *Jumuʿah* in the great hall of Khosrau, and this was the first *Jumuʿah* to be held in Iraq. That was in the month of Safar. In it, was the battle of Jalula in which Yezdajird the son of Khosrau was defeated and he retreated back to Rayy. In it, Takrit was opened, ʿUmar travelled and took al-Bait al-Maqdis (Jerusalem) and gave his famous *khutbah* in al-Jabiyyah. Kinnasrin, Aleppo, and Antioch were opened by force, Manbij by treaty, and Saruj by force. In that year, Qirqisiya' was opened by treaty. In Rabiʿ al-Awwal, dating was begun from the Hijrah on the advice of ʿAli.

In the year 17 AH, ʿUmar increased the size of the Prophet's Mosque. In it there was drought and famine in the Hijaz and it was called the Year of Destruction, and ʿUmar prayed for rain for people by means of al-ʿAbbas.

Ibn Saʿd narrated from Niyar al-Aslami that ʿUmar, when he came out to pray for rain, came out with the cloak of the Prophet, may Allah bless him and grant him peace, upon him.

He narrated that Ibn ʿAwn said: ʿUmar took hold of the hand of al-ʿAbbas and raised it up, saying, 'O Allah, we approach You by means of the uncle of Your Prophet (asking) that You drive away from us the drought, and that You give us to drink from the rain,' and they didn't leave before they were given to drink. The sky poured down upon them for days. In that year Ahwaz was taken by treaty.

In the year 18 AH, Jundaysabur was opened [to Islam] by treaty, and Hulwan by force. In it, was the plague of Emaus; Urfa (Edessa) and Sumaysat were opened by force; Harran, Nasibin and a part of Mesopotamia by force, and it has been said, by treaty; and Mosul and its environs by force.

In the year 19 AH, Cæsarea was opened by force.

In the year 20 AH, Egypt was opened by force. It is also said that all of Egypt was opened by treaty except for Alexandria which was opened by force. ʿAli ibn Rabah said, 'The whole of the *Maghrib* (northwestern Africa) was opened by force.' In that year Tustar was opened, Caesar (Heraclius), the great man of the Byzantines, died. In it also, ʿUmar expelled the Jews from Khaybar and Najran, and he apportioned Khaybar and Wadi'l-Qurra' (between those who had been present there at the original battles of the Prophet, may Allah bless him and grant him peace).

In the year 21 AH, Alexandria was opened by force, and Nahawand, after which the Persians could not muster an army, and Barqah and other places.

In the year 22 AH, Azerbaijan was opened by force, and it has been said, by treaty, and Dinawr by force, Masabdhan and Hamadan by force, and Tripoli of North Africa, Rai, ʿAskar and Qumas.

In the year 23 AH, there were the openings [to Islam] of Kirman, Sijistan, Makran in the mountainous lands, and also Isfahan and its environs.

In the end of this year there was the death of Sayyiduna ʿUmar, may Allah be pleased with him, after his return from the Hajj; he was killed as a martyr.

Saʿid ibn al-Musayyab said: When ʿUmar returned from Mina (to Makkah), he made his camel kneel down in the watercourse, then he threw himself down, raised his hands to the sky and said,

'O Allah! I am advanced in years, my strength has weakened, and my subjects have increased, so take me to You without (my) being wasteful or falling short.' Dhu'l-Hijjah had not gone before he was killed. Al-Hakim narrated it.

Abu Salih as-Saman said: Ka'b al-Ahbar said to 'Umar, 'I find you in the Tawrah killed as a martyr.' He said, 'How can I be a martyr when I am in the peninsula of the Arabs?'

Aslam said: 'Umar said, 'O Allah provide me with martyrdom in Your way, and make my death to be in the city of Your Messenger.' Al-Bukhari narrated it.

Ma'dan ibn Abi Talhah: 'Umar gave a *khutbah* and said, 'I saw (in a dream) as if a cock pecked at me once or twice, and I can only believe that it means that my term has come. There are people who tell me to appoint a successor, and Allah will not cause His *deen* to go to waste nor His *khilafah*. If the matter is hastened for me, then the *khilafah* is a matter of consultation between these six whom the Messenger of Allah, may Allah bless him and grant him peace, was pleased with when he died.' Al-Hakim narrated it.

Az-Zuhri said: 'Umar would not permit a captive who had reached the age of puberty to enter Madinah until al-Mughirah ibn Shu'bah wrote to him – and he was the governor of Kufa – mentioning to him a slave who had a number of crafts and asking permission that he enter Madinah, saying, 'He has many trades which are useful to people. He is a blacksmith, engraver and carpenter.' He gave permission to him to send him to Madinah. Al-Mughirah put a demand for revenue on him (the slave) of one hundred dirhams per month, so the slave came to 'Umar to complain of the severity of that imposition. He ['Umar] said, 'Your demand for revenue is not that much,' and he [the slave] turned away in anger and threateningly. 'Umar waited some days and then called him and said, 'Have I not been informed that you say, "If I wished, I could make a mill which will grind by means of the wind."' Then he turned his face to 'Umar with a frown and said, 'I will make for you a mill which people will talk about.' When he turned away, ᶜUmar said to his companions, 'The slave threatened me just now.' After a while Abu Lu'lu'ah wrapped his garments around a dagger with two heads (to the blade) whose handle was in the middle of it, hid in one of the corners of the mosque in the darkness of the last part of the night, and there he waited until ᶜUmar came out waking people up for the prayer. When he drew near to him, he stabbed him three times. Ibn Saᶜd narrated it.

ᶜAmr ibn Maymun al-Ansari said: Abu Lu'lu'ah, the slave of al-Mughirah, stabbed ᶜUmar with a dagger which had two heads, and he stabbed, along with him, twelve other men of whom six died, then a man from Iraq threw a robe over him. When he became tangled up in it, he killed himself.

Abu Rafiᶜ said: Abu Lu'lu'ah, the slave of al-Mughirah, used to make mills. Al-Mughirah used to demand as revenue from him four dirhams a day. He met ᶜUmar and said, '*Amir al-Mu'minin*, al-Mughirah is being very heavy on me, so speak to him.' He said, 'Behave well towards your master,' – and ᶜUmar's intention was to speak to al-Mughirah about it – so he (the slave) became angry and said, 'His justice encompasses all of the people except for me,' and he secretly decided to kill him. He took a dagger, sharpened it and poisoned it. ᶜUmar used to say, 'Straighten your ranks,' before he pronounced the *takbir*. He came and stood opposite him in the rank, stabbed him in his shoulder and side, and ᶜUmar fell. Then he stabbed thirteen other men with him, of whom six died. ᶜUmar was carried to his family. The sun was about to rise so ᶜAbd ar-Rahman ibn ᶜAwf led the people in prayer with the two shortest *surahs*. ᶜUmar was brought some *nabidh* (a drink made from dates left to soak in water) and he drank it and it came out of his wound, but it wasn't yet distinct (from the blood). So they gave him some milk to drink, and it came out of his wound and they said, 'There's no great harm with you.' He said, 'If there is any harm in killing, then I have been killed.' People began to praise him, saying, 'You were such and such and you were such and such.' He said, 'By Allah, I wish that I had gone out of it, independent of others, with nothing against me and nothing for me, and that the companionship of the Messenger of Allah, may Allah bless him and his family and grant them peace, was secure for me.' Ibn ᶜAbbas praised him, so he said, 'Even if I had that gold which would fill the earth, I would ransom myself by it from the terror of the rising. I have made it (the *khilafah*) a matter of consultation between ᶜUthman, ᶜAli, Talhah, az-Zubayr, ᶜAbd ar-Rahman ibn ᶜAwf and Saᶜd.' He ordered Suhayb to lead people in prayer, and gave the six a period of three (days in which to decide). Al-Hakim narrated it.

Ibn ᶜAbbas said: Abu Lu'lu'ah was a Magian.

ᶜAmr ibn Maymun said: ᶜUmar said, 'Praise be to Allah Who did not make my decree of death to be at the hands of a man who claimed Islam.' Then he said to his son, 'ᶜAbdullah, look and see what debts I have.' They calculated it and found it to be eighty-six thousand or thereabouts. He said, 'If the wealth of the family of ᶜUmar is enough, then pay it. If it is not, then ask among Bani ᶜAdi, and if their wealth is not enough, then ask among Quraysh. Go to the Mother of the Believers, ᶜA'ishah, and say, "ᶜUmar asks permission to be buried with his two companions."' He went to her and she said, 'I wanted it' – meaning the burial plot – 'for myself, but I will definitely prefer him over myself, today.' ᶜAbdullah came and said, 'She has given permission,' so he praised Allah. Someone said to him, 'Make bequest, *Amir al-Mu'minin*, and appoint a successor.' He said, 'I see no-one with more right to this command than these six with whom the Prophet, may Allah bless him and grant him peace, was pleased when he died,' and he named the six, and said, 'ᶜAbdullah ibn ᶜUmar will be present with them but he has no part in the command. If the office should fall to Saᶜd, then he it is, and if not, then let whoever of you is appointed seek help from him, for I did not remove him (from his office as *amir* of Kufa) because of any incapacity or treachery.' Then he said, 'I counsel the *khalifah* after me to have fearful obedience of Allah; I counsel him to pay particular care to the *Muhajirun* and the *Ansar*, and I counsel him to treat the people of the provinces well,' and other similar counsels. When he died, we went walking with him, ʿAbdullah ibn ʿUmar called out the greeting and said, 'ʿUmar seeks permission to enter.' ʿA'ishah said, 'Bring him in.' He was brought in and placed there with his two companions.

When they finished burying him and had returned, that group gathered and ʿAbd ar-Rahman ibn ʿAwf said, 'Delegate your authority to three among you.' Az-Zubayr said, 'I delegate my authority to ʿAli.' Saʿd said, 'I delegate my authority to ʿAbd ar-Rahman.' Talhah said, 'I delegate my authority to ʿUthman.' He continued: so there remained these three. ʿAbd ar-Rahman said, 'I don't want it. Which of you two will be quit of this matter and we will entrust it to him (the remaining one)? And Allah is his witness and Islam, let him consider in himself who is the best of them and let him be eager for the benefit of the *ummah*.' The two Shaykhs, ʿAli and ʿUthman were silent. ʿAbd ar-Rahman said, 'Delegate me and, Allah is my witness, I will not fail you in choosing the best of you.' They said, 'Yes.' Then he went apart with ʿAli and said, 'You have that precedence in Islam and kinship with the Prophet, may Allah bless him and grant him peace, which you know. Allah is your witness; if I give you authority, will you be just, and if I give authority (to ʿUthman) over you, will you hear and obey?' He said, 'Yes.' Then he went apart with the other and said to him the same thing. When he had their agreement, he pledged allegiance to ʿUthman and ʿAli pledged allegiance to him.

There is in the *Musnad* of Ahmad that ʿUmar said: If my term overtakes me, and Abu ʿUbaydah al-Jarrah is still alive, then I would appoint him as *khalifah*. If my Lord asked me, I would say, 'I heard the Prophet, may Allah bless him and grant him peace, saying, "Every Prophet has a trustworthy (companion), and my trustworthy (companion) is Abu ʿUbaydah ibn al-Jarrah."' If my term overtakes me, and Abu ʿUbaydah al-Jarrah has died, I would appoint Muʿadh ibn Jabal as *khalifah*. If my Lord asked me, 'Why did you appoint him as *khalifah*?' I would say, 'I heard the Prophet, may Allah bless him and grant him peace, saying, "He will be raised up on the Day of Resurrection a distance in front of the men of knowledge."' They had both died during his *khilafah*.

Also in the *Musnad* there is from Abu Rafiʿ that someone spoke to ʿUmar at his death about the appointment of a *khalifah*, so he said, 'I have seen among my companions an unfortunate eagerness. If one of two men had reached me, and then I had entrusted this command to him, I would have been sure of him: Salim the freed slave of Abu Hudhayfah and Abu ʿUbaydah ibn al-Jarrah.'

ʿUmar was struck on the Wednesday, four days before the end of Dhu'l-Hijjah, and he was buried on Sunday, the day of the new moon of al-Muharram, the Sacred (month). He was sixty-three years old. It has also been said that he was sixty-six, sixty-one, sixty (which al-Waqidi considered the weightiest). It has been said that he was fifty-nine, fifty-five and fifty-four. Suhayb performed the (funeral) prayer over him in the mosque.

In the *Tahdhib* of al-Mazini, there is that the engraving on the seal-ring of ʿUmar was, 'Death is enough of an admonisher, ʿUmar.'

At-Tabarani narrated that Tariq ibn Shihab said: Umm Ayman said, on the day ʿUmar was killed, 'Today Islam has been rent.'

ʿAbd ar-Rahman ibn Yasar narrated. He said, 'I witnessed the death of ʿUmar ibn al-Khattab and the sun was eclipsed on that day.' The men who transmitted (this *hadith*) were trustworthy.

The things in which he was first

Al-ʿAskari said: He was the first to be called '*Amir al-Mu'minin*', the first to date events from the Hijrah, the first to take a *bait al-mal* (see the chapter on Abu Bakr), the first to establish as a *sunnah* the standing (for prayer) in the month of Ramadan, the first who patrolled at night, the first who punished satire, the first who punished wine-drinking with eighty (lashes), the first who declared *al-mut'ah* (temporary marriage) *haram* (rather the Prophet, may Allah bless him and grant him peace, forbade it on the Day of Khaybar – see the *Muwatta'* of Imam Malik), the first to forbid the sale of female slaves who had borne children to their masters, the first to assemble for prayers over the dead with four *takbirs*, the first to have a register, the first to make conquests, the first to survey the Sawad (the cultivated land of Iraq), the first to convey food from Egypt upon the Aylah Sea (Gulf of 'Aqabah) to Madinah, the first who dedicated *sadaqah* (purely for the sake of Allah) in Islam, and the first who adjusted the division of inheritances (in cases where the calculated portions add up to more than the total inheritance), the first to take the *zakat* of horses, the first to say, 'May Allah lengthen your life,' (he said it to 'Ali) and the first to say, 'May Allah help you,' (he said it to 'Ali). This is the end of what al-'Askari mentioned.

An-Nawawi said in his *Tahdhib* that he was the first to adopt the whip. Ibn Sa'd mentions it in the *Tabaqat*, and he said: It used to be said, after him, 'The whip of 'Umar is more terrible than your sword.' He (an-Nawawi) continued: He was the first to appoint *qadis* in the provinces, the first who established the provinces of (the cities of) Kufa, Basra, and of Mesopotamia, Syria, Cairo (Egypt), and Mosul.

Ibn 'Asakir narrated that Isma'il ibn Ziyad said: 'Ali ibn Abi Talib passed by the mosques in Ramadan and in them there were lamps, so he said, 'May Allah illuminate 'Umar in his grave, as he has illuminated our mosques for us.'

Section: Ibn Sa'd said: 'Umar appointed a meal (flour) house and put flour in it, parched barley meal, dates, raisins and necessities, in order to help the traveller whose journey was interrupted (through need or other causes), and he established between Makkah and Madinah on the road that which would be useful to travellers whose journeys were interrupted. He demolished the Mosque of the

Prophet, added to it, expanded it and floored it with pebbles. He was the one who evicted the Jews from the Hijaz (and sent them) to Syria, and evicted the people of Najran (and sent them) to Kufa. He was the one who moved the Station of Ibrahim back (from the Ka'bah) to where it is today, and it used to be adjoining the House.

Some accounts of him and of his judgements

Al-'Askari narrated in *al-Awa'il*, at-Tabarani in *al-Kabir*, and al-Hakim by way of Ibn Shihab that 'Umar ibn 'Abd al-'Aziz asked Abu Bakr ibn Sulayman ibn Abi Hathamah what was the reason that it used to be written, 'From the Khalifah of the Messenger of Allah, may Allah bless him and grant him peace,' in the time of Abu Bakr, then later 'Umar used to write at first, 'From the Khalifah of Abu Bakr'? Then who was the first to write, 'From the *Amir al-Mu'minin* (the Commander of the Believers)'? He said, 'Ash-Shifa, who was one of the women of the *Muhajirun*, told me that Abu Bakr used to write, "From the Khalifah of the Messenger of Allah," and 'Umar used to write, "From the Khalifah of the Khalifah of the Messenger of Allah," until one day 'Umar wrote to the governor of Iraq, to send him two strong men whom he could ask about Iraq and its inhabitants. He sent to him Labid ibn Rabi'ah and 'Adi ibn Hatim, and they came to Madinah and entered the mosque where they found 'Amr ibn al-'As. They said, 'Get permission for us (to visit) the *Amir al-Mu'minin*.' 'Amr said, 'You two, by Allah, have hit upon his name!' Then 'Amr went in to him and said, 'Peace be upon you, *Amir al-Mu'minin*.' He said, 'What occurred to you about this name? You must explain what you have said.' He told him and said, 'You are the *amir* (commander) and we are the *mu'minun* (the believers).' Thus letters have continued to be written with that from that day.

An-Nawawi said in his *Tahdhib*: 'Adi ibn Hatim and Labid ibn Rabi'ah named him thus when they came as a deputation from Iraq. It has been said that al-Mughirah ibn Shu'bah named him with this name. It has also been said that ⁽Umar said to people, 'You are the believers and I am your *amir*,' and so he was called *Amir al-Mu'minin*, and before that he was known as the Khalifah of the Khalifah of the Messenger of Allah, but they changed from that expression because of its length.

Ibn ⁽Asakir narrated that Mu⁽awiyah ibn Qurrah said: It used to be written 'From Abu Bakr the Khalifah of the Messenger of Allah,' and then when it was ⁽Umar ibn al-Khattab they wanted to say, 'The Khalifah of the Khalifah of the Messenger of Allah.' ⁽Umar said, 'This is lengthy.' They said, 'No. But we have appointed you as *amir* over us, so you are our *amir*.' He said, 'Yes, and you are the believers, and I am your *amir*.' Then it became written *Amir al-Mu'minin*.

Al-Bukhari narrated in his *Tarikh* that Ibn al-Musayyab said: The first to write the date was ⁽Umar ibn al-Khattab two and a half years into his *khilafah*, and it was written down as the sixteenth year of the Hijrah, through the advice of ⁽Ali.

As-Salafi narrated in *at-Tuyuriyyat* with a *sahih isnad* from Ibn ⁽Umar from ⁽Umar that he wished to record the *sunan* (customary practices of the Prophet, may Allah bless him and grant him peace, and of his companions), so he sought Allah's choice in the matter (through the supplication known as the *istikharah*) for a month. Then he arose one morning with a clear resolve and said, 'I remembered a people who were before you who wrote a book, and then they turned to it and abandoned the Book of Allah.'

Ibn Sa⁽d narrated that Shaddad said: The first words that ⁽Umar would say when he ascended the *minbar* were, 'O Allah, I am severe, so make me gentle, I am weak, so strengthen me, and I am miserly, so make me generous."

Ibn Sa⁽d and Sa⁽id ibn Mansur and others narrated by different routes thatt ⁽Umar said, 'I have placed myself in respect to Allah's property in the same relation as the guardian of the orphan to his (the orphan's) wealth. If I am in good circumstances, I will refrain from it, and if I am in need I will eat of it in moderation, and if (again later) I am in good circumstances, I will repay."

Ibn Sa'd narrated that Ibn 'Umar said that when 'Umar ibn al-Khattab was in need, he used to go to the man in charge of the *bait al-mal* and seek a loan from him. Often he might be in difficulty and the man in charge of the public treasury would come to him, seek repayment of the debt and would oblige him to pay it, and 'Umar would be evasive to him. Then, often 'Umar would receive his stipend and so pay his debt.

Ibn Sa'd narrated that al-Bara' ibn Ma'rur said that 'Umar went out one day until he came to the *minbar* and he had been suffering from a complaint. The good qualities of honey were mentioned to him, and there was a receptacle (made of kidskin) of it in the *bait al-mal*. He said, 'If you give me permission I will take it, but if not then it is *haram* for me.' They gave him permission.

He narrated that Salim ibn 'Abdullah said that 'Umar used to insert his hand into the saddle sore of his camel and say, 'I fear that I will be asked about what is (wrong) with you.'

He narrated that Ibn 'Umar said: When 'Umar meant to forbid people from some wrong action, he would come to his family and say, 'If I come to know of anyone who becomes involved in something I have forbidden, I will double the punishment for him.'

We have narrated in more than one way that 'Umar ibn al-Khattab went out one night to patrol Madinah – and he used to do that a lot – when he came upon one of the women of the Arabs whose door was bolted against her (locking her in) and she was saying:

'This night, whose stars creep slowly, is wearisome and makes me sleepless,
    Because I have no bedfellow with whom to sport,
For, by Allah, if Allah's punishments were not feared,
    His rights would have been removed from this couch.
However, I fear a Watchful One Who is in charge of our selves

    And Whose recorder is not negligent for an instant.
Fear of my Lord and modesty prevent me, and I honour my husband (too much),
    That his noble station should be conferred (on another).'

So he (ʿUmar) wrote to his governors about military expeditions that no-one should be absent for more than four months.

Ibn Saʿd narrated from Zadan that Salman said that ʿUmar said to him, 'Am I a king or a *khalifah*?' Salman said to him, 'If you collect a dirham from the land of the Muslims, or less or more, then you put it to an improper use, you are a king, not a *khalifah*.' ʿUmar took warning from it.

He narrated that Sufyan ibn Abi'l-ʿArja' said: ʿUmar ibn al-Khattab said, 'By Allah, I do not know whether I am a *khalifah* or a king, for if I am a king then this is a tremendous matter.' Someone said, '*Amir al-Muʾminin*, there is a distinction between the two of them.' He said, 'What is it?' He said, 'A *khalifah* does not take except what is due and he does not use it except in the right way, and you, praise be to Allah, are like that. The king treats people unjustly, and takes from this one and gives to that one.' ʿUmar was silent.

He narrated that Ibn Masʿud, may Allah be pleased with him, said: ʿUmar mounted a horse and his robe disclosed his thigh. The people of Najran saw on his thigh a black mole and said, 'This is the one whom we find in our Book will exile us from our land.'

He narrated from Saʿd al-Hari that Kaʿb al-Ahbar said to ʿUmar, 'We find you in the Book of Allah at one of the gates of *Jahannam* preventing people from falling into it. When you die, they will carry on plunging into it until the Day of Resurrection.'

He narrated that Abu Mashʿar said: Our shaykhs told us that ʿUmar said, 'This matter will not be correct but with the severity that has no haughtiness in it, and with the gentleness that has no weakness in it.'

Ibn Abi Shaybah narrated in his *Musannaf* that Hakim ibn ʿUmayr said: ʿUmar ibn al-Khattab said, 'Let not the *amir* of an army or a raiding party whip anyone for a *hadd* punishment until he arrives at Darb (Derbe near the Cilician Gates, a mountain pass through which the Muslims passed returning from raids into Byzantine territory) so that the rage of the *shaytan* does not carry him to the point that he joins with the *kuffar*.'

Ibn Abi Hatim narrated in his *tafsir* that ash-Sha'bi said: The Byzantine Emperor wrote to 'Umar ibn al-Khattab, 'My messengers have come to me from you claiming that among you there is a tree which is not like anything else among trees: it produces something like the ears of the ass, it opens out (to reveal) something like a pearl, it becomes green so that it is like the green emerald, it reddens until it is like the red ruby, then later it ripens and matures so that it becomes like the sweetest honey-cake ever eaten, then later it dries until it becomes a defence (against want) for the house-dweller and a provision for the traveller. If my messengers have told me the truth, I can only imagine that this is one of the trees of the Garden.' 'Umar wrote to him, 'From the slave of Allah, 'Umar, the *Amir al-Mu'minin*, to Caesar, the king of the Byzantines. Truly your messengers have told you the truth. This tree, which is with us, is the tree which Allah made to grow over Maryam when she gave birth to 'Isa her son. So fear Allah and do not take 'Isa as a god apart from Allah, for truly, "*The likeness of 'Isa with Allah is as the likeness of Adam, He created him from dust, ...*"' (Qur'an 3: 59) to the end of the *ayah*.

Ibn Sa'd narrated from Ibn 'Umar that 'Umar ordered his governors, so they recorded their properties, and among them was Sa'd bin Abi Waqqas. Then 'Umar shared with them in their properties and took a half and gave them a half.

He narrated that ash-Sha'bi said that when 'Umar used to appoint a governor he would record his property.

He narrated that Abu Imamah ibn Sahl ibn Hunayf said: 'Umar remained some time not eating anything at all from the property of the *bait al-mal*, until poverty and constriction came upon him in that. He sent for the Companions of the Prophet, may Allah bless him and grant him peace, to seek their advice. He said, 'I have occupied myself with this command, so what is fitting for me from it?' ᶜAli said, 'The midday and evening meals.' ᶜUmar took that.

He narrated from Ibn ᶜUmar that ᶜUmar performed the Hajj in the year twenty-three (AH) and spent sixteen dinars upon his Hajj. He said, 'ᶜAbdullah we have been extravagant with this property.'

ᶜAbd ar-Razzaq narrated in the *Musannaf* that Qatadah and ash-Shaᶜbi said: A woman came to ᶜUmar and said, 'My husband stands at night (in prayer) and fasts during the day.' ᶜUmar said, 'You have praised your husband excellently well.' Kaᶜb ibn Sawwar said, 'She was complaining.' ᶜUmar said, 'How?' He said, 'She claims that she has no share in her husband (in his time).' He said, 'If you understood that much, then you decide between them.' He said, '*Amir al-Mu'minin*, Allah has permitted him four (wives). So she has one day of every four days, and one night of every four nights.'

He narrated that Ibn Jarir said: One I trust informed me that ᶜUmar, while he was patrolling, heard a woman saying:

> 'This night stretches out and is grievous,
>> and that I have no intimate to sport with makes me sleepless,
>
> For, if it were not for fear of Allah Whom nothing is like,
>> his rights would have been removed from this couch.'

ᶜUmar said, 'What is wrong with you?' She said, 'You sent my husband on an expedition some months ago, and I long for him.' He said, 'Do you mean to do wrong?' She said, '(I seek) the refuge of Allah!' He said, 'So restrain yourself; it is only (a matter of) the post to him.' He sent a message to him. Then he went to Hafsah and said, 'I want to ask you about a matter which concerns me, so dispel it for me. How long does a woman long for her husband?' She lowered her head and was shy. He said, 'Truly Allah is not shy of the truth.' She gestured with her hand, indicating three months, and if that is not possible, then four months. ʿUmar wrote that armies must not be kept on service for more than four months.

He narrated from Jabir ibn ʿAbdullah that he came to ʿUmar to complain to him of the treatment he received from his womenfolk. ʿUmar said to him, 'We also find that, so much so that when I intend (going out for) some necessity, she says to me, "You are only going to the girls of Bani so-and-so to look at them."' ʿAbdullah ibn Masʿud said to him, 'Has it not reached you that Ibrahim, peace be upon him, complained to Allah about Sarah's character and it was said to him, "She has been created from a rib so have the enjoyment of her company as long as you don't see in her any unsoundness in her *deen*."'

He narrated that ʿIkrimah ibn Khalid said: One of ʿUmar ibn al-Khattab's sons went in to see him. He had combed and oiled his hair and dressed up in the very best clothing. ʿUmar struck him with a whip until he made him weep. Hafsah asked him, 'Why did you strike him?' He said, 'I saw that his self had made him conceited, and I wanted to make it (his self) small for him.'

He narrated from Maʿmar from Layth ibn Abi Salim that ʿUmar said, 'Do not name yourselves with the name al-Hakam (the ruler and judge) nor Abu'l-Hakam (possessor of judgement) for truly Allah, He is al-Hakam (the ruler) and don't call a road a *sikkah*.'[10]

Al-Bayhaqi narrated in *Shuʿab al-Iman* that ad-Dahhak said: Abu Bakr said, 'By Allah, I wish that I were a tree by the side of the road by which a camel passed, and it took me into its mouth, chewed me, swallowed me, passed me out as dung, and that I were not a man.' ʿUmar said, 'Would that I were my family's ram, which they were fattening as much as seemed right to them, until when I became as fat as could be, some people whom they love visit them, and they sacrifice me for them, make some of me into roasted meat,

---

[10] *Sikkah* is literally both a 'row' and a 'plough' and it is possible there is a reference to the tradition that 'The *sikkah* (plough) has not entered the abode of a people but that it humiliated them.'

some of me into sun-dried meat, then eat me, and that I were not a human being.'

Ibn ᶜAsakir narrated that Abu'l-Bakhtari said: ᶜUmar ibn al-Khattab used to give the *khutbah* on the *minbar*. Al-Hussein ibn ᶜAli, may Allah be pleased with him, stood up before him and said, 'Come down from my father's *minbar*.' ᶜUmar said, 'It is the *minbar* of your father and not the *minbar* of my father. Who told you to do this?' ᶜAli stood and said, 'By Allah, no-one told him to do this. I will certainly cause you (al-Hussein) some pain, traitor.' He (ᶜUmar) said, 'Don't hurt the son of my brother, for he has told the truth, it is the *minbar* of his father.'

Al-Khateeb narrated in *Adab ar-Rawi* from Malik by his route from Ibn Shihab that Abu Salamah ibn ᶜAbd ar-Rahman and Saᶜid ibn al-Musayyab narrated that ᶜUmar ibn al-Khattab and ᶜUthman ibn ᶜAffan were arguing over a certain question until an onlooker said, 'They will never reach an agreement.' Yet they only separated on the best and most beautiful terms.

Ibn Saᶜd narrated that al-Hasan said: The first *khutbah* which ᶜUmar delivered, he praised Allah and then said, 'Right. I have been tested by you and you have been tested by me, and I have succeeded to the *khilafah*, amongst you, after my two companions. Whoever is here present, we will manage their affairs in person, and whoever is not here with us, we will appoint over him strong and trustworthy people. Whoever acts excellently well, we will increase him in excellent treatment, and whoever acts wrongly we will punish, and may Allah forgive us and you.'

He narrated from Jubayr ibn al-Huwayrith that ᶜUmar ibn al-Khattab, may Allah be pleased with him, sought the advice of the Muslims on the recording of a register. ᶜAli said to him, 'Divide up every year what is collected for you of property, and don't keep any of it.' ᶜUthman said, 'I see much wealth, which is sufficient for the people and if it is not counted so that whoever takes is distinguished from whoever does not take, I am afraid that the matter will become confused.' Al-Walid ibn Hisham ibn al-Mughirah said, '*Amir al-Mu'minin*, I went to Syria and I saw that its kings had recorded registers and organised the troops, so record registers and organise the troops.' He took his advice, and he called ʿAqil ibn Abi Talib, Makhramah ibn Nawfal and Jubayr ibn Mutʿim, who were genealogists of Quraysh, and said, 'Record people according to their ranks.' They recorded them beginning with Banu Hashim, then they followed with Abu Bakr and his people, then ʿUmar and his people, according to the order of their *khilafahs*. When ʿUmar saw it, he said, 'Begin with the close relatives of the Prophet, may Allah bless him and grant him peace, the closest, then the next closest until you place ʿUmar where Allah placed him.'

He narrated that Saʿid ibn al-Musayyab said: ʿUmar recorded the register in al-Muharram of the year 20 AH.

He narrated that al-Hasan said: ʿUmar wrote to Hudhayfah, 'Give the people their stipends and their provisions.' He wrote back to him, 'We have done that and a great deal remains.' ʿUmar wrote to him, 'It is their spoils which Allah has given them. It is not ʿUmar's nor ʿUmar's family's. Divide it up among them.'

Ibn Saʿd narrated that Jubayr ibn Mutʿim said: While ʿUmar was standing on the mountain of ʿArafah he heard a man calling out, saying, 'Khalifah of Allah!' Another man heard him, and they were taking provisions for the way, so he said, 'What is wrong with you, may Allah split your uvulas?' I went towards the man and shouted at him. Jubayr continued: Then the next morning, I was standing with ʿUmar at al-ʿAqabah (the major pillar of stones in Mina) and he was stoning it, when there came a stray pebble and split (the skin on) ʿUmar's head. I turned that way and heard a man from the mountain saying, 'I make it known, by the Lord of the Kaʿbah, that ʿUmar will not stand in this place after this year,' and it was the one who had called out among us the day before, and that disturbed me greatly.

He narrated that ʿA'ishah, may Allah be pleased with her, said: At the time of the last Hajj which ʿUmar performed with the Mothers of the Believers (the wives of the Prophet, may Allah bless him and grant him peace), when we returned from ʿArafah, I passed by al-Muhassab and I heard a man upon his camel saying, 'Where was ʿUmar, the *Amir al-Mu'minin*?' I heard another man saying, 'Here was the *Amir al-Mu'minin*.' He made the camel kneel down upon its breast, then he raised his voice in a wail saying:

'Upon you peace from an *imam* and may the hand of Allah bless that much-rent skin,

Whoever hurries on or mounts the two wings of the ostrich, in order to overtake what you sent ahead the day before, will be outstripped.

You decided matters, then after them you left behind trials and misfortunes in their sleeves, not yet unloosed.'

That rider did not move and it was not known who he was, and we used to say that he was one of the Jinn, for ʿUmar came back from that Hajj, was stabbed by the dagger and died.

He narrated that ʿAbd ar-Rahman ibn Abza said that ʿUmar said, 'This authority is among the people of Badr as long as one of them remains, then it is among the people of Uhud as long as one of them remains, and among such and such, and such and such, and there is no part in it for a freed captive, nor the son of a freed captive, nor those who became Muslims at the Opening (of Makkah to Islam).'

He narrated from an-Nakhaʿi that a man said to ʿUmar, 'Will you not appoint ʿAbdullah ibn ʿUmar as *khalifah*?' He said, 'May Allah fight you! By Allah, I never wanted this of Allah. Shall I appoint as *khalifah* a man who did not know how to divorce his wife properly?'

He narrated from Shaddad ibn Aws that Kaʿb said: There was among the Tribe of Isra'il a king whom, when we remember him we are reminded of ʿUmar, and when we remember ʿUmar we are reminded of him. He had by his side a prophet who received revelation. Allah revealed to the prophet, peace be upon him, to say to him, 'Make your covenant and write your testament to me, for you are dead after three days.' The prophet informed him of that. When it was the third day, he fell down (dead) between the wall and the couch. He came to his Lord and said, 'O Allah, if You knew that I was just in my rule; that when matters differed, I followed Your guidance; and I was such and such, and such and such, then increase my life-span until my infant son grows up and my nation increases.' Allah revealed to the prophet that, 'He has said such and such – and it is true – and I have added fifteen years to his life-span. That is enough for his infant son to grow up and his nation to increase.' When ʿUmar was stabbed, Kaʿb said, 'If ʿUmar were to ask his Lord, Allah would definitely let him stay.' ʿUmar was told about that. He said, 'O Allah take me back to You without (my) being powerless and incapable or blameworthy.'

He narrated from Sulayman ibn Yasar that the Jinn wailed in mourning for ʿUmar.

Al-Hakim narrated that Malik ibn Dinar said: A voice was heard on the mountain of Tabalah when ʿUmar, may Allah be pleased with him, was killed:

'Let whoever would weep, weep for Islam,

    For they are on the point of being thrown to the ground and (their) appointed time has not been exceeded,

And the world has declined and the best of it has gone, turning its back,

    Whoever is sure of the promise has become weary of it.'

Ibn Abi'd-Dunya narrated that Yahya ibn Abi Rashid al-Basri said: ʿUmar said to his son, 'Be economical with my shroud, for if there is good for me with Allah, He will exchange it for me for that which is better than it. If I have been otherwise, He will strip me and be very fast in stripping me. Be economical in the grave you dig for me, for if there is good for me with Allah, He will expand it for me as far as my sight can reach. If I have been otherwise, He will tighten it upon me until my ribs interlace. Let not a woman go out with me (to the grave), and do not attribute to me a purity that I do not have, for Allah has more knowledge of me. When you go out (with me to the grave) then hasten your pace, for if there is good for me with Allah, you will send me on to what is better for me. If I am otherwise, you will throw an evil you have been carrying down from your necks.'

Section

Ibn ᶜAsakir narrated from Ibn ᶜAbbas that al-ᶜAbbas said: I asked Allah, one year after ᶜUmar had died, to show me him in a dream. I saw him after a year and he was wiping the sweat from his brow, so I said, 'May my father and my mother be your ransom, *Amir al-Mu'minin*! How is it with you?' He said, 'This is the time I have just finished. The house of ᶜUmar had almost been violently demolished if it had not been that I met a pitying, compassionate one (*Ra'uf Rahim*. Note that these are two names that Allah gave to His Messenger, may Allah bless him and grant him peace, in the penultimate *ayah* of Surat at-Tawbah. *Ar-Ra'uf ar-Rahim* are names of Allah).'

He also narrated from Zayd ibn Aslam that ᶜAmr ibn al-ᶜAs saw ᶜUmar in his sleep and asked, 'How have you done?' He asked, 'When did I leave you?' He answered, 'Twelve years ago.' He said, 'I have only finished my accounting now.'

Ibn Saᶜd narrated that Salim ibn ᶜAbdullah ibn ᶜUmar said: I heard a man of the *Ansar* saying, 'I asked Allah to show me ᶜUmar in my sleep, then I saw him after ten years, and he was wiping sweat from his brow. I said, '*Amir al-Mu'minin*, what have you done?' He said, 'Right now I have finished, and if it were not for the mercy of my Lord I would have been destroyed.'

Al-Hakim narrated that ash-Shaᶜbi said: ᶜAtikah bint Zayd ibn

ʿAmr ibn Nufayl eulogised ʿUmar, saying:

'Eye! let your tears and weeping be abundant,
    and do not weary over the noble *imam*.

The fate of the inspired horseman distressed me
    on the day of combat and harsh reproach;

The protection of the *deen*, the helper against fate,
    succour of the troubled and the distressed.

Say to the people of hardship and misfortune,
    "Die! since fate has given us to drink the cup of division and disunion."'

Those of the Companions who died during his days

During the *khilafah* of ʿUmar, may Allah be pleased with him, those of the notable companions who died were: ʿUtbah ibn Ghazwan, al-ʿAla' ibn al-Hadrami, Qais ibn as-Sakan, Abu Quhafah the father of as-Siddiq, may Allah be pleased with him, Saʿd ibn ʿUbadah, Suhayl ibn ʿAmr, Ibn Umm Maktum the *mu'adhdhin*, ʿAyyash ibn Abi Rabiʿah, ʿAbd ar-Rahman the brother of az-Zubayr ibn al-ʿAwwam, Qais ibn Abi Saʿsaʿah one of those who memorised all of the Qur'an, Nawfal ibn al-Harith ibn ʿAbd al-Muttalib, his brother Abu Sufyan, Mariyah the mother of the Sayyid Ibrahim (the son of the Prophet, may Allah bless him and grant him peace, who died in infancy), Abu ʿUbaydah ibn al-Jarrah, Muʿadh ibn Jabal, Yazid ibn Abi Sufyan, Shurahbil ibn Hasanah, al-Fadl ibn al-ʿAbbas, Abu Jandal ibn Suhayl, Abu Malik al-Ashʿari, Safwan ibn al-Muʿattal, Ubayy ibn Kaʿb, Bilal the *mu'adhdhin*, Usayd ibn al-Hudhayr, al-Bara' ibn Malik the brother of Anas, Zaynab bint Jahsh, ʿIyad ibn Ghanam, Abu'l-Haytham ibn at-Tayyihan, Khalid ibn al-Walid, al-Jarud the chief of Bani ʿAbd al-Qais, an-Nuʿman ibn Muqarran, Qatadah ibn an-Nuʿman, al-Aqraʿ ibn Habis, Sawdah bint Zamʿah, ʿUwaym ibn Sa'idah, Ghilan ath-Thaqafi, Abu Mihjan ath-Thaqafi, and other Companions, may Allah be pleased with all of them.

͑Uthman ibn ͑Affan
may Allah be pleased with him

͑Uthman ibn ͑Affan ibn Abi'l-͑As ibn Umayyah ibn ͑Abd Shams ibn ͑Abd Manaf ibn Qusayy ibn Kilab ibn Murrah ibn Ka͑b ibn Lu'ayy ibn Ghalib al-Qurashi al-Amawi (al-Makki and then later al-Madani) Abu ͑Amr, and it has been said Abu ͑Abdullah and Abu Layla.

He was born in the sixth year after the Elephant, and he accepted Islam very early on, being one of those whom as-Siddiq called to Islam. He emigrated on both emigrations: the first to Abyssinia and the second to Madinah.

He married Ruqayyah the daughter of the Messenger of Allah, may Allah bless him and grant him peace, before prophethood, and she died with him during the nights of the Battle of Badr. He was held back from Badr, because of her becoming ill, with the permission of the Messenger of Allah, may Allah bless him and grant him peace, who assigned a portion of the spoils to him and rewarded him, and so he is counted among the people of Badr because of that.

A messenger brought the good news of the victory of the Muslims at Badr on the same day that they buried her in Madinah. The Messenger of Allah, may Allah bless him and grant him peace, married him to her sister Umm Kulthum after her, and she later died [while married] with him in the ninth year of the Hijrah.

The men of knowledge said: We don't know of anyone who married two daughters of a prophet apart from him, and for that reason he is known as Dhu'n-Nurayn – the Possessor of Two Lights.

He was one of the first outstrippers (*as-Sabiqun al-Awwalun*), the first of the *Muhajirun*, one of the ten for whom it was witnessed that they were destined for the Garden, and one of the six with whom the Messenger of Allah, may Allah bless him and grant him peace, was pleased when he died. He was one of the Companions who memorised all of the Qur'an, and indeed Ibn ʿAbbad said, 'None of the *khulafa'* memorised all of the Qur'an except for him and al-Ma'mun.'

Ibn Saʿd said: The Messenger of Allah, may Allah bless him and grant him peace, appointed him as his deputy in charge of Madinah during the military expeditions to Dhat ar-Riqaʿ and Ghatafan.

One hundred and forty-six *hadith* of his have been narrated from the Messenger of Allah, may Allah bless him and grant him peace.

The following related *hadith* from him: Zaid ibn Khalid al-Juhani, Ibn az-Zubayr, as-Sa'ib ibn Yazid, Anas ibn Malik, Zaid ibn Thabit, Salamah ibn al-Akwaʿ, Abu Umamah al-Bahili, Ibn ʿAbbas, Ibn ʿUmar, ʿAbdullah ibn Mughaffal, Abu Qatadah, Abu Hurayrah and other Companions, may Allah be pleased with them, and a great number of others of the Followers (of them Abban ibn ʿUthman, ʿUbaydullah ibn ʿAdi, Humran and others).

Ibn Saʿd narrated that ʿAbd ar-Rahman ibn Hatib said: I saw none of the companions of the Messenger of Allah, may Allah bless him and grant him peace, who, when he narrated a *hadith*, narrated it more completely and more excellently than ʿUthman ibn ʿAffan, unless it was a man who was in awe of the *hadith*.

He narrated that Muhammad ibn Sirin said that ʿUthman was the most knowledgeable of them in the rites of the Hajj, and then after him, Ibn ʿUmar.

Al-Bayhaqi narrated in his *Sunan* that ʿAbdullah ibn ʿUmar ibn Abban al-Juʿfi said: My maternal uncle Hussein al-Juʿfi said, 'Do you realise why ʿUthman was called the Possessor of Two Lights?' I said, 'No.' He said, 'No-one has ever been united to two daughters of a prophet since Allah created Adam (nor will be) until the Hour arises other than ʿUthman, and for that reason he was called the Possessor of Two Lights.'

ʿUthman ibn ʿAffan

Abu Nuʿaym narrated that al-Hasan said: ʿUthman was only called the Possessor of Two Lights because no-one is known of who closed his door upon two daughters of a prophet other than him.

Khaythamah narrated in *Fadaʾil as-Sahabah* and Ibn ʿAsakir that ʿAli ibn Abi Talib was asked about ʿUthman and he said: That was a man who is called in the Highest Assembly the Possessor of Two Lights. He was the son-in-law of the Messenger of Allah, may Allah bless him and grant him peace, with two of his daughters.

Al-Malini narrated with an *isnad* in which there is some weakness that Sahl ibn Saʿd said: It is said about ʿUthman 'the Possessor of Two Lights' because he will pass from one abode to another in the Garden and there will gleam forth for him two flashes of lightning, and it is for that reason that is said about him.

He said: He was given the *kunyah* of Abu ʿAmr in the *Jahiliyyah*, then in the time of Islam, Ruqayyah gave birth to ʿAbdullah for him, and he took his *kunyah* from him (Abu ʿAbdullah).

His mother was Arwa bint Kurayz ibn Rabiʿah ibn Habib ibn ʿAbd Shams (ibn ʿAbd Manaf) and her mother was Umm Hakim al-Baydaʾ bint ʿAbd al-Muttalib ibn Hashim and she was the twin sister of the father of the Messenger of Allah, may Allah bless him and grant him peace. The mother of ʿUthman was the daughter of the paternal aunt of the Prophet, may Allah bless him and grant him peace.

Ibn Ishaq said: He was the first to accept Islam after Abu Bakr, ʿAli and Zaid ibn Harithah.

Ibn ʿAsakir narrated by various routes that ʿUthman was of middle stature – he was not short, nor was he tall – with a beautiful face, a fair complexion tinged with red, on his face the marks of smallpox, with a full beard, large-limbed, broad-shouldered, plump in the shank, long in the forearms, hair covering both his forearms, curly-haired but balding to the fore of his head, the most beautiful of people in the fore-teeth, his locks fell beneath his ears and he coloured them with yellow, and he had strengthened his teeth with gold.

Ibn ʿAsakir narrated that ʿAbdullah ibn Hazm al-Mazini said: I saw ʿUthman ibn ʿAffan and I have never seen a man or a woman with a more beautiful face than him.

He narrated that Musa ibn Talhah said: ʿUthman ibn ʿAffan was the most beautiful of people.

Ibn ʿAsakir narrated that Usamah ibn Zaid said: The Messenger of Allah, may Allah bless him and grant him peace, sent me to ʿUthman's house with a dish in which was meat. I went in, and there was Ruqayyah, may Allah be pleased with her, seated. I began to look at the face of Ruqayyah one time and another time at the face of ʿUthman. When I returned, the Messenger of Allah, may Allah bless him and grant him peace, questioned me and asked me, 'Did you go in to them?' I said, 'Yes.' He said, 'Have you seen a couple more beautiful than them?' I said, 'No, Messenger of Allah.'

Ibn Saʿd narrated that Muhammad ibn Ibrahim ibn al-Harith at-Taymi said: When ʿUthman bin ʿAffan became a Muslim, his paternal uncle, al-Hakam ibn Abi'l-ʿAs ibn Umayyah took hold of him, bound him with rope, and said, 'Do you wish to leave the religion of your fathers for an innovated *deen*? By Allah, I will not leave you until you give up that which you are involved in.' ʿUthman said, 'By Allah, I will not give it up nor abandon it.' When al-Hakam saw his firmness in his *deen* he left him.

Abu Yaʿla narrated that Anas said: The first one to emigrate with his family to the Abyssinians was ʿUthman ibn ʿAffan. The Prophet, may Allah bless him and grant him peace, said, 'May Allah accompany the two of them. ʿUthman is the first to emigrate with his family for the sake of Allah since Lut.'

Ibn ʿAdi narrated that Aʾishah, may Allah be pleased with her, said: When the Prophet, may Allah bless him and grant him peace, married away his daughter Umm Kulthum, he said to her, 'Your husband, of all men, is the one who most resembles your grandfather Ibrahim and your father Muhammad.'

Ibn ʿAdi and Ibn ʿAsakir narrated Ibn ʿUmar said: The Messenger of Allah, may Allah bless him and grant him peace, said, 'We find a resemblance in ʿUthman to our father Ibrahim.'

The *hadith* related on his merit apart from what have already been quoted

The two Shaykhs narrated from ʿA'ishah, may Allah be pleased with her, that the Prophet, may Allah bless him and grant him peace, gathered his garments around him when ʿUthman entered and said, 'Should I not feel shy of a man of whom the angels are shy?'

Al-Bukhari narrated from Abu ʿAbd ar-Rahman as-Sulami that when ʿUthman was besieged, he looked out over them and said, 'I adjure you by Allah, and I adjure none but the Companions of the Prophet, may Allah bless him and grant him peace, do you not know that the Messenger of Allah, may Allah bless him and grant him peace, said, "Whoever equips the Army of Difficulty (of Tabuk) then there is the Garden for him"? And I equipped it. Do you not know that the Messenger of Allah, may Allah bless him and grant him peace, said, "Whoever has the well of Rumah dug, then the Garden is for him"? And I had it dug.' They affirmed what he said.

At-Tirmidhi narrated that ʿAbd ar-Rahman ibn Khabbab said: I witnessed the Prophet, may Allah bless him and grant him peace, urging (people to) support the Army of Difficulty, and then ʿUthman ibn ʿAffan said, 'Messenger of Allah, I will be responsible for one hundred camels with their saddle blankets and their saddles, in the way of Allah.' Then he further urged people to support the army and ʿUthman said, 'Messenger of Allah, I will be responsible for two hundred camels with their saddle blankets and their saddles, in the way of Allah.' Then he further urged people to support the army and ʿUthman said, 'Messenger of Allah, I will be responsible for three hundred camels with their saddle blankets and their saddles, in the way of Allah.' Then the Messenger of Allah, may Allah bless him and grant him peace, came down (from the *minbar*) saying, 'There will be nothing at all against ʿUthman whatever he does after this.'

At-Tirmidhi narrated that Anas said, and al-Hakim, who declared it *sahih*, narrated that ʿAbd ar-Rahman ibn Samurah said: ʿUthman came to the Prophet, may Allah bless him and grant him peace, with one thousand dinars when he equipped the Army of Difficulty and poured them into his lap. The Messenger of Allah, began turning them over, saying, 'Nothing ʿUthman does after this day will harm him,' twice.

At-Tirmidhi narrated that Anas said: When the Messenger of Allah, may Allah bless him and grant him peace, ordered the Pledge of Allegiance of Ridwan (at Hudaybiyyah) ʿUthman ibn ʿAffan was the messenger of the Messenger of Allah, may Allah bless him and his family and grant them peace, to the people of Makkah. So people pledged allegiance. The Prophet, may Allah bless him and his family and grant them peace, said, 'ʿUthman ibn ʿAffan is upon the business of Allah and the business of His Messenger,' and he struck one of his two hands upon the other, so that the hand of the Messenger of Allah, may Allah bless him and grant him peace, was better for ʿUthman than their hands were for them themselves.

At-Tirmidhi narrated that Ibn ʿUmar said: The Messenger of Allah, may Allah bless him and grant him peace, mentioned a *fitnah* (a trial or sedition) and said, 'This one will be killed wrongfully in it,' about ʿUthman.

At-Tirmidhi, al-Hakim, who declared it *sahih*, and Ibn Majah narrated that Murrah ibn Kaʿb said: I heard the Prophet, may Allah bless him and grant him peace, mentioning a trial which he thought to be near. A man passed by, muffled up in his garment, and he (the Prophet) said, 'This one on that day will be upon the guidance.' I stood up and went to him and it was ʿUthman ibn ʿAffan. I turned, faced him (the Prophet) and said, 'This one?' He said, 'Yes.'

At-Tirmidhi and al-Hakim narrated that ʿA'ishah, may Allah be pleased with her, related that the Prophet, may Allah bless him and grant him peace, said, 'ʿUthman, perhaps Allah will robe you in a garment, so if the hypocrites wish to strip it off you, do not take it off until you meet me.'

At-Tirmidhi narrated that ʿUthman said, on the day of the house (the site of his siege), 'The Prophet, may Allah bless him and grant him peace, made a covenant with me and I will be patient with it.'

Al-Hakim narrated that Abu Hurayrah said: ʿUthman bought the Garden from the Prophet, may Allah bless him and grant him peace, twice: when he had the well of Rumah dug and when he equipped the Army of Difficulty.

Ibn ʿAsakir narrated that Abu Hurayrah, may Allah be pleased with him, said that the Prophet, may Allah bless him and grant him peace, said, 'ʿUthman, of my companions, most resembles me in character.'

At-Tabarani narrated that ʿAsmah ibn Malik said: When the daughter of the Messenger of Allah, may Allah bless him and his family and grant them peace, died under (the roof of) ʿUthman, the Messenger of Allah, may Allah bless him and grant him peace, said, 'Get ʿUthman married. Even if I had a third (daughter) I would have got him married, and I did not get him married except through revelation from Allah.'

Ibn ʿAsakir narrated that ʿAli, may Allah be pleased with him said: I heard the Prophet, may Allah bless him and grant him peace, say to ʿUthman, 'Even if I had forty daughters I would marry them to you, one after another, until none of them remained.'

Ibn ʿAsakir narrated that Zaid ibn Thabit said: I heard the Prophet, may Allah bless him and grant him peace, saying, 'ʿUthman passed by me while one of the angels was with me, and he said, "A martyr whose people will kill him. We are shy of him."'

Abu Yaʿla narrated from Ibn ʿUmar that the Prophet, may Allah bless him and grant him peace, said, 'The angels are shy of ʿUthman, just as they are shy of Allah and His Messenger.'

Ibn ʿAsakir narrated from al-Hasan that the modesty of ʿUthman was mentioned in his presence. He said, 'If he were in the middle of the house – and the door locked – then he put off his clothes in order to pour water over himself, modesty would prevent him from raising (straightening) his backbone.'

His *khilafah*

He was pledged allegiance as *khalifah* three nights after the burial of ⁽Umar. It is related that people got together, during those days, with ⁽Abd ar-Rahman ibn ⁽Awf, advising him and talking confidentially with him. Not one person of judgement who sat alone with him saw any to equal ⁽Uthman. When ⁽Abd ar-Rahman sat to pledge allegiance, he praised Allah and said, during his speech, 'I saw that people refuse anybody but ⁽Uthman.' Ibn ⁽Asakir narrated it from al-Miswar ibn Makhramah. In another narration, 'Now! ⁽Ali, I have researched among people and I don't see them regarding anyone equal to ⁽Uthman. Therefore, do not make a way against yourself.' He took the hand of ⁽Uthman and said, 'We pledge allegiance to you according to the *Sunnah* of Allah, the *Sunnah* of His Messenger and the *Sunnah* of the two *khalifahs* after him.' ⁽Abd ar-Rahman pledged allegiance to him and the *Muhajirun* and the *Ansar* pledged allegiance to him.

Ibn Sa⁽d narrated that Anas said: ⁽Umar sent for Abu Talhah al-Ansari an hour before he died and said, 'You be among fifty of the *Ansar* along with this group, the companions of the counsel, because they, as I believe, will gather in a house. Stand at that door with your companions, allow no-one to enter, and do not leave them to allow the third day to pass without their appointing one of themselves to the command.'

There is in the *Musnad* of Ahmad that Abu Wa'il said: I said to ⁽Abd ar-Rahman ibn ⁽Awf, 'How could you have sworn allegiance to ⁽Uthman and neglected ⁽Ali?' He said, 'Where was my wrong action? I started with ⁽Ali and I said, "Shall I swear allegiance to you according to the Book of Allah, the *Sunnah* of His Messenger and the conduct of Abu Bakr and ⁽Umar?" He said, "In what I am able." Then later I offered the same to ⁽Uthman and he said, "Yes."'

ᶜUthman ibn ᶜAffan

It has been related that ᶜAbd ar-Rahman said to ᶜUthman in private, 'If I don't pledge allegiance to you who would you point out to me?' He said, 'ᶜAli.' He said to ᶜAli, 'If I don't pledge allegiance to you who would you point out to me?' He said, 'ᶜUthman.' Then he called for az-Zubayr and said, 'If I don't pledge allegiance to you who would you point out to me?' He said, 'ᶜAli or ᶜUthman.' Then later he called for Saᶜd and said, 'Whom would you indicate to me? because, as for me and you, we don't want it.' He said, 'ᶜUthman.' Then ᶜAbd ar-Rahman sought the counsel of all the notables and saw that most of them were inclined to ᶜUthman.

Ibn Saᶜd and al-Hakim narrated that Ibn Masᶜud, may Allah be pleased with him, said, when ᶜUthman was pledged allegiance, 'We have charged with command the best of those remaining and we have not been negligent.'

In this year of his *khilafah*, Rayy was opened [to Islam], and it had been opened previously and subsequently lost. In that year many nosebleeds occurred among people, so that it was known as, 'The year of the nosebleeds.' ᶜUthman was afflicted by nosebleeds to such an extent that he stayed away from the Hajj and deputed someone in his place. In that year many Byzantine fortresses were taken. In it ᶜUthman appointed Saᶜd ibn Abi Waqqas as governor of Kufa and removed al-Mughirah.

In the year 25 AH, ᶜUthman removed Saᶜd from Kufa and appointed al-Walid ibn ᶜUqbah ibn Abi Muᶜayt – and he was a Companion, and a brother of ᶜUthman on his mother's side – and that was the first thing for which he was disliked; because he appointed his relatives to posts of authority. *It has been told as a tale* that al-Walid led them in prayer for the dawn prayer with four *rakaᶜat* when he was drunk, and that then he turned to them and said, 'Shall I do more (*rakaᶜat*) for you?'

In the year 26 AH, ᶜUthman enlarged and extended *al-Masjid al-Haram*, and bought sites (adjoining it) for the enlargement. In the same year Sabur (possibly Shahpur) was opened.

In the year 27 AH, Muʿawiyah went on a military expedition to Cyprus, taking the armies by sea. ʿUbadah ibn as-Samit was with them and his wife, Umm Haram bint Milhan al-Ansariyah (of the *Ansar*). She fell from her riding beast, and died there as a martyr, and the Prophet, may Allah bless him and grant him peace, had foretold this army for her. He had supplicated for her that she should be of them. She was buried in Cyprus. In that same year Arrajan and Darabjird were opened. ʿUthman removed ʿAmr ibn al-ʿAs from Egypt and appointed ʿAbdullah ibn Saʿd ibn Abi Sarh over it, who led an expedition against northern Africa and opened it [to Islam], both on the plains and in the mountains, and every man in the army received one thousand dinars, and it has also been said, three thousand dinars. Then Andalusia was opened in this same year.

An observation

Muʿawiyah had pressed ʿUmar ibn al-Khattab very persistently about raiding Cyprus and doing so by sea, so ʿUmar wrote to ʿAmr ibn al-ʿAs, 'Describe the sea to me and the one who travels on it.' He wrote to him, 'I have seen a great creation, which a small creation mounts. If it is still, it pierces the hearts, and if it moves, it awes the intellects. In it the intellects grow in littleness, and wrong actions in muchness, and in it they are like grubs upon a timber. If it leans over, it sinks, and if it is swift, it enters into the wave and dives therein.' When ʿUmar read the letter he wrote to Muʿawiyah, 'By Allah I will never convey a Muslim upon it.' Ibn Jarir said, 'Muʿawiyah carried out the expedition against Cyprus during the time of ʿUthman, and its people made a treaty with him on the basis of their paying the *jizyah*.'

In the year 29 AH, Persepolis was opened by force of arms, and Fasa and other places. In that year, ʿUthman added to the mosque of Madinah, extended it, and rebuilt it with sculpted stone, making its pillars of stone and its roof of teak. He made its length one hundred and sixty cubits and its breadth one hundred and fifty cubits.

In the year 30 AH, Jur was opened and many provinces of the land of Khurasan; Naysabur was opened by treaty, and it has been said, by force. Tus and Sarkhas were both opened by treaty, and similarly Marw and Bayhaq. When these extensive provinces were taken, ʿUthman's revenues became abundant, and wealth came to him from every direction, until he established treasuries and made provisions to flow abundantly. He would order for a man one hundred thousand purses in each of which there were four thousand ounces (of silver).

In the year 31 AH, Abu Sufyan ibn Harb, the father of Muʿawiyah, died, and also al-Hakam ibn Abi'l-ʿAs the paternal uncle of ʿUthman, may Allah be pleased with him.

In the year 32 AH, al-ʿAbbas ibn ʿAbd al-Muttalib, the paternal uncle of the Prophet, may Allah bless him and grant him peace, died, and ʿUthman led the (funeral) prayer over him. In that year ʿAbd ar-Rahman ibn ʿAwf died, one of the ten from the first outstrippers who had once given away as *sadaqah* forty thousand and an entire caravan which had come from Syria, just as it was. In that year, ʿAbdullah ibn Masʿud al-Hudhali died, one of the four reciters, one of the earliest in Islam, and one of the men of knowledge among the Companions who were famous for the vast extent of their knowledge. In that year the wise and abstinent Abu'd-Darda' al-Khazraji died; he had been appointed to the position of *Qadi* of Damascus under Muʿawiyah. In that year Abu Dharr Jundub ibn Jinadah al-Ghifari, the truthful in speech, died. In that year, Zaid ibn ʿAbdullah ibn ʿAbd-Rabbihi al-Ansari died, the one who was shown the *adhan* in a dream.

In the year 33 AH, al-Miqdad ibn al-Aswad died at his land at al-Jurf, and he was carried to Madinah (for burial). In that year, Abdullah ibn Saʿd ibn Abi Sarh mounted a military expedition against Abyssinia.

In the year 34 AH, the people of Kufa ejected Saʿid ibn al-ʿAs and were pleased with Abu Musa al-Ashʿari.

In the year 35 AH, there occurred the killing of ʿUthman.

Az-Zuhri said: ʿUthman ruled the *khilafah* for twelve years. For six years he ruled without people criticising him at all. To Quraysh he was preferable to ʿUmar ibn al-Khattab, because ʿUmar was severe against them, but when ʿUthman ruled over them he was gentle with them and made his connections close with them. Then later he flagged in their affair, and appointed his relatives and family in the last six (years of his rule). He decreed for Marwan the *khums* (the fifth share of the spoils of *jihad* that goes to the ruler) of North Africa, and he gave his relatives and family wealth. In that he was interpreting the 'making close connections (with family)' which Allah has ordered. He said, 'Abu Bakr and ʿUmar gave up and abandoned what of that was theirs (by right), and I have taken it and divided it among my relatives,' but people rejected and repudiated that from him. [It was his *ijtihad*]. Ibn Saʿd narrated it.

Ibn ʿAsakir narrated by another route that az-Zuhri said: I said to Saʿid ibn al-Musayyab, 'Can you tell me how was the killing of ʿUthman? What were people up to and what was he up to? And why did the Companions of Muhammad, may Allah bless him and grant him peace, fail to help him? Ibn al-Musayyab said, "ʿUthman was killed unjustly, whoever killed him was wrongdoing, and whoever failed to help him is free of blame.' I said, 'How was that?' He said, 'When ʿUthman was appointed, a group of the Companions disliked his appointment, because ʿUthman used to love his people. He ruled people for twelve years. He used to appoint people from Bani Umayyah who had not kept company with the Prophet, may Allah bless him and grant him peace. His *amirs* used to produce matters which the Companions of Muhammad, may Allah bless him and grant him peace, would repudiate. ʿUthman used to ask people to have good will for them and he would not remove them. That was in the year 35 AH. During the six last years he chose in preference the tribe of his paternal uncle. He appointed them and did not let anyone share with them. He ordered them to fear Allah, he appointed ʿAbdullah ibn Abi Sarh in charge of Egypt and he remained in control there for years. The people of Egypt came to complain of him and to complain of his wrongdoing. There had been slights before from ʿUthman to ʿAbdullah ibn Masʿud, Abu Dharr and ʿAmmar ibn Yasir. Banu Hudhayl and Banu Zuhrah had what they had in their hearts because of the state of Ibn Masʿud. Banu Ghifar, their allies and whoever was angry because of Abu Dharr, had in their hearts what they had in them. Banu Makhzum were furious at ʿUthman because of the condition of ʿAmmar ibn Yasir.

'The people of Egypt came to complain of Ibn Abi Sarh, so he wrote a letter to him in which he threatened him, but Ibn Abi Sarh refused to accept what ʿUthman forbade him, he struck one of those of the people of Egypt who came to him from ʿUthman, one of those who had gone to ʿUthman, and he killed him. Seven hundred men left Egypt and dwelt in the mosque (of Madinah). They complained to the Companions at the times of the prayers about what Ibn Abi Sarh had done. Talhah ibn ʿUbaydullah stood and addressed ʿUthman very severely. ʿA'ishah, may Allah be pleased with her, sent a message to him saying, "The Companions of Muhammad, may Allah bless him and grant him peace, came to you and they asked you to remove this man and you refused? This one has killed a man from among them so treat them with justice (in their complaint) against your governor." ʿAli ibn Abi Talib came to him and said, "They are only asking you for a man in place of (in retaliation for) a man and they have claimed from him (retaliation for the spilling of) blood. Remove him from over them and give a (just) decision between them. If there is anything due against him, be just to them." He (ʿUthman) said to them (the Egyptians), "Choose from amongst yourselves a man whom I shall appoint over you in his (Ibn Abi Sarh's) place." The people indicated to him Muhammad ibn Abi Bakr. They said, "Appoint Muhammad ibn Abi Bakr over us." He wrote his covenant and appointed him.

A number of the *Muhajirun* and *Ansar* went with them to look into that (dispute) which was between the people of Egypt and Ibn Abi Sarh. Muhammad went and those with him. When they were about three days' journey from Madinah they came upon a black slave on a camel beating the camel so much that it was as if he was pursuing or being pursued. The Companions of Muhammad, may Allah bless him and grant him peace, said to him, "What is your story? What is your business? It is as if you were fleeing or pursuing someone." He said to them, "I am the slave of the *Amir al-Mu'minin* and he has directed me to the governor of Egypt." A man said to him, "This (Muhammad ibn Abi Bakr) is the governor of Egypt." He said, "It is not this one I want." Muhammad ibn Abi Bakr was told of his affair and so he sent a man in search of him who took him and brought him to him. He said, "Slave, who are you?" He began to say, one time, "I am the slave of the *Amir al-Mu'minin*," and another time, "I am the slave of Marwan," until one man recognised that he was the slave of ʿUthman. Muhammad said to him, "To whom are you sent?" He said, "To the governor of Egypt." He said, "With what?" He said, "With a message." He said, "Do you have a letter with you?" He said, "No." They searched him and didn't find a letter with him. He had with him an ewer which was dry, in which was something which moved about, so they moved it about to bring it out but it didn't come out. They broke the ewer and there was a letter in it from ʿUthman to Ibn Abi Sarh. Muhammad gathered those with them of the *Muhajirun*, the *Ansar* and others, then he opened the letter in their presence. There was in it, "When Muhammad, so-and-so, and so-and-so come to you, then find a way to kill them, and declare his letter to be false. Consider yourself confirmed in your governorship until my advice on it comes to you, and imprison whoever tries to come to me to accuse you of wrongdoing. My advice on that will certainly come to you, if Allah wills."

'When they read the letter they were terrified. Then they became resolved and returned to Madinah. Muhammad sealed the letter with the signet rings of the group who were with him, and then entrusted the letter to a man who was with them. Then they went to Madinah. There they gathered together Talhah, az-Zubayr, ʿAli, Saʿd, and whoever there was of the Companions of Muhammad, may Allah bless him and his family and grant them peace. He broke (the seals of) the letter in their presence, and told them of the story of the slave. They read out the letter to them, and none of the people of Madinah was left who was not enraged at ʿUthman. It only increased those who were angry because of Ibn Masʿud, Abu Dharr and ʿAmmar ibn Yasir in fury and rage. The Companions of Muhammad rose and kept to their houses. There was no-one among them who was not incoherent when he read the letter. The people besieged ʿUthman in the year 35 AH, and Muhammad ibn Abi Bakr raised Bani Taym and others against him.

'When ʿAli saw that, he sent for Talhah, az-Zubayr, Saʿd, ʿAmmar and a group of the Companions, all of whom were at Badr. Then he went in to ʿUthman, with him the letter, the slave and the camel. ʿAli said to him, "This slave is your slave?" He said, "Yes." He said, "And the camel is your camel?" He said, "Yes." He said, "Then you wrote this letter?" He said, "No," and he swore an oath, "By Allah I did not write this letter, I did not order it, and I had no knowledge of it." ʿAli said, "The seal is your seal?" He said, "Yes." He said, "How does your slave go out on your camel, with a letter upon which is your seal, and you know nothing about it?" He swore again, "By Allah, I did not write this letter, I didn't order it, and I never directed this slave to go to Egypt." As for the handwriting, they recognised that it was that of Marwan, and they came to doubt as to ʿUthman. They demanded that he should give them Marwan and he refused, while Marwan was with him in the house. The Companions of Muhammad, may Allah bless him and grant him peace, left him in anger, and in doubt about his affair. They knew that ʿUthman would not swear an oath that was false, but people said, "ʿUthman will never be free of guilt in our hearts unless he hands Marwan over to us for questioning, so that we know the situation of the letter, and how he could order the killing of a man of the Companions of Muhammad, may Allah bless him and grant him peace, without right. If ʿUthman wrote it, we will remove him from office. If Marwan wrote it as if it had been written by ʿUthman, then we will have to look seriously at what we shall do in the case of Marwan."

'They stuck to their houses, and ʿUthman refused to send Marwan out to them, for he feared that he would be killed. People continued laying siege to ʿUthman, and they prevented water (from reaching him). He looked over the people (from an upper floor) and said, "Is ʿAli among you?" They said, "No." He said, "Is Saʿd among you?" They said, "No." He was silent and then he said, "Will no-one reach ʿAli and ask him to get us water to drink?" That reached ʿAli, so he sent him three water-skins full of water, but they almost didn't reach him. Because of them a number of the freed slaves of Banu Hashim and Banu Umayyah were wounded in the course of the water getting to him.

'It reached ʿAli that it was intended to kill ʿUthman, and he said, "We only want Marwan from him. As for the killing of ʿUthman, no!" He said to al-Hasan and al-Hussein, "Go with your two swords and stand at the door of ʿUthman and allow no-one to reach him." Then az-Zubayr sent his son, Talhah sent his son and a number of the Companions of the Prophet, may Allah bless him and grant him peace, sent their sons to prevent people getting to ʿUthman, and to demand the surrender of Marwan. When people saw that, they shot arrows against the door of ʿUthman until al-Hasan ibn ʿAli was reddened with blood at his door, an arrow struck Marwan while he was in the house. Muhammad ibn Talhah was smeared with blood and also Qanbar, the freed slave of ʿAli, was wounded in the head.

'Muhammad ibn Abi Bakr was afraid that Banu Hashim would

become angry because of the state of al-Hasan and al-Hussein and provoke a tumult. He took the hands of two men and said to them, "If Banu Hashim come and see blood on the face of al-Hasan they will remove these people from around ʿUthman and what we wanted will be rendered useless. Let us go and scale the wall of the house and kill him, without anyone knowing about it." Muhammad and his two men got over the wall from the house of a man of the *Ansar* and entered ʿUthman's house, without any of those who were with him (ʿUthman) knowing, because everyone with him was up above the houses (on the roofs). There was no-one with him but his wife. Muhammad said to the two of them, "Stay where you are, because his wife is with him, until I first enter. When I have taken hold of him, then you come in and strike him until you have killed him." Muhammad went in and took hold of his beard, and ʿUthman said to him, "By Allah, if your father could see you, your behaviour to me would cause him great distress," and so his hand slackened (and he held back), and then the two men entered and struck him until they had killed him.

'They went out in flight by the same way that they had come in, and his wife cried out, but her cry was not heard in the house because of the commotion in the house. His wife went up to the people and said, "The *Amir al-Mu'minin* has been killed!" The people entered and they found him slaughtered. The news reached ʿAli, Talhah, az-Zubayr, Saʿd and whoever was in Madinah and they went out – and their intellects had gone, because of the news which had come to them – until they came in to ʿUthman and found him killed. They repeated again and again, "Truly we belong to Allah and truly we are returning to Him." ʿAli said to his two sons, "How was the *Amir al-Mu'minin* killed while you two were at the door?" He raised his hand and slapped al-Hasan, struck the chest of al-Hussein, abused Muhammad ibn Talhah and ʿAbdullah ibn az-Zubayr, and went out – enraged – until he came to his house.

'The people came rushing to him, saying to him, "We will pledge allegiance to you, so stretch out your hand, for there must be an *amir*." ᶜAli said, "That is not your business. It only belongs to the people of Badr. Whoever the people of Badr are pleased with is the *khalifah*." Not one of the people of Badr remained without coming to ᶜAli and they said to him, "We see no-one who has more right to it than you. Stretch out your hand and we will pledge allegiance to you." They pledged allegiance to him. Marwan and his son fled.

ᶜAli came to the wife of ᶜUthman and said to her, "Who killed ᶜUthman?" She said, "I don't know. Two men I don't know came in to him, and along with them was Muhammad ibn Abi Bakr." She told ᶜAli and the people of what Muhammad had done, so ᶜAli called for Muhammad and asked him about what the wife of ᶜUthman had said. Muhammad said, "She did not lie. By Allah, I did come into him, I did want to kill him, then he reminded me of my father and I stood back from him, turning in penitence to Allah, exalted is He. By Allah, I did not kill him, and I did not hold him." His wife said, "He has told the truth. But he did bring the two of them in.'"

Ibn ᶜAsakir narrated that Kinanah, the freed slave of Safiyyah, and others said: An Egyptian, who was blue-eyed with a ruddy complexion, called Himar killed ᶜUthman.

Ahmad narrated that al-Mughirah ibn Shuᶜbah said that he entered upon ᶜUthman while he was besieged and said, 'You are the *imam* of the people, and what you see has happened to you. I offer you three courses; one of them, that you come out and fight them, for there are numbers (of men) and strength with you; you are in the right and they are in the wrong; or we should cut a door for you other than the door over which they stand guard, then sit on your mount and take yourself to Makkah, for they will not consider it lawful to kill you when you are there; or else you should take yourself to Syria, for they are the people of Syria and among them is Muᶜawiyah.' ᶜUthman said, 'As for me going out and fighting, I will not be the first *khalifah* of the Messenger of Allah, may Allah bless him and grant him peace, in his *ummah* to spill (their) blood; and as for me going to Makkah, I heard the Messenger of Allah, may Allah bless him and grant him peace, saying, "A man of Quraysh will wrangle and dispute in Makkah; there will be upon him half the punishment of the world," and I shall not be him; and as for me taking myself to Syria, then I will never separate myself from the Abode of the Hijrah and the neighbourhood of the Messenger of Allah, may Allah bless him and grant him peace.'

Ibn ʿAsakir narrated that Abu Thawr al-Fahmi said: I entered upon ʿUthman while he was besieged and he said, 'I have hidden ten (things) with my Lord: I was the fourth of four in Islam; I equipped the Army of Difficulty; the Messenger of Allah, may Allah bless him and grant him peace, married me his daughter and then later she died, and he married me his other daughter, and I did not court (her) and I didn't wish (for it); I have never placed my right hand upon my private parts since I pledged allegiance with it to the Messenger of Allah, may Allah bless him and grant him peace; and no *Jumuʿah* has passed me by since I accepted Islam without my freeing a slave, unless there was something with me (of debt), then I would free him (or her) after that; and I never committed adultery in *Jahiliyyah* or Islam; and I never stole in *Jahiliyyah* or Islam; and I memorised the entire Qur'an in the time of the Messenger of Allah, may Allah bless him and grant him peace.'

ʿUthman was killed in the middle of the Days of *Tashriq* (the days of the ʿEid of Hajj) in the year 35 AH; and it has been said that he was killed on the day of *Jumuʿah*, the 18th of Dhu'l-Hijjah. He was buried on the night before Saturday, between the sunset and night prayers, in Hawsh Kawkab in al-Baqiʿ (the cemetery of Madinah) and he was the first to be buried in it (Hawsh Kawkab). It was said that his killing was on Wednesday, and it was said that it was Monday six days before the end of Dhu'l-Hijjah. On the day he was killed, he was eighty-two years old. It has also been said that he was eighty-one years old, eighty-four, eighty-six, eighty-eight or eighty-nine, and it was said that he was ninety. Qatadah said: Az-

Zubayr prayed the funeral prayer over him and buried him and he had requested him to do that.

Ibn ᶜAdi and Ibn ᶜAsakir narrated from Anas in a *marfuᶜ hadith*, 'Allah has a sword sheathed in its scabbard as long as ᶜUthman is alive. Then when he is killed, that sword will be drawn and it will not be sheathed until the Day of Resurrection.'

Ibn ᶜAsakir narrated that Zaid ibn Abi Habib said: It has reached me that all of the mounted group who went to ᶜUthman went mad.

He narrated that Hudhayfah said: The first of the trials was the killing of ᶜUthman, and the last of the trials is the emergence of the Dajjal. By the One in Whose hand is my self, a man will not die, in whose heart there is the weight of grain of love for the killing of ᶜUthman, but that he will follow the Dajjal if he reached him (his time), and if he did not reach him he would affirm him in his grave.

He narrated that Ibn ᶜAbbas said: If people had not sought (retaliation) for the blood of ᶜUthman they would have been stoned with stones from heaven.

He narrated that al-Hasan said: ᶜUthman was killed while ᶜAli was away in some land he owned. When it reached him he said, 'O Allah, I did not approve (of it) and I did not abet (it).'

Al-Hakim narrated, and he declared it *sahih*, that Qais ibn ᶜAbbad said: I heard ᶜAli on the Day of the (battle of the) Camel saying, 'O Allah I am clear before You of having taken part in the (shedding of the) blood of ᶜUthman. My intellect was shaken on the day of ᶜUthman's killing, my soul was repulsed, and they came to me to pledge allegiance to me and I said, "By Allah, I am ashamed to take the allegiance of a people who killed ᶜUthman, and I am ashamed before Allah to be sworn allegiance while ᶜUthman is not yet buried," so they went away. When the people returned and asked me to accept their allegiance, I said, "O Allah, I am afraid of what I am proceeding to do." Then the determination (of the people) came, I was sworn allegiance, they said, "*Amir al-Mu'minin*!" and it was as if my heart was rent asunder. I said, "O Allah, take from me for the sake of ʿUthman until You are contented.'"

Ibn ʿAsakir narrated that Abu Khaldah al-Hanafi said: I heard ʿAli saying, 'Banu Umayyah claim that I killed ʿUthman. No, by Allah Whom there is no god but He! I did not kill him, I did not abet it, I forbade it but they disobeyed me.'

He narrated that Samurah said: Islam was in a well fortified fortress, and they made a breach in Islam with the killing of ʿUthman which will not be closed until the Day of Resurrection. The *khilafah* was among the people of Madinah and they drove it out and it did not return to them.

He narrated that Muhammad ibn Sirin said: The piebald horses (of the angels) were never missing from the battles and the armies until the killing of ʿUthman. There was no disagreement on the new moons until the killing of ʿUthman. This redness which is on the horizons was never seen until the killing of al-Hussein.

ʿAbd ar-Razzaq narrated in the *Musannaf* that Humayd ibn Hilal said: ʿAbdullah ibn Salam came upon those who were besieging ʿUthman and said, 'Do not kill him, for, by Allah, any man of you who kills him will meet Allah without a hand. The sword of Allah will remain sheathed, and by Allah, if you kill him, Allah will draw it out and He will never sheathe it again. A prophet was never killed but that seventy thousand were killed because of him, nor a *khalifah* but that thirty-five thousand were killed because of him before they were again united.'

Ibn ʿAsakir narrated that ʿAbd ar-Rahman ibn Mahdi said: There were two qualities that ʿUthman had which neither Abu Bakr nor ʿUmar had: his self-collectedness until he was killed, and his uniting the people upon a single *mushaf* (written copy of the Qur'an).

Al-Hakim narrated that ash-Shaʿbi said: I have not heard a better elegy upon ʿUthman than the words of Kaʿb ibn Malik when he said:

> Then he restrained his hands and closed his door,
>   And he was certain that Allah is not forgetful,

He said to the people of the house, 'Do not kill them!
    May Allah pardon every man who does not fight."

So how you have seen Allah pour out upon them
    Enmity and hatred after harmony with each other!

And how you have seen the good turning back from people
    After him, the way the driving winds turn (the clouds) back!'

Section

Ibn Sa'd narrated that Musa ibn Talhah said: I saw 'Uthman going out on the day of *Jumu'ah*, upon him two yellow garments. He would sit on the *minbar*, then the *mu'adhdhins* would call to the prayer while he would talk, asking people about their prices and their sick.

He narrated that 'Abdullah ar-Rumi said: 'Uthman would take care of his *wadu'* (water for *wudu*) at night himself. Someone said to him, 'If only you would tell one of the servants then they would take care (of it for) you.' He said, 'No! The night is for them to rest in.'

Ibn 'Asakir narrated that 'Amr ibn 'Uthman ibn 'Affan said: The engraving on the seal-ring of 'Uthman was, 'I trust in the One Who created and completed (His creation).'

Abu Nu'aym narrated in *ad-Dala'il* from Ibn 'Umar that Jahjah al-Ghifari stood up against 'Uthman while he was (upon the *minbar*) delivering the *khutbah*, and he took his staff from his hand and broke it over his knee. The year did not pass until Allah sent gangrene in his foot and he died from it.

The things in which 'Uthman was first

Al-'Askari said in *al-Awa'il* (The Firsts): He was the first to grant lands (taken in *jihad*), and the first who enclosed pastures (for the animals paid in *zakat* and for the horses and camels for *jihad*), the first to lower his voice in the *takbir*, the first to perfume the mosque (of Madinah), the first to command the first call to prayer on the *Jumu'ah*, the first to provide for the *mu'adhdhins*, the first to be speechless in the *khutbah*, and then he said, 'People, the first time of mounting is hard, after today there are other days, and if I live you will have the *khutbah* in its proper manner. We were never public speakers and Allah will teach us.' He was the first to place the *khutbah* on the *'Eid* before the prayer, the first to entrust to the people the payment of their own *zakat*, the first to take charge of the *khilafah* during the life of his mother, the first to appoint a chief of police, and the first to set apart an enclosure in the mosque from fear that there should happen to him what happened to 'Umar. This is what al-'Askari mentioned and he also said: The first disagreements in the *ummah* in which some would accuse others of errors were in his time, concerning things for which they blamed him. Before that they used to disagree about *fiqh* and no-one would accuse others of errors.

I say: Of his firsts there remain that he was the first of this *ummah* to emigrate with his family for the sake of Allah, as has preceded, and he was the first to unite people on one manner of recitation.

Ibn 'Asakir narrated that Hakim ibn 'Abbad ibn Hanif said: The first reprehensible thing that appeared in Madinah when the world was overflowing (with wealth) and the fatness of people reached a limit, was the flying of pigeons and archery with crossbows (firing clay bullets, for bets), so 'Uthman appointed a man from Banu Layth in the eighth year of his *khilafah* who clipped them (the wings of the pigeons) and broke the crossbows.

The notables who died during the time of 'Uthman

There died during the time of 'Uthman the following notable people: Suraqah ibn Malik ibn Jushum, Jabbar ibn Sakhr, Hatib ibn Abi Balta'ah, 'Iyad ibn Zuhayr, Abu Usayd as-Sa'idi, Aws ibn as-Samit, al-Harith ibn Nawfal, 'Abdullah ibn Hudhafah, Zaid ibn Kharijah the one who spoke after death, Labid the poet, al-

Musayyab the father of Sa'id, Mu'adh ibn 'Amr ibn al-Jamuh, Ma'bad ibn al-'Abbas, Mu'ayqib ibn Abi Fatimah ad-Dawsi, Abu Lubabah ibn 'Abd al-Mundhir, Nu'aym ibn Mas'ud al-Ashja'i and others of the Companions.

Apart from the Companions there were Hutay'ah the poet and Abu Dhu'ayb the poet of the tribe of Hudhayl.

͑Ali ibn Abi Talib
may Allah be pleased with him

͑Ali ibn Abi Talib, may Allah be pleased with him – and the name of Abu Talib was ͑Abd Manaf – ibn ͑Abd al-Muttalib – and his name was Shaybah – ibn Hashim – and his name was ͑Amr – Ibn ͑Abd Manaf – and his name was al-Mughirah – ibn Qusayy – and his name was Zaid – ibn Kilab ibn Murrah ibn Ka͑b ibn Lu'ayy ibn Ghalib ibn Fihr ibn Malik ibn Nadr ibn Kinanah. He was Abu'l-Hasan and he was Abu Turab, a *kunyah* which the Prophet, may Allah bless him and grant him peace, gave him.

His mother was Fatimah bint Asad ibn Hashim and she was the first Hashimi woman to give birth to a Hashimi child. She accepted Islam and emigrated.

͑Ali, may Allah be pleased with him, is one of the ten for whom it is witnessed that the Garden is for them, he was the brother of the Messenger of Allah, may Allah bless him and his family and grant them peace, by the act of taking brothers (undertaken between the *Muhajirun* and the *Ansar* in Madinah); he was his son-in-law through (marriage to) Fatimah, the mistress of the women of the worlds, may Allah be pleased with her; he was one of the first to embrace Islam, one of the lordly learned ones, one of the famously courageous ones, one of those mentioned for being abstinent, one of the recognised deliverers of the *khutbah*, one who memorised the entire Qur'an and recited it before the Prophet, may Allah bless him and grant him peace, and Abu'l-Aswad ad-Du'ali and ͑Abd ar-Rahman as-Sulami, in turn, recited it before him. He was the first *khalifah* from Bani Hashim, the father of the two grandsons (of the Prophet, may Allah bless him and grant him peace). He accepted Islam very early on; rather, Ibn ᶜAbbas, Anas, Zaid ibn Arqam, Salman al-Farisi and a whole group of others said that he was the first to accept Islam, and some of them relate that there is a consensus on that.

Abu Yaᶜla narrated that ᶜAli, may Allah be pleased with him, said, 'The Messenger of Allah, may Allah bless him and grant him peace, was sent (on his prophetic mission) on Monday and I accepted Islam on the Wednesday.' His age when he accepted Islam was ten years old. It has been said that it was nine, eight, and it has even been said that it was less than that. Al-Hasan ibn Zaid ibn al-Hasan said: He didn't ever worship idols, because of his youth. Ibn Saᶜd narrated it.

When he, may Allah bless him and grant him peace, told him to remain some days behind after him in Makkah, in order to repay some things entrusted to and deposited with the Prophet, may Allah bless him and grant him peace, and for him then to join his family, he did that.

He was present with the Messenger of Allah, may Allah bless him and his family and grant them peace, at Badr, Uhud and all the rest of the battles except for Tabuk, because the Prophet, may Allah bless him and grant him peace, made him his deputy in Madinah. In all of the battles there are famous stories about him, and the Prophet, may Allah bless him and grant him peace, gave him the standard on many occasions.

Saᶜid ibn al-Musayyab said: On the day of Uhud, ᶜAli received sixteen wounds.

It is well established in the two *Sahih* collections, 'That he, may Allah bless him and grant him peace, gave him the standard on the day of Khaybar and told that victory would be at his hands.' The accounts of his bravery and stories of him in the wars are famous.

ᶜAli, as an old man, was stout, balding over the forehead, with much hair, of middle stature inclining to shortness, full-bellied, with an extremely full beard which filled between his two shoulders and was white as if it were cotton, and he was very tawny complexioned.

Jabir ibn ᶜAbdullah said: ᶜAli carried the gate upon his back on the day of Khaybar until the Muslims ascended upon it and conquered it. They tried to drag it afterwards and it was only possible for forty men to carry it. Ibn ᶜAsakir narrated it.

Ibn Ishaq in *al-Maghazi* and Ibn ᶜAsakir narrated from Abu Rafiᶜ that: ᶜAli took hold of the gate of the fortress, the fortress of Khaybar; he used it as a shield to protect himself, and it continued in his hand while he fought until Allah gave us the victory. I certainly saw eight of us struggling to turn that gate over and we were not able to turn it.

Al-Bukhari narrated in *al-Adab* that Sahl ibn Saᶜd said: The name that ᶜAli, may Allah be pleased with him, loved the most was 'Abu Turab ('Dusty One' or literally 'Father of Dust'), and he rejoiced in being called by it. No-one named him Abu Turab except for the Prophet, may Allah bless him and grant him peace. That was because one day, when he was angry with Fatimah, he went out and laid down against the wall of the mosque, and then the Prophet, may Allah bless him and grant him peace, came and his back was covered in dust. The Prophet, may Allah bless him and grant him peace, began to rub the dust from his back saying, 'Sit down Abu Turab.'

He related five hundred and eighty-six *hadith* from the Prophet, may Allah bless him and his family and grant them peace.

His three sons, al-Hasan, al-Hussein and Muhammad ibn al-Hanafiyyah, related from him, and Ibn Masᶜud, Ibn ᶜUmar, Ibn ᶜAbbas, Ibn az-Zubayr, Abu Musa, Abu Saᶜid, Zaid ibn Arqam, Jabir ibn ᶜAbdullah, Abu Imamah, Abu Hurayrah, and a great number of other Companions and Followers, may Allah be pleased with all of them.

The *hadith* related on his merit

Imam Ahmad ibn Hanbal said: Those merits which have been related about ʿAli, may Allah be pleased with him, have not been related about any of the Companions of the Messenger of Allah, may Allah bless him and grant him peace. Al-Hakim narrated it.

The two Shaykhs narrated from Saʿd ibn Abi Waqqas that: The Messenger of Allah, may Allah bless him and his family and grant them peace, deputised ʿAli ibn Abi Talib (as his *khalifah* in Madinah in the Battle of Tabuk. He said, 'Messenger of Allah, will you leave me behind with the women and children?' He said, 'Are you not pleased to be in the same relation to me as Harun was to Musa, except that there is no prophet after me?' Ahmad and al-Bazzar narrated it in *hadith* of Abu Saʿid al-Khudri, and at-Tabarani narrated it in a *hadith* from Asma' bint Qais, Umm Salamah, Habashi ibn Jinadah, Ibn ʿUmar, Ibn ʿAbbas, Jabir ibn Samurah, al-Bara' ibn ʿAzib and Zaid ibn Arqam.

They both narrated from Sahl ibn Saʿd said that the Messenger of Allah, may Allah bless him and his family and grant them peace, said on the day of Khaybar, 'I will give the standard tomorrow to a man at whose hands Allah will give victory, who loves Allah and His Messenger, and whom Allah and His Messenger love.' The people spent the night wondering about and discussing who would be given it. When people awoke in the morning they went to the Messenger of Allah, may Allah bless him and his family and grant them peace, and all of them were hoping that they would be given it. He said, 'Where is ʿAli ibn Abi Talib?' They said, 'He is complaining of an ailment in his eyes.' He said, 'Send for him.' They brought him. The Messenger of Allah, may Allah bless him and his family and grant them peace, spat in his eyes and supplicated for him and he was healed to such an extent that it was as if he had not had a pain. Then he gave him the standard.

At-Tabarani narrated this *hadith* from Ibn ʿUmar, ʿAli, Ibn Abi Layla, ʿImran ibn Husayn and al-Bazzar narrated it from Ibn ʿAbbas.

Muslim narrated that Sa'd ibn Abi Waqqas said: When this *ayah* was revealed, '*Let us call our sons and your sons …*' (Qur'an 3: 61) then the Messenger of Allah, may Allah bless him and his family and grant them peace, called for 'Ali, Fatimah, al-Hasan, al-Hussein and said, 'O Allah, these are my family.'

At-Tirmidhi narrated from Abu Surayhah or Zaid ibn Arqam that the Prophet, may Allah bless him and grant him peace, said, 'He for whom I am his master (*mawla*), then 'Ali is his master.' Ahmad narrated it from 'Ali, Abu Ayyub al-Ansari, Zaid ibn Arqam and 'Amr ibn Dhi Murr, Abu Ya'la narrated it form Abu Hurayrah, at-Tabarani narrated it from Ibn 'Umar, Malik ibn Huwayrith, Habashi ibn Jinadah, Jarir, Sa'd ibn Abi Waqqas, Abu Sa'id al-Khudri, Anas, and al-Bazzar narrated it from Ibn 'Abbas, 'Ammarah, and Buraydah, and in most of them there is the addition, 'O Allah, befriend whoever befriends him and be an enemy to whoever is his enemy.'[11]

Ahmad narrated that Abu't-Tufayl said: 'Ali gathered people together in the year 35 AH in the court (of the mosque) and said to them, 'I adjure you by Allah, of every Muslim man who heard the Messenger of Allah, may Allah bless him and grant him peace, saying on the day of Ghadir Khumm what he said when he arose.' Thirty men stood up and bore witness that the Messenger of Allah, may Allah bless him and grant him peace, said, 'He for whom I am his master, then 'Ali is his master. O Allah, befriend whoever befriends him and be an enemy to whoever is his enemy.'

At-Tirmidhi narrated, as did al-Hakim who declared it *sahih* that Buraydah said: The Messenger of Allah, may Allah bless him and grant him peace, said, 'Allah has told me to love four and informed me that He loves them.' It was said, 'Messenger of Allah, name them for us.' He said, ''Ali is of them,' – saying that three times – 'And Abu Dharr, Miqdad and Salman.'

---

[11] The Arabic equally translates as, 'O Allah befriend whomever he befriends and be an enemy to whomever he is an enemy.'

At-Tirmidhi, an-Nasa'i and Ibn Majah narrated that Habashi ibn Jinadah said: The Messenger of Allah, may Allah bless him and grant him peace, said, 'Ali is from me and I am from ⁽Ali.'

At-Tirmidhi narrated that Ibn ⁽Umar said: The Messenger of Allah, may Allah bless him and grant him peace, made pacts of brotherhood between his companions, so ⁽Ali came with his eyes full of tears and said, 'Messenger of Allah, you made pacts of brotherhood between your companions and you did not make brotherhood between me and anyone.' The Messenger of Allah, may Allah bless him and grant him peace, said, 'You are my brother in the world and in the hereafter.'

Muslim narrated that ⁽Ali said: By the One Who split the grain and created the soul, the Unlettered Prophet promised me that no-one would love me except for a believer and that no-one would hate me except for a hypocrite.

At-Tirmidhi narrated that Abu Sa⁽id al-Khudri said: We used to recognise the hypocrites by their hatred of ⁽Ali.

Al-Bazzar narrated as did at-Tabarani in *al-Awsat* from Jabir ibn ⁽Abdullah and at-Tirmidhi and al-Hakim narrated from ⁽Ali that both of them said: The Messenger of Allah, may Allah bless him and grant him peace, said, 'I am the Madinah of knowledge and ⁽Ali is its (the Madinah's) gate.' This is a good (*hasan*) *hadith* as is the correct position, not *sahih* as al-Hakim said, nor fabricated as a group of them said including Ibn al-Jawzi and an-Nawawi. I have explained its status in *at-Ta⁽aqqubat ⁽ala'l-mawdu⁽at*.

Al-Hakim narrated and he declared *sahih* that ⁽Ali said: The Messenger of Allah, may Allah bless him and grant him peace, sent me to the Yemen, so I said, 'Messenger of Allah, you have sent me, and I a youth, to judge between them, and I don't know what the nature of judgement is.' He struck my chest with his hand and said, 'O Allah, guide his heart and make firm his tongue.' (⁽Ali said), 'By the One Who split the grain, I have not had any doubt about passing judgement (in a dispute) between two (people).'

Ibn Sa'd narrated from 'Ali that someone said to him, 'Why is it that you have the most *hadith* of the companions of the Messenger of Allah, may Allah bless him and grant him peace?' He said, 'I was such that when I asked him, he informed me, and when I was silent, he began (to teach) me.'

He narrated that Abu Hurayrah said: 'Umar ibn al-Khattab said, ''Ali is the best of us in judicial decision.'

Al-Hakim narrated that Ibn Mas'ud, may Allah be pleased with him, said: We used to say among ourselves that the best of the people of Madinah in judicial decision was 'Ali.

Ibn Sa'd narrated that Ibn 'Abbas said: When a trustworthy person relates to us a *fatwa* of 'Ali, we do not go beyond it.

He narrated that Sa'id ibn al-Musayyab said: 'Umar ibn al-Khattab used to seek refuge with Allah from every difficult question or case for which there is no Abu Hasan (in which he was not present).

He narrated that he (Sa'id ibn al-Musayyab) also said: None of the Companions would say, 'Ask me (about anything you like)!' except for 'Ali.

Ibn 'Asakir narrated that Ibn Mas'ud said: The most knowledgeable of the people of Madinah in the laws of inheritance and in judicial decisions is 'Ali ibn Abi Talib.

He narrated about 'A'ishah, may Allah be pleased with her, that 'Ali was mentioned in her presence and she said, 'As for him, he is the most knowledgeable, of those who remain, in the *Sunnah*.'

Masruq said: The knowledge of the Companions of the Messenger of Allah, may Allah bless him and grant him peace, culminated in 'Umar, 'Ali, Ibn Mas'ud and 'Abdullah, may Allah be pleased with them.

'Abdullah ibn 'Ayyash ibn Abi Rabi'ah said: 'Ali had whatever you will of a cutting tooth in knowledge, he had excellence by reason of his family relations, priority in (accepting) Islam, his acquaintanceship with the Messenger of Allah, may Allah bless him and his family and grant them peace, discernment (*fiqh*) in the *Sunnah*, courage in war, and liberality with property.

At-Tabarani narrated in *al-Awsat* with a weak *isnad* that Jabir ibn ᶜAbdullah said: The Prophet, may Allah bless him and grant him peace, said, 'People are from all sorts of different stocks, and I and ᶜAli are from one stock.'

At-Tabarani and Ibn Abi Hatim narrated that Ibn ᶜAbbas said: Allah did not reveal an *ayah* beginning, 'O you who believe ...' but that ᶜAli is its *amir* and its eminence. Allah reproached the Companions of Muhammad in more than one place but He never mentioned ᶜAli but with approval.

Ibn ᶜAsakir narrated that Ibn ᶜAbbas said: There has not been revealed about anyone in the Book of Allah what has been revealed about ᶜAli.

Ibn ᶜAsakir narrated that Ibn ᶜAbbas said: Three hundred *ayat* were revealed about ᶜAli.

Al-Bazzar narrated that Saᶜd said: The Prophet, may Allah bless him and grant him peace, said to ᶜAli, 'It is not permitted for anyone to be in a state of *junub* (requiring the complete washing of the body known as *ghusl*) in this mosque apart from me and you.'

At-Tabarani narrated as did al-Hakim who declared it *sahih* that Umm Salamah, may Allah be pleased with her, said: When the Messenger of Allah, may Allah bless him and his family and grant them peace, became angry, none dared to speak to him except for ᶜAli.

At-Tabarni and al-Hakim narrated from Ibn Masᶜud, may Allah be pleased with him, that the Prophet, may Allah bless him and grant him peace, said, 'Looking at ᶜAli is an act of worship.' Its *isnad* is *hasan*.

At-Tabarani and al-Hakim narrated it in *hadith* of ᶜImran ibn Husayn.

Ibn ᶜAsakir narrated it in *hadith* of Abu Bakr as-Siddiq, ᶜUthman ibn ᶜAffan, Muᶜadh ibn Jabal, Anas, Thawban, Jabir ibn ᶜAbdullah and ʿA'ishah, may Allah be pleased with them.

At-Tabarani narrated in *al-Awsat* that Ibn ʿAbbas said: ʿAli had eighteen excellences which no-one else of this *ummah* had.

Abu Yaʿla narrated that Abu Hurayrah said: ʿUmar ibn al-Khattab said, 'ʿAli was given three qualities the gift of any one of which I should prefer over high-bred camels.' He was asked, 'And what are they?' He said, 'He married him his daughter Fatimah; his dwelling at the mosque, wherein what is not permitted to me in it is permitted to him; and the standard on the day of Khaybar.' Ahmad narrated the like of it is from Ibn ʿUmar with a *sahih isnad*.

Ahmad and Abu Yaʿla narrated with a *sahih isnad* that ʿAli said: I have not been afflicted with swelling of the eye nor a headache since the Messenger of Allah, may Allah bless him and grant him peace, drew his hand over my face and spat lightly in my eyes on the day of Khaybar when he gave me the standard.

Abu Yaʿla and al-Bazzar narrated that Saʿd ibn Abi Waqqas said: The Messenger of Allah, may Allah bless him and grant him peace, said, 'Whoever harms ʿAli, harms me.'

At-Tabarani narrated with a *sahih isnad* from Umm Salamah that the Messenger of Allah, may Allah bless him and grant him peace, said, 'Whoever loves ʿAli, loves me, and whoever loves me, loves Allah. Whoever hates ʿAli, hates me and whoever hates me, hates Allah.'

Ahmad and al-Hakim, who declared it *sahih*, narrated that Umm Salamah heard the Prophet, may Allah bless him and grant him peace, saying, 'Whoever reviles ʿAli, reviles me.'

Ahmad and al-Hakim narrated with a *sahih isnad* from Ibn Abi Saʿid al-Khudri that the Prophet, may Allah bless him and grant him peace, said to ʿAli, 'You will fight for the sake of the Qur'an, as I fought for the sake of its revelation.'

Al-Bazzar, Abu Yaʿla and al-Hakim narrated that ʿAli said: The Messenger of Allah, may Allah bless him and his family and grant them peace, called me and said, 'ʿAli, there is in you a resemblance to

'Isa; the Jews hated him so much that they slandered his mother, and the Christians loved him so much that they gave him a degree which wasn't his.' Now surely, two (sorts) will be destroyed because of me: a lover who goes beyond the limits, who praises me immoderately for what is not in me, and one who hates (me), whose hatred of me brings him to slander me.

At-Tabarani narrated in *al-Awsat* and *as-Saghir* that Umm Salamah said: I heard the Prophet, may Allah bless him and grant him peace, saying, ''Ali is with the Qur'an and the Qur'an is with 'Ali; they will not separate until they come to me to drink from the Pool.'

Ahmad and al-Hakim narrated with a *sahih isnad* from 'Ammar ibn Yasir that the Prophet, may Allah bless him and grant him peace, said to 'Ali, 'The most grievous of people are two men: the fair-complexioned one of Thamud who hamstrung the female camel, and the one who will strike you, 'Ali, upon this' – meaning his cranium above the forehead – 'until this becomes moistened from it (from the blood)' – meaning his beard. This has been narrated in *hadith* of 'Ali, Suhayb, Jabir ibn Samurah and others.

Al-Hakim narrated, and he declared it *sahih*, that Abu Sa'id al-Khudri said: People complained about 'Ali so that the Messenger of Allah, may Allah bless him and grant him peace, rose among us delivering an address and said, 'Do not complain about 'Ali for, by Allah, he is somewhat rough for the sake of Allah, or in the way of Allah.'

The pledge of allegiance to 'Ali for the *khilafah* and what came about from that

Ibn Sa'd said: 'Ali was pledged allegiance as *khalifah* the morning after the killing of 'Uthman in Madinah. All of the Companions, may Allah be pleased with them, who were there pledged allegiance. It is said that Talhah and az-Zubayr pledged allegiance with displeasure and unwillingly. Then they went to Makkah, and

'A'ishah, may Allah be pleased with her, was there. They took her and went with her to Basra seeking retaliation for the blood of 'Uthman. That reached 'Ali so he went to Iraq and at Basra met Talhah, az-Zubayr, 'A'ishah and whoever was with them, which is known as the Battle of the Camel, and which occurred in Jumada al-Akhirah of the year 36 AH. Talhah, az-Zubayr and others were killed there, the dead reaching thirteen thousand. 'Ali spent fifteen nights at Basra and then he went to Kufa.

Then Mu'awiyah ibn Abi Sufyan and those with him in Syria came out against him. That reached 'Ali and he went out to meet him. They met at Siffin in Safr of the year 37 AH. The fighting continued there for some days, until the people of Syria raised the *mushafs* calling to that which is in them, which was a trick of 'Amr ibn al-'As. People hated the war and they called each other to negotiate and appointed two arbiters. 'Ali appointed Abu Musa al-Ash'ari and Mu'awiyah appointed 'Amr ibn al-'As. They signed a decree between them that they should meet at the beginning of the year at al-Adhruh where they would consider seriously the command of the *ummah*. People separated, Mu'awiyah returning to Syria and 'Ali to Kufa.

Then (a group known as) the *Khawarij* (the seceders – literally 'those who go out') from among his companions and those with him, went out against him. They said, 'There is no judgement but (that) of Allah', and they set up a military camp at Harura'. He sent Ibn 'Abbas to them, who argued with them and convinced them, so that many of them returned. A group of them stayed firm, went to an-Nahrawan and obstructed the roadway. 'Ali went to them there and killed them at an-Nahrawan, killing Dhu'th-Thudayyah.[12] That was in the year 38 AH.

People gathered in al-Adhruh in Sha'ban of this year, among them Sa'd ibn Abi Waqqas, Ibn 'Umar and other Companions. 'Amr

---

[12] Literally, 'the possessor of the little breast', a man who had been foretold to be among the *Khawarij* by the Prophet, may Allah bless him and grant him peace.

allowed Abu Musa al-Ash'ari to go first, as a trick he had devised. He (Abu Musa) spoke and removed 'Ali from office. Then 'Amr spoke and confirmed Mu'awiyah in office and pledged allegiance to him. People split up over this. 'Ali disagreed with his companions to such an extent that he began to bite his fingers saying, 'I am disobeyed and Mu'awiyah is obeyed?'

Three men of the *Khawarij* hastened to act: 'Abd ar-Rahman ibn Muljam al-Muradi, al-Burk ibn 'Abdullah at-Tamimi and 'Amr ibn Bukayr at-Tamimi. They gathered in Makkah and made a covenant with each other that they three would kill: 'Ali ibn Abi Talib, Mu'awiyah ibn Abi Sufyan and 'Amr ibn al-'As, and that they would give the slaves (of Allah) rest from them. Ibn Muljam said, 'I will take 'Ali for you.' Al-Burk said, 'I will take Mu'awiyah for you.' 'Amr ibn Bukayr said, 'I will suffice you for 'Amr ibn al-'As.' They made a covenant on that one night, either the eleventh or the seventeenth of Ramadan, and then each of them directed himself to the land in which his intended victim was. Ibn Muljam went to Kufa, met his companions of the *Khawarij* and told them secretly of what they intended to do.

On the night preceding the *Jumu'ah* of the seventeenth of Ramadan of the year 40 AH, 'Ali woke up before dawn. He said to his son al-Hasan, 'This night I saw the Messenger of Allah, may Allah bless him and his family and grant them peace, and I said, "Messenger of Allah, what distress and argumentation I have received from your *ummah*!" He said to me, "Supplicate Allah against them." I said, "O Allah, give me in exchange for them what is better for me than they are, and give them in exchange for me what is worse for them than I am."'

Then the *mu'adhdhin* Ibn adh-Dhabbah came in to 'Ali and said, 'The prayer.' 'Ali went out the door crying out, 'People, the prayer, the prayer!' Ibn Muljam stood before him, struck him with the sword, and it hit the top of his forehead reaching the brain. People rushed upon him from every side, and he was held and bound. 'Ali lingered for the *Jumuʿah* and Saturday, and died the night before Sunday. Al-Hasan, al-Hussein and ʿAbdullah ibn Jaʿfar washed his body, al-Hasan led the prayer over him, then he was buried in the house of the Amirate in Kufa at night. Later they cut off the limbs of Ibn Muljam, he was put in a reed basket, and they burnt him in a fire.

All of the above are the words of Ibn Saʿd. He summarised all of these events and battles excellently well, and he didn't expand on them greatly as others did. This is more befitting to this occasion. He said, may Allah bless him and grant him peace, 'When my companions are mentioned, restrain yourselves (from speaking)', and he said, 'It is sufficient for my Companions (to mention) their killing.'

There is in *al-Mustadrak* that as-Suddi said: ʿAbd ar-Rahman ibn Muljam fell passionately in love with a woman of the *Khawarij* called Qatam, and he married her and gave her as a dowry three thousand dirhams and the killing of ʿAli. Al-Farazdaq said about that:

'I have not seen a dowry sent by a liberally generous one,
    Like the dowry of Qatam, of human beings (slaves) and beasts:

Three thousand, a slave, a maidservant
    And the striking of ʿAli with the penetrating sword.

There is no dowry dearer than ʿAli even if it were very expensive,
    And no assassination but that it is less than the assassination by Ibn Muljam.'

Abu Bakr ibn ʿAyyash said: The grave of ʿAli was concealed so that the *Khawarij* would not dig up his body; and Sharik said: His son al-Hasan carried him to Madinah. Al-Mubarrad said from Muhammad ibn Habib: The first to be transferred from one grave to another was ʿAli, may Allah be pleased with him.

Ibn ʿAsakir narrated that Saʿid ibn ʿAbd al-ʿAziz said: When ʿAli ibn Abi Talib, may Allah be pleased with him, was killed, they carried him to bury him with the Prophet, may Allah bless him and grant him peace. While they were journeying with him at night, the camel on which he was bolted. No-one knew where it had gone, and they couldn't overtake it. For that reason the people of Iraq say, 'He is in the clouds.' Others say, 'The camel arrived in the lands of Tayy, where they took him and buried him.'

When ʿAli was killed he was sixty-three years old. It has been said that he was sixty-four, sixty-five, fifty-seven and fifty-eight. He had nineteen women slaves.

Some fragments of accounts of ʿAli, his judgements and his words

Saʿid ibn Mansur said in his *Sunan*: Hushaym narrated to us: Hajjaj narrated to us: A Shaykh from Fazarah told me: I heard ʿAli saying, 'Praise belongs to Allah Who made our enemy ask us about something that had occurred to him in the matter of his *deen*. Muʿawiyah wrote to me, asking me about the ambiguous hermaphrodite.[13] I wrote to him that he should make him inherit according to how he urinates.' Hushaym said the same from Mughirah from ash-Shaʿbi from ʿAli.

Ibn ʿAsakir narrated that Al-Hasan said: When ʿAli came to Basra, Ibn al-Kawwa' and Qais ibn ʿAbbad stood before him and said to him, 'Will you not inform us about this course which you are set upon, taking charge of the *ummah*, so that some of them are striking others; is it a covenant of the Messenger of Allah, may Allah bless him and grant him peace, which he made with you? Tell us, for you are the trusted one in whom we have confidence about that which you have heard.'

He said, 'As for my having a covenant about that from the Prophet, may Allah bless him and grant him peace, then no. By Allah, if I was the first to affirm him, I will not be the first to attribute a lie to him. If I had had a covenant from the Prophet, may Allah bless

---

[13] i.e. does the hermaphrodite inherit property as a man or as a woman?

him and grant him peace, about that, I would never have allowed the brother of Bani Taym ibn Murrah (Abu Bakr) and ʿUmar ibn al-Khattab to stand upon his *minbar*; I would have fought them with my own hand, even if I could find nothing but this garment of mine. However, the Messenger of Allah was not killed, and he did not die suddenly, rather he lingered in his illness for days and nights, with the *muʾadhdhin* coming to him to announce the time of the prayer to him. He would order Abu Bakr, who would lead the people in prayer, while he knew my standing. One of his wives wanted to turn him away from Abu Bakr, and he refused and became angry. He said, "You are the female companions of Yusuf! Tell Abu Bakr to lead the people in prayer!" When Allah took His Prophet, may Allah bless him and grant him peace, we considered our affairs and we chose for our worldly affairs he whom the Prophet of Allah, may Allah bless him and grant him peace, was satisfied with for our *deen*. The prayer is the root of Islam and it is the *amir* of the *deen*, and the support of the *deen*, so we pledged allegiance to Abu Bakr, for he was worthy of that, no two of us disagreed about him, none of us bore testimony against others, and nor did we deny his privilege. I discharged what was due to Abu Bakr, acknowledged the obedience that was his right, went on military expeditions with him in his troops. I would take when he gave me, go on military expeditions when he sent me on them, and I would lash with my whip for the *hadd* punishment for him.

'When he died, ʿUmar undertook it (the *khilafah*) and he took it according to the *Sunnah* of his companion (Abu Bakr) and that which he knew of his affair. We pledged allegiance to ʿUmar, no two of us disagreeing about him, nor any of us bearing testimony against any others, nor did we deny his privilege. I discharged what was due to ʿUmar, acknowledged the obedience that was his right, and went on military expeditions with him in his armies. I would take when he gave me, go on military expeditions when he sent me on them, and I would lash with my whip for the *hadd* punishment for him.

'When he died, I recalled within myself my close relationship (to the Prophet, may Allah bless him and grant him peace), my priority, my precedence and my merit, thinking that no-one would hold another equal to me. However, he (ᶜUmar) was afraid that, if the *khalifah* after him would do a wrong action, it would attach to him in his grave. He withdrew himself and his son from it, for if there had been any partiality in him he would have preferred his son for it (the *khilafah*). He quit himself of it, passing it on to a group of six from Quraysh of whom I was one. When the group met, I thought that they would not consider anyone equal to me. ᶜAbd ar-Rahman ibn ᶜAwf took a compact from us that we would listen to and obey whomever Allah gave authority over us. Then later he took the hand of ᶜUthman ibn ᶜAffan and put his hand in his.

'I considered my affair, and (saw that) my obedience had preceded my oath of allegiance, and my covenant had been taken for another. We therefore pledged allegiance to ᶜUthman. I discharged what was due to him, acknowledged the obedience that was his right, and went on military expeditions with him in his armies. I would take when he gave me, go on military expeditions when he sent me on them, and I would lash with my whip for the *hadd* punishment for him.

'When he was struck down I considered my affair. The two *khalifahs*, who had taken hold of it through the covenant of the Messenger of Allah, may Allah bless him and grant him peace, to the two of them regarding [or in respect of] the prayer, had gone. This one, with whom the covenant had been taken, had been killed. The people of the two Harams (Makkah and Madinah) pledged allegiance to me, and the people of these two provinces (Kufa and Basra). One sprang into it who is not the like of me, his relationship not as my relationship, nor his knowledge like my knowledge, nor does he have priority like my priority, and I have more right to it than him.'

Abu Nuᶜaym narrated in *ad-Dala'il* from Jaᶜfar ibn Muhammad that his father said: Two men were brought before ʿAli in a dispute, and so he sat at the base of a wall. A man said to him, 'The wall will fall down!' ʿAli said, 'Carry on. Allah suffices as a guardian.' He passed judgement between them, stood up and then the wall fell down.

There is in *at-Tuyuriyyat* with its *isnad* from Jaʿfar ibn Muhammad that his father said: A man said to ʿAli ibn Abi Talib, 'We hear you saying in the *khutbah*, "O Allah, set us right with that which You set right the *khalifahs* who followed the right course and were guided," so who are they?' His eyes filled with tears and he said, 'They are my two beloveds, Abu Bakr and ʿUmar, the two *imams* of guidance, the two shaykhs of Islam, the two men of Quraysh, who are to be taken as exemplars after the Messenger of Allah, may Allah bless him and grant him peace. Whoever takes them as exemplars will be protected (from error), and whoever follows their footsteps will be guided on the straight path, and whoever clings to them is of the party of Allah.'

ʿAbd ar-Razzaq narrated that Hujr al-Madari said: ʿAli ibn Abi Talib said to me, 'What will you do when you are ordered to curse me?' I said, 'Will that happen?' He said, 'Yes.' I said, 'What should I do?' He said, 'Curse me, but do not forsake me.' He (Hujr) said: Muhammad ibn Yusuf, the brother of al-Hajjaj – and he was the *amir* of Yemen – ordered me to curse ʿAli, so I said, 'The *amir* has told me to curse ʿAli, so you curse him! may Allah curse him!' No-one understood it except for one man.

At-Tabarani narrated in *al-Awsat* and Abu Nuʿaym in *ad-Dala'il* from Zadhan that ʿAli was relating a *hadith* and a man accused him of lying. ʿAli said to him, 'Shall I supplicate against you if you are lying?' He said, 'Supplicate!' He supplicated against him and he did not leave before his eyesight went.

He narrated that Zirr ibn Hubaysh said: Two men sat eating the morning meal, one of them having five small loaves and the other three small loaves. When they had placed the meal in front of them a man passed by them and greeted them. They said, 'Sit down and eat.' He sat down, ate with them and they ate equally of the eight loaves. The man stood, tossed down eight dirhams and said, 'Take them in place of what I have eaten from you two, and what I have consumed of your food.' The two of them quarrelled. The man who had the five loaves said, 'I have five dirhams and you have three.' The man who had the three loaves said, 'I will not be content unless the dirhams are divided in two halves between us.' They raised it before the *Amir al-Mu'minin* ᶜAli, and told him their story. He said to the man who had the three loaves, 'Your companion has offered you what he offered you. His bread was more than your bread, so be content with the three.' He said, 'By Allah, I will not be content with him except with the bitter truth.' ᶜAli said, 'There is nothing for you, in bitter truth, except for one dirham and he has seven dirhams!' The man said, 'Glory be to Allah!' He said, 'That's it!' He said, 'Show me the reason in the bitter truth so that I can accept it.' ᶜAli said, 'Do the eight loaves not have twenty-four third parts? You ate them and you were three persons, not knowing who ate more or less, so we will assume that you ate equally.' He continued, 'You ate eight thirds but you only had nine thirds. Your companion ate eight thirds and he had fifteen thirds, of which he ate eight leaving seven which the man who had the dirhams ate, and he ate one of your nine. You have one (dirham) for your one (third of a loaf) and he has seven.' The man said, 'I am now content.'

Ibn Abi Shaybah narrated in the *Musannaf* that ᶜAta' said: A man was brought to ᶜAli and two men bore witness against him that he had stolen. He took up (another) thing from people's affairs and threatened false witnesses, saying, 'If I am brought a false witness, I will do such and such with him.' Then he sought for the two witnesses but could not find them, so he let the man go.

ᶜAbd ar-Razzaq narrated in the *Musannaf*: Ath-Thawri narrated to us from Sulayman ash-Shaybani from a man that a man was brought to ᶜAli. Someone said, 'This man claims that he had a wet dream about my mother.' He said, 'Go and stand him in the sun and strike his shadow.'

Ibn ᶜAsakir narrated by way of Jaᶜfar ibn Muhammad from his father that the seal-ring of ᶜAli was silver and that its engraving was, 'Blessed as the One Who Decrees is Allah.'

He narrated that ᶜAmr ibn ᶜUthman ibn ᶜAffan said: The engraving on the seal-ring of ᶜAli was, 'Sovereignty belongs to Allah.'

He narrated that al-Mada'ini said: When ᶜAli entered Kufa, one of the wise men of the Arabs came to see him and said, 'By Allah, *Amir al-Mu'minin*, you have ornamented the *khilafah* and it has not ornamented you. You have raised it up and it has not raised you up. It was in more need of you than you were of it.'

He narrated from Mujammiᶜ that ᶜAli used to sweep out the *bait al-mal* and then perform a prayer, hoping that it would be evidence for him that he had not stored wealth within (keeping it) away from the Muslims.

Abu'l-Qasim az-Zujaji said in his *Amali*: Abu Jaᶜfar Muhammad ibn Rustum at-Tabari narrated to us: Abu Hatim as-Sijistani narrated to us: Yaᶜqub ibn Ishaq al-Hadrami narrated to me: Saᶜid ibn Salim al-Bahili narrated to me: My father narrated to us from my grandfather from Abu'l-Aswad ad-Du'ali – or he said: from my grandfather Abu'l-Aswad from his father that he said: I entered upon the *Amir al-Mu'minin* ᶜAli ibn Abi Talib, may Allah be pleased with him, and saw him with his eyes lowered, deep in thought. I said, 'What are you thinking about *Amir al-Mu'minin*?' He said, 'I have heard in this city of yours mistakes (in the use of Arabic), and I want to make a book on the principles of Arabic.' I said, 'If you do this, you will give life to us, and this language will remain among us.' Later, after three days I came to him, and he gave me a page in which was, 'In the name of Allah, the Merciful, the Compassionate. The word is noun, verb and particle. The noun is that which tells you about the named thing. The verb is that which tells you about the movement of the named thing. The particle is that which tells you of a meaning which is neither a noun nor a verb.' He said, 'Follow this up and add to it what occurs to you. Know, Abu'l-Aswad ad-Du'ali, that things are threefold: a substantive, a pronoun, and a thing which is neither a substantive nor a pronoun. The men of knowledge only have differing degrees of excellence in recognition of what is neither substantive nor pronoun.' Abu'l-Aswad said: I compiled some things on it and I showed them to him. The particles of *nasb* (which put the noun governed by them in the accusative) were in it. Of them I mentioned *inna, anna, laita, la'alla,* and *ka'anna* but I did not mention *lakinna*. He said to me, 'Why did you leave it out?' I said, 'I did not reckon it to be one of them.' He said, 'It is one of them so add it in among them.'

Ibn ꜥAsakir narrated that Rabiꜥah ibn Najid said: ꜥAli said, 'Be among people as the bee is among birds, for there is no bird that doesn't regard it (the bee) as insignificant. If the birds knew what blessing there is in its belly, they would not do that to it. Mix with people with your tongues and your persons, and be separate from them in your actions and your hearts; because a man has what he earns, and on the Day of Resurrection he will be with whomever he loves.'

He narrated that ꜥAli said: Be more concerned for the acceptance of your action than you are for the action; for, an action with fearful obedience will not be little. How could an action which is accepted be little?

He narrated that Yahya ibn Juꜥdah said: ꜥAli ibn Abi Talib said, 'Carriers of the Qur'an (memorisers of it)! act according to it! for the knowledgeable man (ꜥalim) is only one who knows, then acts according to what he knows, and whose knowledge is in accord with his action. There will be people whose knowledge will not pass below their collarbones (i.e. to their hearts), whose inner selves are at variance with their appearances, and whose actions are at variance with their knowledge. They will sit in circles competing for superiority with each other, to such an extent that a man will become angry at the man who sits beside him because he sits beside another and leaves him. Those, their actions in these assemblies of theirs will not rise up to Allah.'

He narrated that ʿAli said: *At-tawfiq* (being directed by Allah to the right course) is the best leader, good character is the best associate, the intellect is the best companion, courtesy the best inheritance, and there is no loneliness worse than conceit.

He narrated that al-Harith said: A man came to ʿAli and said, 'Tell me about the decree.' He said, 'It is a dark path; do not travel it.' He said, 'Tell me about the decree!' He said, 'A deep ocean; do not enter it.' He said, 'Tell me about the decree!' He said, 'The secret of Allah which is concealed from you; do not investigate it!' He said, 'Tell me about the decree!' He said, 'Questioner! Did Allah create you for what He wills or for what you will?' He said, 'Of course, for what He wills.' He said, 'Then He will make use of you for what He wills.'

He narrated that ʿAli said: Calamities have endings. Whoever suffers misfortune must go to the end of them. It is only right for an intelligent man, when some misfortune occurs to him, that he should submit to it until its time ends, because in trying to repulse it before the natural ending of its time there is increase in its unpleasantness.

He narrated that it was said to ʿAli, 'What is generosity?' He said, 'That which comes from the man as an initiative. As for that which comes in response to a request, it is only shame and feigning generosity.'

He narrated from ʿAli that a man came to him, spoke well of him, praised him excessively, and something about him had already reached him (ʿAli) before that. He said, 'I am not as you say. And I am better than what you believe within your self.'

He narrated that ʿAli said: The recompense of disobedience is weakness in worship, constriction in livelihood and shortcoming in pleasure.' Someone asked, 'What is a shortcoming in pleasure?'

He said, 'When one obtains the fulfilment of a permitted appetite something intervenes which prevents one having the desire fulfilled.'

He narrated from ᶜAli ibn Rabiᶜah that a man said to ᶜAli, and the man used to hate him, 'May Allah establish you!' ᶜAli said, '… upon your heart.'

He narrated that ash-Shaᶜbi said: Abu Bakr used to speak poetry (i.e. compose it), ᶜUmar used to speak poetry, ᶜUthman used to speak poetry, but ᶜAli was more poetical than the three.

He narrated that Nabit al-Ashjaᶜi said: ᶜAli ibn Abi Talib, may Allah be pleased with him, said,

'When hearts enclose despair
    And the wide breast is constricted with their worry,

And calamities take up their abode and are at rest,
    And misfortunes take up residence in their places,

And no way is seen to remove the harm,
    And the cunning one does not gain freedom by his trickery,

A helper comes to you, right upon your despair,
    Whom the Near, the Answerer brings,

And all misfortunes, when they reach their limit,
    Near deliverance is joined with them.'

He narrated that ash-Shaᶜbi said: ᶜAli ibn Abi Talib said to a man whom he disliked keeping the company of another man,

'Do not accompany an ignorant brother;
    Beware of him!

How many an ignorant man has destroyed
    A forbearing man when he took him as his brother.

A man is measured by another man
    If he walks along with him.

'Ali ibn Abi Talib

One thing has measures and
> Similarities for another thing.

The measure of a sandal is another sandal,
> When it is placed beside it.

For the heart there is an indication
> Of the heart when it meets it.'

He narrated that al-Mubarrad said: Written on the sword of ʿAli ibn Abi Talib, may Allah be pleased with him, was:

'People have an eagerness for the world and (want) to manage it,
> And its purity is mixed for you with impurity.

They are not provided it with intelligence after it had been divided up,
> But rather they are provided it in measured portions.

How many a courteous and intelligent man it does not help!
> A fool attains his world through (his) shortcoming.

If it had been from strength or conquest,
> Then hawks would have flown off with the sparrows' provisions.'

He narrated that Hamzah ibn Habib az-Zayyat said: ʿAli ibn Abi Talib used to say:

'Do not disclose your secret except to yourself,
> For every sincere one has a sincere advisor.

I have seen deviating men
> Who do not leave alone an unblemished skin (without trying to attack it).'

He narrated that ʿUqbah ibn Abi's-Sahba' said: When Ibn Muljam struck ʿAli, al-Hasan went in to see him, weeping. ʿAli said to him, 'My son, memorise from me four and four.' He said, 'What are they, father?' He said, 'Intelligence is the wealthiest of riches, the greatest poverty is folly, the loneliest solitude is conceit, and the noblest of noble qualities is good character.' He said, 'And the other four?' He said, 'Beware of keeping the company of a fool, for he wants to benefit you and he harms you; beware of befriending a liar, for he will make the remote seem near to you and the near seem remote; beware of befriending a mean person for he will sit inactively however much you are in need of him; and beware of befriending an immoral person, for he will sell you for a trifling sum.'

Ibn ʿAsakir narrated from ʿAli that a Jew came to him and said to him, 'When did our Lord come into existence?' ʿAli's face flushed with anger and he said, 'He was not, and then He was? He *is*, without existence. He *is*, without cause. He *is*, without anything before Him nor any end. All ends fall short of Him, for He is the end of every end.' Then the Jew accepted Islam.

Ad-Darraj narrated in his well known *Juz'* with an unknown *isnad* from Maysarah that the Qadi Shurayh said: When ʿAli was setting out to Siffin, he found that he was missing a coat of armour of his. When the war was over and he returned to Kufa, he came across the armour in the hands of a Jew. He said to the Jew, 'The armour is mine; I have not sold it or given it away.' The Jew said, 'It is my armour and it is in my hand.' He said, 'Let us go to the *qadi*.' ʿAli went first, sat beside Shurayh, and said, 'If it was not because my opponent is a Jew, I would have sat beside him in the gathering, but I heard the Prophet, may Allah bless him and grant him peace, saying, "Humiliate them, since Allah has humiliated them."' Shurayh said, 'Speak, *Amir al-Muʾminin.*' He said, 'Yes. This armour, which this Jew has, is my armour; I did not sell it and I did not give it away.' Shurayh said, 'What do you say, Jew?' He said, 'It is my armour and it is in my possession.' Shurayh said, 'Do you have any evidence, *Amir al-Muʾminin?*' He said, 'Yes. Qanbar and al-Hasan will witness that the armour is mine.' Shurayh said, 'A son's witness is not acceptable on behalf of his father.' ʿAli said, 'A man from the Garden, and his testimony is not acceptable? I heard the Prophet, may Allah bless him and grant him peace, saying, "Al-Hasan and al-Hussein are the two lords of the youth of the people of the Garden."' The Jew said, 'The *Amir al-Mu'minin* brought me before his *qadi*, and his *qadi* gave judgement against him. I witness that this is the truth, and I witness that there is no god but Allah and I witness that Muhammad is the messenger of Allah, and that the armour is your armour.'

His commentary on the Qur'an

As for his words in commentary on the Qur'an, there are many.

Ibn Sa'd narrated that 'Ali said, 'By Allah, an *ayah* has not been revealed without me knowing about what it was revealed, where it was revealed, and about whom it was revealed. My Lord has given me a very intelligent heart and a true and articulate tongue.'

Ibn Sa'd and others narrated that Abu't-Tufayl said: 'Ali said, 'Ask me about the Book of Allah, because there is no *ayah* but that I know whether it was revealed at night or in daytime, on the plain or in the mountain.'

Ibn Abi Dawud narrated that Muhammad ibn Sirin said: When the Prophet, may Allah bless him and grant him peace, died, 'Ali was slow to pledge allegiance to Abu Bakr. Abu Bakr met him and said, 'Do you dislike my (having the) authority?' He said, 'No, but I have sworn not to don my mantle, except for the prayer, until I have collected together the Qur'an.' They claimed that he wrote it in the order of its revelation. Muhammad (ibn Sirin) thus said, 'If that book were come across, there would be knowledge in it.'

Some fragments of his astonishingly concise words

'Ali, may Allah be pleased with him, said, 'Precaution is bad opinion.'

He said, 'The close one (i.e. the near relative) is the one whom affection renders close even if his kinship makes him distant. The distant one is the one whom enmity makes far even though his kinship makes him a near relative. There is nothing nearer to the body than the hand, and yet the hand, if it is corrupt, is cut off and if it is cut off, then it is cauterised.' Abu Nuʿaym narrated it.

He said, 'Take five things from me: Let none of you fear anything but his wrong action; let him hope for nothing but his Lord; let someone who does not know, not be shy of learning; and let someone who does not know, not be shy of saying, "Allah knows best"; and patience has the same relation to *iman* as does the head to the body: when patience goes then *iman* goes, for when the head goes, then the body goes.' Saʿid ibn Mansur narrated it in his *Sunan*.

He said: The real *faqih* is the one who does not make people despair of the mercy of Allah; who does not grant them licence to disobey Allah; who does not make them feel secure from the punishment of Allah; who does not abandon the Qur'an longing for something other than it; because there is no good in worship in which there is no knowledge, there is no knowledge unless there is understanding along with it, and there is no recitation if there is no reflection in it. Ibn ad-Daris narrated it in the *Fada'il al-Qur'an*.

He said: The coolest thing for my liver, when I am asked about what I don't know, is to say, 'Allah knows best.' Ibn ʿAsakir narrated it.

He said: Whoever wants to give people what is due from him, let him love for them what he loves for himself. Ibn ʿAsakir narrated it.

He said: Seven things are from the *shaytan*: strong anger, strong sneezing, strong yawning, vomiting, nosebleeds, secret discourse, and falling asleep during *dhikr* (remembrance of Allah).

He said: Eat the pomegranate with its pulp for it is *the* stomachic (literally: the tan of the stomach). Saʿid ibn Mansur narrated it.

He said: A time will come to people in which the believer will be more humiliated than a female slave. Saʿid ibn Mansur narrated it.

Abu'l-Aswad ad-Du'ali said, eulogising ʿAli,

'Eye, woe to you! Come to our aid;
    Do you not weep for the *Amir al-Mu'minin*?

Umm Kulthum (the daughter of ʿAli and Fatimah, and the wife of ʿUmar) weeps over him
    With her tears, and she has seen death.

Say to the *Khawarij* wherever they are
    – and may the eyes of the envious not find rest –

"Is it in the month of fasting that you have distressed us,
    Through the best of men altogether?

You have killed the best of those who mounted steeds
    And tamed them, and of those who mounted ships,

Of those who wore sandals and cut them to measure,
    And who recited the Mathani (the Fatihah) and the Clear (Book).

All the qualities of good were in him,
    And the love of the Messenger of the Lord of the Worlds."

Quraysh knew, wherever they were,
    That you (ʿAli) were the best of them in standing and in *deen*.

When I looked towards the face of Abu Hussein
    I saw the full moon over the onlookers.

Before his killing we were in good;
    We would see the *mawla* of the Messenger of Allah among us.

He was establishing the truth without doubting concerning it,
    And he was just to enemies and close relatives.

He would not conceal any knowledge that he had,
    And he did not have the character of the haughty ones.

It is as if when people lost ʿAli,

> They were ostriches bewildered in a land for years.
>
> Do not rejoice at our affliction Mu'awiyah ibn Sakhr,
> For the rest of the *khulafa'* are from us.

Those notable people who died during his time

The following notable people died during the days of 'Ali, either natural deaths or by being killed: Hudhayfah ibn al-Yaman, az-Zubayr ibn al-'Awwam, Talhah, Zaid ibn Suhan, Salman al-Farisi, Hind ibn Abi Halah, Uways al-Qarani, Khabbab ibn al-Aratt, 'Ammar ibn al-Yasir, Sahl ibn Hunayf, Suhayb ar-Rumi, Muhammad ibn Abi Bakr as-Siddiq, Tamim ad-Dari, Khawwat ibn Jubayr, Shurahbil ibn as-Samt, Abu Maysurah al-Badri, Safwan ibn 'Assal, 'Amr ibn 'Anbasah, Hisham ibn Hakim, Abu Rafi' the freed-slave of the Prophet, may Allah bless him and grant him peace, and others.

Al-Hasan ibn ʿAli
may Allah be pleased with him

Al-Hasan ibn ʿAli ibn Abi Talib, may Allah be pleased with him, Abu Muhammad, the grandson of the Messenger of Allah, may Allah bless him and grant him peace, his descendant and the last of the *khulafa'* by his (the Prophet's, may Allah bless him and grant him peace) explicit words.

Ibn Saʿd narrated that ʿImran ibn Sulayman said: Al-Hasan and al-Hussein are two of the names of the people of the Garden. The Arabs did not use these names in the *Jahiliyyah*.

Al-Hasan, may Allah be pleased with him, was born in the middle of Ramadan in the third year of the Hijrah. Hadith have been related from him from the Prophet, may Allah bless him and grant him peace. ʿA'ishah, may Allah be pleased with her, related *hadith* from him, and a great number of the Followers, of them his son al-Hasan, Abu'l-Hawra' Rabiʿah ibn Sinan, Ash-Shaʿbi, Abu Wa'il and Ibn Sirin.

He resembled the Prophet, may Allah bless him and grant him peace. The Prophet, may Allah bless him and grant him peace, named him al-Hasan, slaughtered a sheep for him on his seventh day, shaved off his hair and ordered that the weight of the hair in silver should be given away as *sadaqah*. He was the fifth of the family of the mantle (when the Prophet, may Allah bless him and grant him peace, said, 'O Allah, these are my family.').

Abu Ahmad al-ʿAskari said: This name was not known in the *Jahiliyyah*.

Al-Mufaddal said: Allah veiled the names of al-Hasan and al-

Hussein until the Prophet, may Allah bless him and grant him peace, used them to name his two grandsons.

Al-Bukhari narrated that Anas said: No-one more resembled the Prophet, may Allah bless him and grant him peace, than al-Hasan ibn ᶜAli.

The two Shaykhs narrated that al-Bara' said: I saw the Prophet, may Allah bless him and grant him peace, with al-Hasan upon his shoulder, saying, 'O Allah, I love him, so love him.'

Al-Bukhari narrated that Abu Bakrah said: I heard the Prophet, may Allah bless him and grant him peace, upon the *minbar*, with al-Hasan by his side looking at the people one time and looking at him one time, saying, 'This son of mine is a chief, and it is likely that through him Allah will make peace between two parties of the Muslims.'

Al-Bukhari narrated that Ibn ᶜUmar said: The Prophet, may Allah bless him and grant him peace, said, 'They are my two descendants (literally 'my two sprigs of basil' or 'my two sweet-smelling plants [or flowers]') in the world,' meaning al-Hasan and al-Hussein.

At-Tirmidhi and al-Hakim narrated that Abu Saᶜid al-Khudri said: The Messenger of Allah, may Allah bless him and grant him peace, said, 'Al-Hasan and al-Hussein are the two lords of the youth of the people of the Garden.'

At-Tirmidhi narrated that Usamah ibn Zaid said: I saw the Prophet, may Allah bless him and grant him peace, and al-Hasan and al-Hussein were upon his hips (one on each), and he said, 'These are my two sons and the two sons of my daughter. O Allah, I love them, so love them and love whoever loves them.'

He narrated that Anas said: The Prophet, may Allah bless him and grant him peace, was asked, 'Who of the people of your house are most beloved to you?' He said, 'Al-Hasan and al-Hussein.'

Al-Hakim narrated that Ibn ᶜAbbas said: The Prophet, may Allah bless him and grant him peace, approached carrying al-Hasan on his shoulder. A man met him and said, 'What a blessed mount you have, boy!' The Prophet, may Allah bless him and grant him peace, replied, 'And what a blessed rider is he.'

Ibn Sa'd narrated that 'Abdullah ibn az-Zubayr said: The one most like the Prophet, may Allah bless him and grant him peace, of his family and the most beloved to him is al-Hasan ibn 'Ali. I saw him come while he was prostrate and mount his shoulders – or he said, 'his back' – and he did not make him get down until he himself got down. I saw him while he was bowing in prayer and he would separate his legs for him so that he could pass through the other side.'

Ibn Sa'd narrated that Abu Salamah ibn 'Abd ar-Rahman said: The Prophet, may Allah bless him and grant him peace, used to put forth his tongue for al-Hasan ibn 'Ali, then when the infant saw the redness of the tongue, he would be merry with him.

Al-Hakim narrated that Zuhayr ibn al-Arqam said: Al-Hasan ibn 'Ali stood to deliver the *khutbah*, and a man from Azd Shanu'ah stood up and said, 'I witness that I saw the Prophet, may Allah bless him and grant him peace, place him in his lap (*hubwah* denotes sitting on the haunches with the legs drawn in to the belly, often with a cloth wrapped around the legs and the back in support), saying, "Whoever loves me, let him love him, and let the one who is present convey it to whoever is absent," and if it were not for high regard for the Messenger of Allah, may Allah bless him and grant him peace, I would not have related it to anyone.'

Al-Hasan, may Allah be pleased with him, had many virtues: he was lordly, forbearing, possessing tranquillity, gravity and modesty; he was liberally generous, much praised; he disliked seditions and the sword; he married a great deal; and he would bestow upon a single man as much as one hundred thousand.

Al-Hakim narrated that 'Abdullah ibn 'Ubayd ibn 'Umayr said: Al-Hasan performed the Hajj twenty-five times walking, and the high-bred, riding beasts were led along with him.

Ibn Sa'd narrated that 'Umayr ibn Ishaq said: No-one ever spoke in my presence who it was more preferable, when he talked, that he should not be silent than al-Hasan ibn ᶜAli. I never heard from him an improper word except for one time. There was a dispute between al-Hasan and ᶜAmr ibn ᶜUthman about some land. Al-Hasan proposed something which ᶜAmr did not like. Al-Hasan said, 'There is nothing for it with us but to act in spite of him (literally 'that his nose cleave to the dust').' This was the most improper word I ever heard from him.

Ibn Saᶜd narrated that ᶜUmayr ibn Ishaq said: Marwan was the *amir* over us, and he used to abuse ᶜAli every *Jumuᶜah* from the *minbar*, while al-Hasan would listen and make no reply. Then he sent a man to him saying, 'I swear by ᶜAli, by ᶜAli, by ᶜAli, and by you, by you! I don't find any likeness for you except the mule, to which it is said, "Who is your father?" and it replies, "My mother is a mare."' Al-Hasan said to him, 'Return to him and say to him, "By Allah, I will not efface for you anything of what you have said by abusing you. However, you and I have an appointment together before Allah. Then, if you are truthful, may Allah recompense you for your truthfulness. If you are a liar, then Allah is worse in revenge."'

Ibn Saᶜd narrated that Zurayq ibn Sawwar said: There were some words between al-Hasan and Marwan, then Marwan approached him, became very tough on him – and al-Hasan was silent. Marwan blew his nose using his right hand. Al-Hasan said to him, 'Woe to you! Do you not know that the right hand is for the face, and the left for the private parts (and for unclean matters generally)? I am disgusted with you (literally 'filth to you')!' Marwan became silent.

Ibn Saᶜd narrated from Ashᶜath ibn Sawwar that a man said: A man sat down with al-Hasan and he (al-Hasan) said, 'You have sat down with us at the moment we were going to stand. Will you permit?'

Ibn Saᶜd narrated that ᶜAli ibn Zaid ibn Judaᶜan said: Al-Hasan gave forth his property twice for the sake of Allah, and Allah divided up his property and shared it with him three times, to such an extent that he used to give a sandal and keep a sandal with him, or give away a leather sock (known as *khuff*) and keep another sock.

Ibn Sa'd narrated that 'Ali ibn al-Hussein said: Al-Hasan was given to divorcing women, and he did not separate from a woman but that she loved him. He married ninety women.

Ibn Sa'd narrated from Ja'far ibn Muhammad that his father said: Al-Hasan used to marry and divorce so much that I was afraid he would cause enmity towards us among the tribes.

Ibn Sa'd narrated from Ja'far ibn Muhammad that his father said: 'Ali said, 'People of Kufa, do not marry (your womenfolk) to al-Hasan because he is a man much given to divorce.' A man from Hamadan said, 'By Allah, we will marry him (to our womenfolk). Whosoever pleases him he can keep, and whosoever displeases him he can divorce.'

Ibn Sa'd narrated that 'Abdullah ibn Hasan said: Hasan was a man who used to marry women a great deal, and they very rarely found favour with him. There were very few women he married who did not love him and were not passionately attached to him.

Ibn 'Asakir narrated that Juwayriyyah ibn Asma' said: When al-Hasan died, Marwan wept at his funeral prayer. Al-Hussein said to him, 'Do you weep when you forced him to swallow that which you did?' He said, 'I used to do that to one more forbearing than this,' and he pointed towards the mountain. (The mountain was proverbially the epitome of forbearance).

Ibn 'Asakir narrated that al-Mubarrad said: Someone said to al-Hasan ibn 'Ali, 'Abu Dharr says, "Poverty is more beloved to me than wealth, and illness more beloved to me than health."' He said, 'May Allah show mercy to Abu Dharr. As for me, I say, "Whoever is absolutely dependent on the goodness of Allah's choosing for him does not wish to be in any state other than the one which Allah has chosen for him."' This is the limit in research into the subject of contentment with that which destiny turns about.

Al-Hasan, may Allah be pleased with him, took charge of the *khilafah* after the death of his father through the pledge of allegiance of the people of Kufa, and he remained in it for six months and some days. Then Mu'awiyah came out against him – and the matter belongs to Allah – and so al-Hasan sent a message to him to offer to surrender the *khilafah* to him, on condition that the *khilafah* should be his after him, that no-one of the people of Madinah, al-Hijaz and Iraq should be sought out for revenge or retaliation for anything which had happened in the time of his father, and that he would pay off his debts for him. Mu'awiyah agreed to what he asked, they concluded a treaty upon that basis, and the prophetic miracle became evident in his words, may Allah bless him and grant him peace, 'Allah will make peace through him between two groups of the Muslims.' He abdicated from the *khilafah* for him. Al-Balqini sought to prove from his abdication from the *khilafah* – which is the greatest rank – that it is permitted to abdicate from and renounce offices and positions. His abdication from it was in the year 41 AH, in the month of Rabi' al-Awwal. It has also been said that it was in Rabi' al-Akhir, or Jumada al-Ula. His companions said to him, 'O disgrace of the *mu'minin*!' and he would say, 'Disgrace is better than the Fire.'

A man said to him, 'Peace be upon you, humiliator of the believers!' He said, 'I am not the humiliator of the believers, but I disliked to kill you for the sovereignty.'

Then al-Hasan moved from Kufa to Madinah and resided there.

Al-Hakim narrated that Jubayr ibn Nufayr said: I said to al-Hasan, 'People are saying that you want the *khilafah*.' He said, 'The chiefs of the Arabs were with me, at war with whomever I was at war with, and at peace with whomever I was at peace with. I abandoned that desiring the Face of Allah, and to prevent spilling the blood of the *ummah* of Muhammad, may Allah bless him and grant him peace. Now later, shall I take it by force with the help of the herds of goats of the people of al-Hijaz?'

Al-Hasan ibn ʿAli

Al-Hasan, may Allah be pleased with him, died in Madinah through poisoning. His wife, Jaʿdah bint al-Ashʿath ibn Qais poisoned him. Yazid ibn Muʿawiyah suggested secretly to her that she should poison him and that then he would marry her, and she did so. When al-Hasan died, she sent a message to Yazid asking him for the fulfilment of what he had promised her. He said, 'We were not pleased with you for al-Hasan, so should we then be pleased with you for ourselves?' His death was in 49 AH. It has also been said that it was on the fifth of Rabiʿ al-Awwal in the year 50 AH. And it has been said that it was in 51 AH. His brother argued with him to get him to tell him who had given him the (poisoned) drink, but he would not tell him. He said, 'Allah is most severe in revenge if it should be the one I suspect. If not, then no innocent person must be killed in retaliation for me.'[14]

Ibn Saʿd narrated that ʿImran ibn ʿAbdullah ibn Talhah said: Al-Hasan saw as if there were written between his eyes, '*Say, "He Allah is One,"*' (Qur'an 112: 1) and his family rejoiced at that. They told it to Saʿid ibn al-Musayyab and he said, 'If his dream is true, then he has very few days left to live.' He only lived a few days more before he died.

Al-Bayhaqi and Ibn ʿAsakir narrated by way of Abu'l-Mundhir Hisham ibn Muhammad that his father said: Al-Hasan ibn ʿAli was constricted (in his provision), and his stipend was one hundred

---

[14] Contrary to his usual practice, as-Suyuti gives no source for this story. In *Defence Against Disaster*, Qadi Abu Bakr ibn al-Arabi says concerning the allegation that the *Amir al-Mu'minin* Muʿawiyah, may Allah be pleased with him, poisoned al-Hasan, '...it was an unknown business. Only Allah knows about it. How can you assume it without proof and ascribe it to one of His creatures in a distant time when we do not have any sound transmission about it?' (p. 203) The same applies to this story. In the same book, the Qadi exonerates Yazid of a great deal of the slander levelled at him and says, '[Ahmad ibn Hanbal] included him among the men of *zuhd* (doing without the world) of the Companions and Followers... Indeed, he included him in the group of Companions before he proceeded to mention the Followers.'.

thousand a year. Muʿawiyah withheld it from him one year, and he was extremely constricted. He said, 'I called for an ink-pot so that I might write to Muʿawiyah to remind him about myself, and then I controlled (myself). I saw the Messenger of Allah, may Allah bless him and grant him peace, (in a dream) and he said, "How are you, Hasan?" I said, "Well, father." And I complained to him about the withholding of the property from me. He said, "Did you call for an ink-pot to write to a creature like yourself to remind him of that?" I said, "Yes, Messenger of Allah. What should I do?" He said, "Say:

$$\text{اَللّٰهُمَّ اقْذِفْ فِي قَلْبِي رَجَاءَكَ، وَاقْطَعْ رَجَائِي عَمَّنْ سِوَاكَ، حَتَّى لَا أَرْجُوَ أَحَداً غَيْرَكَ .}$$

$$\text{اَللّٰهُمَّ وَمَا ضَعُفَتْ عَنْهُ قُوَّتِي، وَقَصُرَ عَنْهُ عَمَلِي، وَلَمْ تَنْتَهِ إِلَيْهِ رَغْبَتِي، وَلَمْ تَبْلُغْهُ مَسْأَلَتِي، وَلَمْ يَجْرِ عَلَى لِسَانِي، مِمَّا أَعْطَيْتَ أَحَداً مِّنَ الْأَوَّلِينَ وَالْآخِرِينَ مِنَ الْيَقِينِ، فَخُصَّنِي بِهِ يَا رَبَّ الْعَالَمِينَ .}$$

O Allah, cast into my heart hope in You, and cut off my hope in everything other than You, until I don't hope for anyone other than You. O Allah, that for which my strength is too weak, and my action falls short of, my desire does not attain, my supplication does not reach, and what does not flow upon my tongue, of that certainty which You have given anyone of the ancients and the later peoples, then single me out for it, Lord of the Worlds."'

He said, 'Then, by Allah, I had not persisted in it for a week before Muʿawiyah sent me one million and five hundred thousand, and I said, "Praise be to Allah Who does not forget whoever remembers Him and doesn't disappoint whoever supplicates Him." I saw the Prophet, may Allah bless him and his family and grant them peace, in sleep and he said, "Hasan, how are you?" I said, "Well, Messenger of Allah," and I told him my story. He said, "My son, that is how it is for whoever hopes for (something) from the Creator and does not hope for (something) from the creature.'"

There is in *at-Tuyuriyyat* that Sulaym ibn ʿIsa, the Qurʾan reciter of the people of Kufa, said: When death came to al-Hasan he was overcome with agitation and grief. Al-Hussein said to him, 'My brother, what is this agitation and grief? You are going to the Messenger of Allah, may Allah bless him and his family and grant them peace, and ʿAli and they are your two fathers, and to Khadijah and Fatimah and they are your two mothers, and to al-Qasim and at-Tahir and they are your two maternal uncles, and to Hamzah and Jaʿfar and they are your two paternal uncles.' Al-Hasan said to him, 'Brother, I am entering into a matter of Allah's, exalted is He, the like of which I have never entered, and I see a creation of Allah's the like of which I have never seen.'

Ibn ʿAbd al-Barr said: From various sources we relate that when his time came, he said to his brother, 'My brother, your father raised his eyes to this authority and Allah averted him from it and put Abu Bakr in charge of it (the *khilafah*). Later, he raised his eyes to it, but it was turned away from him to ʿUmar. Later again, he had no doubt at the time of the Council that it would not pass him by, but it was turned away from him to ʿUthman. When ʿUthman was killed, then ʿAli was pledged allegiance. Then we were restrained until swords were unsheathed and so it (the *khilafah*) was never undisturbedly his. By Allah, I don't think that Allah will combine prophecy and *khilafah* in us. I don't know but that the fools of Kufa will try to appoint you as *khalifah* and drive you out. I have asked ʿAʾishah, may Allah be pleased with her, that I should be buried with the Messenger of Allah, may Allah bless him and his family and grant them peace, and she said, "Yes." When I die, ask her about that, but I only anticipate that people will try to prevent you. If they do, don't bandy words with them.' When he died, al-Hussein came to the Mother of the Believers, ʿAʾishah, may Allah be pleased with her, and she said, 'Yes, and it is an honour,' but Marwan prevented them. Then al-Hussein and those with him donned their swords, until Abu Hurayrah prevented them, and so he was buried in al-Baqi' by the side of his mother, may Allah be pleased with her.

Glossary of Arabic Terms

adhan – the call to prayer. *mu'adhdhin* – the one who calls to prayer.
Akhirah – what comes later, the next life.
ʿalim pl. *ʿulama'* – a man of knowledge. 'The *ʿalim* is only someone who knows, then acts according to what he knows, and whose knowledge is in accord with his action,' Sayyiduna ʿAli.
amir – commander. *Amir al-Mu'minin* – the Commander of the Believers, a title of respect given to the *khalifah*. *Imarah* – amirate.
Ansar – lit. Helpers, the people of Madinah who welcomed and aided the Messenger of Allah, may Allah bless him and grant him peace. See also *Muhajirun*.
ʿaqiqah – at the birth of a child when the head is shaved and the hair's weight in silver given away as *sadaqah,* and a sheep sacrificed and the meat shared with others and given away.
ʿArafah – the plain upon which the pilgrims stand during the pivotal day of the Hajj in prayer and supplication.
ayah pl. *ayat* – a sign, miracle and a verse of the Qur'an.
al-Bait al-Maqdis – lit. The Purified Dwelling, i.e. the mosque of Jerusalem or all of Jerusalem.
bait al-mal – lit. House of Property, where the collected *zakat* of the Muslims and other revenues are stored while awaiting distribution.
al-Baqiʿ – the graveyard of Madinah where many of the Companions, may Allah be pleased with them, are buried.
Dajjal – lit. Liar, the false Messiah whose appearance marks the imminent end of the world.
deen – the life-transaction, lit. the debt (*dayn*) of exchange between

two parties, in this usage between the Creator and the created.
dhikr – lit. remembrance, mention. In a general sense all acts of worship are *dhikr*. In common usage it has come to mean invocation of Allah by repetition of His names or particular formulae.
dhimmah – obligation or contract, in particular a treaty of protection for non-Muslims living in Muslim territory.
dinar – a gold coin of approximate value $107/£57.4 (2008).
dirham – a silver coin of approximate value $3.18/£1.76 (2008). Note that for *zakat* purposes only, 10 dirhams equals 1 dinar.
Dunya – what is lower and closer to hand, the 'world'. The word is most often an adjective of 'life', thus meaning the 'lower life'.
ʿEid – the celebration at the end of Ramadan and also at the end of the Hajj, marked by a general public prayer, *dhikr* and mutual visiting and hospitality.
faqih pl. *fuqaha'* – a man learned in knowledge of *fiqh* (see below).
fatwa – an authoritative legal opinion or judgement made by a *faqih* who is a Mufti authorised by an *amir*.
fiqh – science of understanding the *shariʿah* in terms of the obligations, recommendations, sunnahs, permitted matters, disapproved and forbidden matters.
fitnah – a trial or affliction whereby one is tried or proved, a temptation, civil war and strife, faction and slaughter. Originally derived from a root meaning 'burning', with the sense of the burning of a metal such as gold to remove the dross.
ghusl – a washing of the entire body in order to enter Islam, after sexual intercourse or ejaculation, or preparatory for the weekly *Jumuʿah* and *ʿEid* prayers.
hadd pl. *hudud* – lit. the limits, Allah's boundary limits for the *halal* and the *haram*. The *hadd* punishments are the specific fixed penalties laid down by *shariʿah* for specified crimes.
hadith pl. *ahadith* – reported speech, particularly of the Prophet Muhammad, may Allah bless him and grant him peace. Not to be confused with *Sunnah*.

Hajj – the yearly pilgrimage to Makkah

halal – permitted by the *shari'ah*

haram – forbidden by the *shari'ah*; also an inviolable place or object.

hasan – lit. good, beautiful, and thus a category of *hadith*, which is reliable, but whose *isnad* is not perfect.

hawd – the 'pond' of the Prophet Muhammad, may Allah bless him and grant him peace, on the Last Day, which is replenished by rivers from the Garden and from which he will give the believers to drink. Whoever drinks from it will not thirst again.

hijab – veil, the covering by adult women of their hair, and all of their bodies excepting the face and hands.

Hijaz – the western area of Arabia which includes Makkah and Madinah.

Hijr – the semi-circular un-roofed enclosure at one side of the Ka'bah, whose wall outlines the shape of the original building built by the Prophets Ibrahim and Isma'il, peace be upon them.

hijrah – emigration in the way of Allah. Islam takes its dating (indicated by AH 'After *Hijrah*') from the Hijrah of the Prophet, may Allah bless him and grant him peace, from Makkah to Madinah.

ihram – state entered to perform Hajj or *'Umrah*, which includes, for males, wearing two pieces of cloth also known as *ihram*.

imam – the one who leads, often a term for the *amir* or *khalifah*. 'Leaders and nobles who order them (the people) and they obey them.' (Sayyiduna Abu Bakr). It is now more often restricted to one who leads people in prayer.

imamah – imamate, the office of *imam*.

iman – belief in the heart and affirmation on the tongue.

insha'Allah – if Allah wills.

iqamah – the act of establishing the prayer, and also the call made immediately prior to prayer in order to summon the people in the mosque.

isnad – chain of transmission of a *hadith*.

Isra' – the Night Journey of the Prophet, may Allah bless him and grant him peace, from Makkah to Jerusalem from whence he went on the *Mi'raj* (the ascension through the heavens).

i'tizal – lit. withdrawal or secession, and thus the theology of that group which withdrew from the circle of Hasan al-Basri, who became know as *Mu'tazilah*.

Jahiliyyah – the Time of Ignorance, before the coming of Islam

jama'ah – the group, particularly referring to the group of people performing the prayer together.

jihad – struggle, particularly warfare to defend and establish Islam.

jinn – unseen beings created of smokeless fire who cohabit the earth with mankind.

jizyah – a tax levied on people of previous revelations who make a contract to live under Muslim rule (see *dhimmah*). The tax was four dinars per adult male per year. It is interesting to note that this sum in present terms (2008) is approximately $428/£230.

Jumada al-Ula – a month of the Muslim lunar calendar.

Jumada al-Akhirah – a month of the Muslim lunar calendar.

Jumu'ah – Friday, and particularly the prayer performed on that day which it is necessary for all adult males to attend if they are able and if its conditions are fulfilled.

junub – condition after sexual intercourse or ejaculation, requiring the complete washing of the body known as *ghusl*.

kafara – he covered over the truth, he showed ingratitude, he disbelieved, thus *kufr* disbelief, *kafir* disbeliever pl. *kafirun/kuffar*.

kalam – lit. speech, but also the science of investigating the tenets of *iman*.

khalifah pl. *khulafa'* – lit. successor, both the rank of Adamic man, one who stands in for Allah in His creation, and a Caliph or successor of the Prophet, may Allah bless him and grant him peace.

khilafah – the office of the *khalifah*.

Khawarij – a sect who believed that committing major wrong actions turns a Muslim into an unbeliever.

al-Khulafa' ar-Rashidun – (see *khalifah* above) the *khulafa'* who took the right way.

khutbah – public address, particularly in the mosque on Friday or one of the ʿ*Eid* prayers.

kunyah – a respectful and affectionate way of calling, such as the 'father of so-and-so', the 'mother of so-and-so' or the 'son or daughter of so-and-so'.

maʿrifah – lit. recognition, which in its first level is a rational knowledge of what is necessary to know about Allah and His Messengers, peace be upon them, and which can then deepen to become gnosis rather than scholastic knowledge.

Maghrib – the West, specifically northwest Africa.

al-Masjid al-Haram – the Inviolable Mosque of Makkah.

marfuʿ – a tradition ascribed to the Prophet, may Allah bless him and grant him peace.

mawla – 'a master', the freed slave but also his former master.

minbar – steps on which the *imam* stands to deliver the *khutbah* on the day of *Jumuʿah*.

Muhajirun – Companions of the Messenger of Allah, may Allah bless him and grant him peace, who accepted Islam outside Madinah and emigrated to Madinah, particularly those who came with him from Makkah.

Muharram – the first month of the Muslim lunar year.

mu'min, pl. *mu'minun* and *mu'minin* – a believer (see *iman* above).

al-Murji'ah – a sect which was characterised by an indulgent attitude towards wrong action in the sense that they felt that 'believers' would not be diminished in their *iman* by the wrong actions they did.

mursal – a *hadith* attributed directly to the Prophet, may Allah bless him and grant him peace, by one of the Followers or Followers of the Followers when it is not known from which Companion it was transmitted.

mushaf – a written copy of the Qur'an.

musnad – a book containing *ahadith* arranged according to their *isnad*, e.g. the author mentions the *Musnad as-Siddiq* which contains *ahadith* narrated by Abu Bakr, may Allah be pleased with him.

mutʿah – a temporary form of marriage common among pre-Islamic Arabs which was prohibited by the Prophet, may Allah bless him and grant him peace.

mutawatir – the strongest *isnad* possible for a *hadith*. This is when a number of Companions have narrated the text of the *hadith* to large numbers of knowledgeable Followers who each in turn transmitted it to numbers of later students, etc., so that there is no possible doubt about the *hadith*.

al-Qadariyyah – sect of Muslims who believe more in man's free-will than in predestination.

qadi – a judge.

ar-Rafidah – a group of the *Shiʿah* known for rejecting Abu Bakr and ʿUmar as well as ʿUthman (as opposed to the Zaydiyyah *Shiʿah* who accept them).

rakʿah pl. *rakaʿat* – a complete unit of *salah* consisting of standing, bowing and two prostrations.

ar-Riddah – the reneging or apostasy of the desert Arabs after the death of the Prophet, may Allah bless him and grant him peace.

Ruh al-Quds – the Spirit of Purity, the angel Jibril.

sabeel – a way, often *jihad*, 'the way of Allah'.

as-Sabiqun al-Awwalun – the First Foremost ones, i.e. those *Muhajirun* and *Ansar* who accepted Islam before the conquest of Makkah and strove with their lives and their wealth in *jihad*.

sadaqah pl. *sadaqat* – giving in the way of Allah, often used synonymously with *zakat*.

sahih – authentic or sound. A technical term of the science of *hadith* which indicates the strength of the *isnad*.

as-Sakinah – lit. tranquillity. The presence of Allah sometimes made clear by a sign, also the feeling of peace of mind and security.

salah – the prayer consisting of standing reciting Qur'an, bowing, prostrating and sitting.

salat at-tarawih – the prayers performed after the *ʿIsha'* (night) prayer during Ramadan.

as-Saqifah – roofed building, particularly the roofed gallery of Bani Sa'idah in which the *Ansar* and some of the *Muhajirun* met after the death of the Prophet, may Allah bless him and grant him peace, to choose a *khalifah*.

shahadah – witnessing and bearing witness that there is no god but Allah and that Muhammad is the Messenger of Allah, may Allah bless him and grant him peace, i.e. the first pillar of Islam.

shari'ah – lit. a road, and in particular the pathway leading down to drinking water at an oasis. It is the legal modality of a people based on the revelation of their Prophet. The last *shari'ah* in history is that of Islam, which abrogates all previous *shari'ahs*.

Shawwal – the month of the Islamic lunar calendar immediately following Ramadan.

Shaykh – lit. an old man. Title of respect used for a man of great knowledge or a leader among his people

shaytan – a devil, particularly Iblis.

Shi'ah – the sect which differed from the Muslims over their allegation of the prior right of 'Ali, may Allah be pleased with him, to the *khilafah*.

shirk – the unforgivable wrong action of associating something in partnership with Allah and worshipping it or them along with Him.

sidq – truthfulness and thus *sadiq* – a truthful one and *siddiq* – one eminently truthful and affirmative of the truth.

siwak and *miswak* – toothstick cut from the 'araq tree.

Sultan – the ruler.

Sunnah pl. *sunan* – lit. a form, the customary practice of a person or group of people. It has come to refer almost exclusively to the practice of the Messenger of Allah, Muhammad, may Allah bless him and grant him peace, but also comprises the customary practice of *al-Khulafa' ar-Rashidun* and of the first generation of Muslims in Madinah. *Sunan* is also a title often used for certain collections of *hadith*.

surah – a large unit of Qur'an linked by thematic content, composed of *ayat*. There are 114 *surahs* in the Qur'an.
takbir – the declaration '*Allahu Akbar* – Allah is Greater'
talbiyah – the cry of the pilgrim to Makkah '*Labbayk Allahumma labbayk …*' – 'At Your service, O Allah, at Your service …'
taqwa or *tuqa* – lit. self-protecting, fearful obedience of Allah in avoiding all that is forbidden and undertaking all that is obligatory. Higher degrees then involve avoiding that which is disapproved of and undertaking that which is recommended, and so on.
at-Tasawwuf – Sufism. It is held by the ʿ*ulama* to be a *fard ʿayn* – a science which is an individual obligation on every Muslim man and woman.
at-tawfiq – being directed to the right direction, the grace of Allah.
ummah – a nation. The *Ummah* of the Prophet, may Allah bless him and grant him peace, are the Muslims.
ʿ*Umrah* – the lesser pilgrimage to Makkah which may be undertaken at any time of the year.
wird or *hizb* – two synonymous terms for a set portion of *dhikr*, *ayat* of Qur'an and supplications to be recited regularly at any time of the day or night. The latter is often used to refer to a portion of one sixtieth of Qur'an.
wudu' – the minor washing of the face and limbs in preparation for the *salah*.
zakat – a wealth tax. It is an act of worship of Allah and one of the *arkan* (indispensable pillars) of Islam. It is levied on certain storable crops, cattle and other livestock, gold and silver, items of trade, etc. and distributed among a number of categories including the needy and the bereft, travellers, the indebted, for the freeing of slaves, and in the way of Allah (*jihad*).

Appendix: On the Imamate

Allah, exalted is He, said: "*You who believe! obey Allah and obey the Messenger and those in command among you.*" (Qur'an 4:59) Al-Qurtubi narrates in commentary on this *ayah*:

When He, glorious is He and exalted, had previously addressed himself to those in authority in the previous *ayah* and had begun with them and ordered them to discharge trusts and to judge justly between people, then He proceeded in this *ayah* to address Himself to their subjects, and He ordered obedience to Himself, mighty is He and majestic, first of all, which means obeying His commands and avoiding His prohibitions, and then obedience to His Messenger secondly in that which he ordered and forbade, and then thirdly obedience to the *amirs*, according to the position of the dominant majority and Abu Hurayrah, Ibn ʿAbbas and others. Sahl ibn ʿAbdullah at-Tustari said, 'Obey the *sultan* in seven things: minting dirhams and dinars, measures and weights, judgements, hajj, *Jumuʿah*, the two ʿ*Eid*s and *jihad*.'

(Al-Qurtubi, *Al-Jamiʿ li ahkam al-Qur'an,* Dar Ihya at-Turath al-Arabi, Beirut, Lebanon, 1405/1985)

Ibn Juzayy al-Kalbi said:
Concerning the Imamate there are two issues.
1. An affirmation of the Imamates of the Four *Khulafa'*, may Allah be pleased with them. The proof of the Imamates of all of them has three aspects:

    a. Each of them united the conditions of the Imamate completely;

b. The Muslims who lived in the time of each one of them were unanimous in pledging allegiance to him and in coming under obedience to him, and consensus is a proof;

c. That companionship (with the Prophet, may Allah bless him and grant him peace) which each of them had, emigration, magnificent deeds, Allah's praise of them, and the Truthful One's bearing witness of the Garden for them.

Moreover the Messenger of Allah, may Allah bless him and grant him peace, indicated the *khilafah* of Abu Bakr and ʿUmar, and he commanded that people model themselves on them. He put Abu Bakr in charge of the Farewell Hajj and made him lead the prayer in his final illness which is an indication of his being appointed *Khalifah*. Then Abu Bakr appointed ʿUmar *Khalifah*, then ʿUmar made the matter the business of consultation among six [people] and they agreed on putting ʿUthman forward. He was wrongfully killed, for which there is the testimony of the Prophet, may Allah bless him and grant him peace, and his promise to him of the Garden for that. Then the man with most right to it was ʿAli because of his noble rank and his sublime virtues.

As for that which happened between ʿAli and Muʿawiyah and those Companions with each of them, then the most fitting thing is to withhold oneself from mentioning it, and that they should be remembered in the best way, and that one should seek the best interpretation for them, because it was a matter of *ijtihad*. As for ʿAli and those with him, they were in the right because they exercised *ijtihad* and were correct [in it] and so they will be rewarded. As for Muʿawiyah and those with him, they exercised *ijtihad* and were mistaken, and they are to be excused. It is required that one respect them and all of the Companions and love them because of the praise of them that occurs in Qur'an and because of their accompanying the Messenger of Allah, may Allah bless him and grant him peace.

He, may Allah bless him and grant him peace, said, "[Beware of] Allah! [Beware of] Allah! concerning my companions. Do not make them a target after me. Whoever loves them, then it is for love of me he loves them. Whoever hates them, it is because of hatred of me that he hates them. Whoever harms them has harmed me, and whoever harms me has harmed Allah."

2. The preconditions of the Imamate are eight:

Islam, maturity (puberty), intellect (sanity), maleness, justice, knowledge, competence, and that his descent should be from Quraysh, but on this [last] there is a difference of opinion, so that if people agree [on pledging allegiance] to one who does not meet all of the conditions then it is permitted, from fear of causing dissension and sedition.

It is not permitted to rise up against people in authority even if they are tyrannical, unless they openly display clear disbelief. It is obligatory to obey them in whatever a man loves and dislikes, unless they order disobedience [to Allah] for there is no obedience due to a creature if it involves disobedience to the Creator.

(Ibn Juzayy al-Kalbi, *al-Qawanin al-Fiqhiyyah,* The Opening (*Fatihah*) concerning what principles of ʿaqidah of the fundamentals of the *deen* are obligatory, chapter 8)

Ibn Rajab al-Hanbali said:

Al-Hasan said about *amirs*, "They take charge of five of our affairs: the *Jumuʿah* and the congregational prayer [*jamaʿah*], the ʿEid, the frontiers, and the *hadd* punishments. By Allah! the *deen* will only be straight and effective by them, even if they are tyrannical and wrongdoing. By Allah! that which Allah puts right by means of them is more than that which they corrupt, although, by Allah! obedience to them is tough, but separating oneself from them is *kufr*."

Al-Khalal narrated in the "*Kitab al-Imarah* – Book of Amirate"

from the *hadith* of Abu Umamah that he said, "The Prophet, may Allah bless him and grant him peace, commanded his companions when they had prayed ʿIsha', 'Assemble, because I have need of you.' When they finished the morning prayer, he asked, 'Have you assembled as I told you?' They answered, 'Yes.' He said three times, 'Worship Allah and do not associate anything with Him! Have you grasped this?' We answered, 'Yes.' He said three times, 'Establish the prayer and produce the *zakah*! Have you grasped this?' We answered, 'Yes.' He said three times, 'Hear and obey!' He said three times, 'Have you grasped this?'" He said, "We had thought that the Messenger of Allah, may Allah bless him and grant him peace, was going to give a long discourse, but then [we saw] that he had collected together the entire affair for us."
(Ibn Rajab al-Hanbali, *Jamiʿ al-ʿulum wa'l-hikam* translated by Abdassamad Clarke and published by Turath Publishing Ltd., as *The Compendium (of knowledge and wisdom)*. In commentary on *hadith* no.28, p.707)

Bibliography

Al-ᶜAwasim min al-Qawasim, published in translation as *Defence Against Disaster* by *Qadi* Abu Bakr ibn al-ᶜArabi. Madinah Press, Cape Town, South Africa. 1416 AH/ 1995. ISBN 0-620-19688-2.

The Return of the Khalifate, Shaykh Abdalqadir as-Sufi. Madinah Press, Cape Town, South Africa. 1417 AH/ 1996. ISBN 1-874 216 215

Osmanli history, 1289-1922: based on Osmanli sources by Professor Mehmet Maksudoglu.

Al-Muqaddimah, Ibn Khaldun.

Al-Qawanin al-Fiqhiyyah, Ibn Juzayy al-Kalbi.

History of the Caliphs, Jalalu'ddin a's Suyuti, translated from the original Arabic by Major H. S. Jarrett, Karimsons (Pakistan).[1]

---

[1] It was originally our intention to edit this work and republish it, but it was soon found to be easier to make an entirely fresh translation. However, there were one or two points for which having access to this book was very useful.